OLYMPIC REVOLUTION

also by David Miller

Father of Football
A Biography of Matt Busby

World Cup 1970

World Cup 1974

The Argentina Story 1978

Running Free
(*with Sebastian Coe*)

Cup Magic

The World to Play For
(*with Trevor Francis*)

Sebastian Coe – Coming Back

England's Last Glory
The Boys of '66

Seoul '88
Official IOC Book of the Games

Sportswriter's Eye
(*Anthology*)

Stanley Matthews
The Authorized Biography

Albertville 1992
Official IOC Book of the Winter Games

IAAF 80
(*joint author*)
Official History of the
International Amateur Athletics Federation

Sebastian Coe – Born to Run
The Authorized Life in Athletics

OLYMPIC REVOLUTION

The Biography of Juan Antonio Samaranch

David Miller

First published in Great Britain in 1992 by
PAVILION BOOKS LIMITED
196 Shaftesbury Avenue, London WC2H 8JL

Designed by Roy Cole

A CIP catalogue record for this book is available from the British Library.

ISBN 1 85145 768 2
2 4 6 8 10 9 7 5 3

Printed and bound in Great Britain by
The Bath Press

This book may be ordered by post direct ftom the publisher. Please contact the Marketing Department, but try your bookshop first.

Contents

Foreword by H.M. The King of Spain

Considero que este libro, significativamente titulado *Olympic Revolution*, supone una contribución muy válida para entender la innovadora y delicada etapa de adaptación al mundo moderno que valerosamente se ha impuesto el Movimiento Olimpico Internacional bajo la presidencia de Juan Antonio Samaranch.

Samaranch es un español ligado toda su vida al deporte y a sus responsabilidades en nuestro país. En 1980 fue elegido en Moscú, Presidente del Comité Olímpico Internacional, primer organismo del deporte mundial, desde el que ha promovido una política de evolución, paralela a la que se ha operado en la sociedad contemporánea, que ha permitido al Movimiento Olímpico ocupar un lugar destacado en la dinámica de nuestro tiempo.

En vísperas de los Juegos de la XXV Olimpia da en Barcelona, quiero felicitar a David Miller por la iniciativa de escribir este libro, que enriquecerá a sus lectores con muchas facetas de la vida deportiva, quizás un tanto desconocidas. Los – resultados y records son la punta visible de un iceberg compuesto por muchos otros elementos fundamentales que no deben caer en el olvido.

Foreword by H.M. The King of Spain

I consider that this book, *Olympic Revolution*, makes a valuable contribution to our understanding of the innovative and difficult phase of adaptation to the modern world on which the International Olympic Committee has embarked with great courage under the Presidency of Juan Antonio Samaranch.

Samaranch is a Spaniard who has been involved with sport all his life and has held the highest sports posts and responsibilities in our land. In 1980, in Moscow, he was elected President of the International Olympic Committee, the foremost body in world sport, a position from which he has promoted a policy of evolution and adaptation parallel to developments in contemporary society. He has enabled the Olympic Movement to play an outstanding role in the dynamics of our time.

On the eve of the Games of the XXV Olympiad in Barcelona, I would like to congratulate David Miller on his initiative in writing this book, which will give its readers fascinating glimpses into many aspects of the sporting world with which they may not be entirely familiar. Results and records are the tip of an iceberg made up of many other fundamental elements which should not be forgotten.

Acknowledgements

I am much indebted to Juan Antonio Samaranch for extensive collaboration in the preparation of this biography of his twelve years, so far, as President of the International Olympic Committee. It is, I think, a mark of the man that he has sought neither to include nor exclude any particular references, entrusting me exclusively with the content, accepting such criticisms as I have seen fit to make. All the opinions expressed are mine and should not in any way be attributed to him other than where they are in direct quotation from him. I am also grateful to the many members of the IOC, the International Federations, the National Olympic Committees, and other members of the Olympic Movement who have generously given me their time for discussion. They include: Henry Adefope, Luciano Barra, Charles Battle, Comte de Beaumont, Anne Beddow, Joseph Blatter, John Boulter, François Carrard, Alain Coupat, Willi Daume, Anita DeFrantz, Lamine Diack, Carlos Ferrer, Jean-Claude Ganga, Raymond Gafner, Anton Geesink, Alex Gilady, Mary Glen Haig, Louis Guirandou-N'Diaye, Kevan Gosper, Joao Havelange, Zhenliang Hé, Robert Helmick, Paul Henderson, Marc Hodler, John Holt, Carl Olaf Homen, Chiharu Igaya, Annie Inchauspé, Fekrou Kidane, Lord Killanin, Un Yong Kim, Ashwini Kumar, Michael Lee, Nada Lekarska, Gert Le Roux, Anselmo Lopez, Lord Luke, Wolf Lyberg, Keba M'Baye, Prince Alexandre de Mérode, Bob Miyakawa, Raoul Mollet, Charles Mukora, Primo Nebiolo, Ichiro Ogimura, Charles Palmer, Dick Palmer, Michael Payne, William Payne, Richard Pound, Mario Vazquez Raña, Leopoldo Rodes, Jacques Rogge, Sonny de Sales, Marta Salsas, Maria Therese Samaranch, Alexandru Siperco, Ivan Slavkov, Vitaly Smirnov, Boris Stankovic, Joe Stutzen, Peter Tallberg, Walter Tröger, Peter Ueberroth, Andres Varela, Michèle Verdier, Jean-Marie Weber, C.K.Wu and Harold Zimman. Françoise Zweifel, the IOC Secretary-General; Gilbert Felli, the sports director; Michael Payne, the marketing director; Alexandra Leclef-Mandl, José Sotelo, Michèle Veillard and Karel Wendl gave willing assistance.

Grateful thanks once more are due to Steve Dobell for attentive editing, Julie Davis for patient supervision and Jane Butterworth for production of the manuscript. *The Times* kindly gave permission for the use of material previously published in their columns. A glossary of acronyms is provided.

David Miller
June 1992

1 Mission

—

There are five universal languages in this world: money, politics, art, sex and sport. The intriguing aspect of the fifth of these is that, increasingly so throughout the past century, it has included elements of the other four. The most universal expression of sport is the Olympic Games. For better or worse, and many would say worse, the Olympic Games over the past thirty years have been inextricably linked with the changing face of global politics and attendant controversies, with man's mounting preoccupation with money. Nor would anyone deny that elements of art and the expression of sexuality, from the extremes of boxing and wrestling to ice dancing, rhythmic gymnastics and springboard diving, are integral aspects of the Games. That abstract, almost ephemeral perception of the Games which until now remains imperishable in the public mind, in combination with the more voyeuristic fascination of a theatrical event with a multitude of unpredictable conclusions, resulted in more than three billion people around the globe watching on their television the last summer Olympic Games in Seoul, South Korea; and probably an even larger audience for the Games about to take place in Barcelona in Spain.

In four years' time, the modern Olympic Games will celebrate a centenary in Atlanta, Georgia, yet throughout an illustrious history it has repeatedly seemed that the titanic structure of the Games had struck, or was about to strike, the iceberg that would bring its demise. Never was this more so than twelve years ago when the Games experienced a second successive boycott, in Moscow, leaving its credibility and its moral security severely damaged. It was at this point that Juan Antonio Samaranch, a Spaniard little known outside the corridors of the Olympic Movement, was elected president of the International Olympic Committee. He has achieved since then a transformation in the prestige and fortunes, in every sense, of the Olympic Games that is truly remarkable. In a recent Spontaneous Awareness survey conducted on behalf of the interested sponsors of international events, the Olympic Games carried twice the impact of the World Cup in football, the second-ranked event, with a recognition factor of 71 per cent. Its global impact was three times greater than that of the Wimbledon Tennis Championships, in third place, and four times that of the Formula One Motor Racing Grand Prix, in fourth. It rated six times higher than the Tour de France and the American Super Bowl and World Series of baseball, ten times higher than the Americas Cup and Davis Cup.

The man who has ridden the hurricanes of the sporting world with such dexterity was born on 17 July 1920 in Barcelona, studied at the local Institute of Business, took only a cursory interest in the family textile company and, by the time he was appointed to the Spanish Olympic Committee in 1954, was wholly dedicated to a career in sport. Moving stealthily, shrewdly and almost anonymously through the ranks of administration, with an eye for detail that left his friends and contemporaries in awe, he was appointed to the International Olympic Committee in 1966. He became a chief of protocol, was appointed a vice-president in 1974 and, adroitly gaining appointment as Spanish Ambassador to the Soviet Union in 1977, based in Moscow, was perfectly placed to conduct a camouflaged campaign for election as IOC President at the commencement of the Games in Moscow in 1980.

He became only the seventh president since Demetrius Vikelas of Greece (1894–96), who was succeeded by Baron Pierre de Coubertin, the French founder (1896–1925), Henri de Baillet Latour of Belgium (1925–1942), Sigrid Edstrom of Sweden (1946–1952), Avery Brundage of the United States (1952–1972), and Lord Killanin, benign leader from Ireland (1972–1980). He would bring to the presidency a guiding hand even more distinctive than that of de Coubertin, whose immortal phrase should touch the soul of any competitor who goes to the starting line at an Olympic Games, whether or not he or she fulfils that principle: 'The important thing in the Olympic Games is not winning but taking part.' In a relentless pursuit of that principle, Samaranch would in twelve years travel three million kilometres, or nearly two million miles.

'Samaranch has made a revolution, though without the support of the IOC he wouldn't have been able to finish his work,' Mario Vazquez Raña, the Mexican president of the Association of National Olympic Committees (ANOC), says. 'There are still many IOC members whose attitudes are the same as were de Coubertin's, and if he returned today, he would immediately die again. Yet we have to think within a new world, for de Coubertin was a hundred years ago. This is the *perestroika* of Samaranch, but it is a tortuous path.' Samaranch himself is under no illusion about the fragility of the organization that he leads, never mind the prestige that he has built around it. The irony is that, though the IOC may technically own the Olympic Games, on the day that any Games begins the events depend on the International Federations (IFs), who administer the individual sports, and upon the National Olympic Committees (NOCs), who provide the competitors. The dispensable body, arguably, is the IOC itself. 'The IOC is in theory very weak,' Samaranch says. 'We are only a part of the Olympic movement. That is why it is essential to achieve a unity of the three arms of the movement: the IOC, the Federations and the NOCs.'

Few doubt the need for the transformation that Samaranch undertook and has achieved. Robert Helmick was President of the United

States Olympic Committee, and a member of the 11-strong IOC executive board, until financial indiscretions involving conflict of interest forced his resignation from both USOC and the IOC in the autumn of 1991 (related in detail in Chapter 13). Yet Helmick, thirty years in the Olympic Movement, reflected a common view during discussions we had at the '91 Pan American Games, when his resignations were yet unforeseen. 'There was a need to break the classic old aura, the traditional European thinking, of which Brundage, though American, was very much a part,' Helmick says. 'Until Samaranch, the executive board membership was predominantly wedded to that point of view. While the world changed, sport hadn't. Now there is a different balance between the three arms of the movement, and the organizing committees (at each city staging the Games) are more influential, shaping the world perception of sport. The Games of Munich, Montreal and Moscow were, on balance, negative. Those of Los Angeles and Seoul were positive, they helped an upturn of the IOC's direction. The Federations and NOCs were no longer subjugated, yet there is no question that the global appearance and feel of sport is set by the IOC more than by any other international body.'

What kind of man is this quiet Catalonian revolutionary who, in the words of Richard Pound of Canada, one of the IOC's foremost thinkers, has shifted the IOC from the typical, kitchen-table amateur sports administration of Brundage thirty years ago to the high-tech boardroom of today? 'In twenty years,' Pound says, 'we moved from an old-fashioned authoritarian to Merlin the Magician.' The initial perception of Samaranch within sport, in the opinion of Alain Coupat, his former *chef de bureau*, who is now with the volleyball federation, was of a man of weakness. 'In fact, he was a seeker of compromise,' Coupat says, 'an opener of mountain passes, wishing always to keep as many options available as possible. He had strong opinions on what the Olympic movement should and should not be, and this attitude has tended to put him in difficult positions in the last few years.'

For a man of immense will and unceasing energy, Samaranch remains inscrutable to the outside world, to all, in fact, but his closest colleagues and friends. Any emotion is invisible. 'I have never, ever, seen him angry, never have a sudden change of mood,' Annie Inchauspé, one of his two personal secretaries at the IOC headquarters in Lausanne, observes. 'Sometimes tired, occasionally upset, but never short. At first, I thought he was very shy, he didn't talk much, but then I saw he was a very straightforward man, easy to work with. Once he trusts you, he lets you get on, to the point of depending on you in every detail of his ceaseless programme of meetings and travelling. He hardly ever rejects an invitation or a request for an appointment, saying, "My time is their time". His only real dislike is formal dinners. He devotes fifty minutes every morning to exercises, reducing that to half an hour only if he has an early flight, his attitude being that the more he travels the more important is the exercise. Even for a 24-hour trip he takes his skipping rope and door-frame elastic stretcher. He will sacrifice his time right round the calendar, except for Christmas with his family in Spain, and skiing in the new year in order to give a break to his two security guards.' So highly does the Spanish government regard his position and his work that in a country plagued by terrorists, he is given 24-hour protection from the moment he steps off a plane at Barcelona, or Madrid.

John Boulter, a former British Olympic athlete based in France, who has worked around the world on international relations for the Adidas sport and leisure-wear company, reflects that Samaranch has noticeably attempted to surround himself with good people, and has unfailingly gone to the assistance of those in trouble; either in sickness, or in political difficulty within their country from time to time, such as Mohamed Mzali of Tunisia, General Ahmed Gadir of Sudan and Ivan Slavkov of Bulgaria. When Louis Guirandou-N'Diaye, IOC member and head of diplomatic training for ambassadors of the Ivory Coast, was poisoned by agents unknown and seriously ill in hospital in Paris, Samaranch was intimately involved in supervising his convalescence.

'When Samaranch arrived as President, he opened all the windows,' Guirandou-N'Diaye, who is now IOC chief of protocol, says. 'He *listened*. He may have his own ideas, but was always ready to hear anyone who had even a small stone to give to the building of the house. He believed in what he was doing, and was committed, yet he knew, as the French say, that the best general cannot win without his troops. He produced Olympism with a human face, now it is something we can all touch. When I was in hospital in Paris, he had me transferred to Lausanne, and visited me every day. Not just your bunch of flowers.'

The impersonal mask conceals emotions. The only time his staff have observed him shaken was when, at a reception in Stockholm in August 1990, the Queen of Sweden asked him if he had heard of the death, on the first night of the invasion of Kuwait, of Sheikh Fahad, brother of the ruler of Kuwait and a widely respected senior official of both the IOC and of FIFA, the international football federation. For a moment, Samaranch stood open-mouthed with shock, literally speechless, because he had regarded Fahad as a good ally and a key figure in the turbulent waters of the Olympic Council of Asia. 'He's a very loyal friend,' Leopoldo Rodes, a Barcelona banker who masterminded the city's successful bid for this year's Games, says. 'He doesn't look that way, and while he can appear abrupt, almost rude at times, he is very sensitive. He has, too, an extraordinary memory, and will recall the details of conversations months or even years later.' At his large but discreet apartment just off the broad Avenida Diagonal in Barcelona, the staff – chauffeur, secretary, housekeeper – have far more affection for him, according to his wife, than for her, never mind the perception of him being a cold man.

François Carrard is a prominent Swiss lawyer, or Maître, co-opted from his profitable practice by Samaranch since three years ago, and is Director-General of the IOC. 'He is more complex than I thought,' Carrard says. 'On one occasion he said to me, "Look at that man, he's small, like me. Beware".' Samaranch does indeed epitomize the ambitious drive of the small man, especially the small Hispanic man, with the Hispanic man's sense of superiority over woman. This is a quality that was to play a critical part in one of the key phases of the twelve-year revolution, the deposing in 1985 of the then all-powerful Director, Monique Berlioux (the detail of which I shall come to in the next chapter). The range of achievements has been comprehensive and profound:

- The loosening of the eligibility code, Rule 26 of the Olympic Charter, thereby to admit professionals and counter-balance the dangerously over-weighing superiority of totalitarian state-sponsored amateurs now outdated by the demise of the USSR.
- The spectacular, and controversial, development of commercialization and marketing in order to place the IOC, and the Olympic Movement, on a secure base.
- The broadening of the election to IOC membership so as to include more athletes, more presidents of International Federations and National Olympic Committees (another controversy) and, for the first time, belatedly, seven women members.
- The formation, at the Congress in Baden-Baden in his second year, of the Commission for the Olympic Movement, replacing and bringing directly under the IOC umbrella the former Tri partite Commission that embraced the three Olympic arms, the new Commission having no fewer than 31 members.
- The stabilization within sport of east-west, communist-capitalist relations in the run-up to the Seoul Games that was to have a domino effect on world affairs.
- The agreement, in January 1992, in Consultation with Boris Yeltsin, on a combined team for the Games of 1992 from the newly independent states, thereby stabilising the Games.
- A campaign, at first tardy, to come to grips with the menace of drugs, culminating in the suspension of Ben Johnson in 1988.
- An innovative approach to the IOC's twenty-year-old cancer involving South Africa, that not only achieved the reinstatement of that blighted country but would influence political thinking and commercial/social action.

- The completion of Killanin's unfulfilled solution to the joint IOC membership of China and Taiwan.
- The firm establishment of continental Olympic Associations.
- First-hand acquaintance with National Olympic Committees by tireless journeying to visit, up to now, all but a few of the 172 member countries.
- The creation through donations of a $35 million Olympic Museum in Lausanne on the shore of Lake Geneva.
- The acceptance by Swiss authorities of IOC territory at Vidy as having international, independent, untaxed status.
- Last, but not least, a transformation in administration at Lausanne, taking residence as the first full-time president, an action which inevitably led to conflict with and the demise of Berlioux.

'The evolution was fascinating,' Coupat recalls, 'the way he wove his spider's web: everywhere, with everybody. He had this beguiling way of letting people talk and not speaking himself, careful to draw every opinion. He was a fantastic manoeuvrer, and at the same time he was establishing an information network. He has a sense of history, of what might be important to the future.'

The manoeuvring was indeed elaborate, though it typified the man. A Spanish colleague claims, extravagantly but believably, that Samaranch had carried an ambition to be President almost from the age of 18; and as Boulter has observed, while offending few, Samaranch has been willing to sup with the devil in the pursuit of information or ulterior objectives. He has contrived, with a touch so deft that people tend not to notice it happening, to combine expediency with honesty and loyalty. 'He wants his collaborators to be in the front line, where a self-promoter would want to do it all himself,' Keba M'Baye of Senegal, the recently retired judge from the International Court of Justice at The Hague, says. 'His has been the classic formula,' Peter Tallberg, president of the International Yacht Racing Union and one of Finland's two IOC members, observes: 'The pursuit of unity by the dividing of rival forces.'

There has been no tedious, seemingly meaningless seminar or conference through which Samaranch would not sit, no posturing gathering of political opportunists that he would not endure, in the pursuit of winning allegiance to the Games' movement. As recently as 1988, he was attending the 'Meeting of Nuclear Weapon-Free Zones', in what was then still East Berlin, as part of his determined campaign to ensure that the eastern European countries would participate in South Korea, never mind the absence of political and diplomatic relations. Though knowing that there existed widespread criticism, especially within the Anglo-Saxon world, of an alleged Latin-Spanish mafia taking control of the key positions in worldwide sport – Havelange (Brazil) in football, Nebiolo (Italy) in athletics, Acosta (Mexico) in volleyball, Vazquez Raña (Mexico) president of the Association of National Olympic Committees (ANOC), Suleiman (Mexico) with the World Boxing Council – Samaranch has always been ready to barter influence in the furtherance of his own objectives.

While doing so, he managed at the same time to maintain an appearance of neutrality. 'One of my first intentions when I took office was not to vote: on elections for the executive board, on host city nominations, on any issue at a Session,' Samaranch says. 'I try to be the Speaker of the House. I say very little at Sessions, where the main speakers are the chairmen of Commissions. Then there are questions, with answers mainly from the chairmen. Then I ask for a decision from the Session. Were I to vote, then there can be seen to be a winner and loser, and I am seen to be one or the other. Brundage, at a vote on skiing, and Killanin, on a proposal regarding China and Taiwan, were both defeated. As far as I can remember, neither I nor the executive board have been defeated on a vote.'

With a sixth sense for the mood of the membership, Samaranch has a number of times withdrawn proposals that he estimated were at risk of defeat. 'He's one of the best chairmen I have ever experienced,' Kevan Gosper, a vice-president from Australia and potential successor, says. 'He absorbs issues and draws conclusions quickly, keeps everyone on-side, yet is very serious. I've not missed an executive board meeting in five years, few of us have. We attend *because* of him, because he gets value from the meeting, yet sometimes it's a seven-day turn-around: a three-day meeting and seventy hours travelling there and back. There's nothing attractive about that. The motivation is the discipline and control that he exercises.'

Part of Samaranch's skill and discipline is that in the two hours, say, between breakfast and a conference starting at 10.30, he regularly arranges no fewer than eight appointments for officials wishing to speak to him personally; and in their allotted fifteen minutes none will feel that their time was wasted, that their request went unheard or that they were hastily dismissed. The man's own patience is extreme. He has spent hours with dictionaries improving his French and English, and will always talk in the other person's mother tongue even where they are bilingual in Spanish. Though he may spend much of his life travelling first class, riding in limousines and meeting heads of state, he is wholly without self-importance off-stage. On routine days at the office in Lausanne, he takes a light lunch in the staff canteen. At last year's Session in Birmingham, he was halted by security men on the bridge between the hotel and conference centre, having left behind his accreditation on the way to the opening ceremony by the Queen. His aides were on the point of vigorous protest when Samaranch objected. 'The man's doing his job,' he observed.

Yet if the mask hides emotion, it also obscures the immense sense of fulfilment that he has. One story reveals the contrast between altruism and vanity. Manfred Ewald, for many years the head of East Germany's triumphant sports machine, commented to Samaranch: 'It doesn't matter who has the power, as long as I have the glory.' To which Samaranch responded: 'The power *is* the glory.' There are not many who begrudge him either. Pound, an Olympic freestyle swimming finalist in 1960, who was elected two years before Samaranch became President, says: 'I had my doubts before he was picked, yet what he has done has been incomparable.'

In 1955, at the age of 35, Samaranch married Maria Theresa Salkisachs-Rowe, partially descended from a family from Cornwall in south-west Britain, known to her friends as Bibis: a sunny and elegant woman with an equanimity as unshakeable as her husband's. 'I had little interest in sport, absolutely not!' she says. 'But sport was part of his personality, and he was involved seven days a week, though at that time he used to maintain his position in the family business. I followed him then exactly as I do now, it was never a problem. The first time we ever went out was to a gymnastics competition. Soon we were going out regularly, but often it was to hockey or some other sport. He started to tell me about the IOC, which to me sounded so impressive. Within a month I knew *everything*! A year after Juan Antonio was elected, he was appointed Delegate for Sports by Franco. Maybe he dreamed about being president, but it's so difficult to get into the IOC, he was just happy to learn. He stood for the executive board in 1968, and missed. I realized he wanted the presidency, though he always said timing was everything. He'd been chief of protocol, and six months or so before the election I began to feel he could be elected, though I wasn't sure. Marc Hodler of Switzerland [president of the International Ski Federation] another candidate, was very down to earth, a stable, practical man. Being in Moscow did help, yet I think it would have happened anyway.

'Is he cold? That's the way he seems outwardly, it's his nature, his brother Paco is completely different. When Juan Antonio wants something, he follows it relentlessly, it receives all his concentration, he lists all the people who can help him, gaining ground a little every day. People have always trusted him because he gives others their opportunity, he delegates and doesn't take the credit for what they do. His objective was to make the IOC strong and respected, important. His greatest satisfaction was the participation of everyone in Seoul. In thirty-five years of the Olympic Games there has always been something that was going to prove the end of the Games: '72, '76, '80, '84, '88. I don't believe in disasters any more.

'I think Juan Antonio's health is good. He travels too much, though in a comfortable way, with secretaries taking care of so much detail. He's so preoccupied with one thing or another, it's unusual to find him happy, yet he's not an *un*happy man, merely always having something on his mind. I don't think the family suffered, because he would always find time for the children, Mo and Juanito. When he's not with me, he rings me two or three times a day: very brief, half a minute, unless I shout, "wait, wait, I have something to tell you!" He was very low when the eastern European countries pulled out of the LA Games. I'm not involved to the extent of him saying, "What would you do?", though I do give my opinion. Sometimes this has influence. He doesn't react, but a month or so later he may say, "My wife said so and so."

'Do I get weary of the life, attending functions and events all over the world? If I was not married to Juan Antonio, it would be a low-key and completely different existence, a quiet time going to the theatre, visiting my brother. Yet it's been wonderful. I need to be pushed, and I'm happy to have been. Being in the public eye is my job with him, and fortunately I'm happy any place. I enjoy reading, photography, fashion-design. It's a pity I never studied, so my work is never used! I don't know whether Juan Antonio will carry on [seek re-election in 1993]. He hasn't said he would like to be there for the centenary. His primary ambition now is the museum. That's his fixation.'

Bibis's weariness of crisis is a common enough complaint. The syndrome had effectively forced the termination of Killanin's presidency at the end of the statutory first eight years. After the terrorist experience of Munich, when he was president-elect, the African boycott of Montreal and the American-led boycott against the Soviet invasion of Afghanistan in 1980, Killanin, the mild-mannered journalist and company director from Dublin, had had enough. Indeed, Killanin had exceeded the prediction of Brundage, who, when he handed over in Munich, had said that the movement would not survive another two Olympic Games. Yet the pressures of office probably contributed to Killanin suffering a mild heart attack; so that although he transparently enjoyed, in his quiet way, the vanities that go with high office, the range of tempestuous controversies and the demands they placed upon the IOC President had become too severe for him to consider re-election. He had, however, provided the bridge between the old and the new.

History should be grateful to Killanin, reflects Coupat, who enjoyed an inner view of the IOC's workings. 'He was the key element in the evolution from this totally closed organization under Brundage to the open regime of Samaranch. He guided the thinking that made the change possible. With his mild manner, it was masterfully done. He *was* indecisive, in the sense of not having the will to make decisions, yet it seemed he did not want to preclude his successor's options in any way because of what he did.' Killanin had been elected President in preference to Comte Jean de Beaumont of France, who had opposed Brundage's re-election in 1968, and failed. It is Killanin's opinion that only Brundage's suspicion of trouble lying ahead in Montreal – on financial grounds – dissuaded him from standing for re-election a fourth time in 1972. As Killanin has said, Brundage was paternalistic, opposed to all public discussion of IOC affairs, opposed to close links with the Federations and NOCs. His rank out-dated dogmatism might well have seen him defeated had he stood again in 1972.

It was thought that de Beaumont, from ancient aristocratic lineage and with all the wealth of a banking family, had a distinct advantage over Killanin, at a time when IOC members were still paying all their own expenses. Brundage boasted the presidency cost him (converted to today's terms) half a million dollars a year. Killanin, strangely, drew more votes than de Beaumont by telling the members that he would only be able to accept office on condition that his expenses were paid, thereby establishing an important precedent: that the presidency was not the preserve of rich men.

If Killanin's election was in a sense close, dependent on a change in principle, that of Samaranch also hung by a thread a mere two months beforehand. He had to leave his Ambassador's residence in the Soviet capital to return to Spain for the crucial meeting of his National Olympic Committee, and their decision on whether or not to accept their government's advice to join the boycott. Had the advice been accepted, Samaranch knew that his ambition would have dissolved and that he might even have had to resign from the IOC itself. The NOC voted by 20 to 13 to go to Moscow, and Samaranch could return to his diplomatic post, confident in the knowledge that his residence behind the Iron Curtain during the previous three years had provided him with an unparalleled advantage in gaining the support of the eastern Europeans. 'In Moscow, he was "*our* Ivan Antonovic" to many Russians and their communist allies,' Alexandru Siperco, the veteran Romanian member, recalls. 'He had the categoric sympathy of the Soviet Union because of his extreme diplomacy. Yet before his election to the executive board and a vice-presidency, he had been a representative from the regime of Franco, with a serious question mark against him. He was an excellent ambassador, and had huge support from Bibis. *She* learned Russian as well as he, and they developed very intimate relations both inside and outside sport, which created such a favourable impression for the election.' Vitaly Smirnov, one of the then USSR's two IOC members and a key figure in the organizing committee of the Moscow Games, recalls that even in a totalitarian country, where sport meant so much, Samaranch never emphasized that he was from the Olympic family.

If he showed tact and subtlety then, there have been characteristics and incidents during his presidency which, inevitably, have drawn criticism. His public-relations compliments for events that are transparently inefficient can look particularly silly: such as his repeated statement that the Calgary Winter Olympic Games of 1988 were 'the best ever', when they had been littered with blatant errors of planning, construction, and administration; and his praise of an opening ceremony at the 1991 World Championships of the International Amateur Athletic Federation which had been seriously marred by electronic failures and long intervals devoid of action. He has, by the catholicity of his public and private behaviour, been able to rise above any criticism of his involvement in administration during Franco's time. The most obvious accusation against him as President, which only history will be able to judge, is the rushed decision in 1986 to separate, from 1994 onwards, the Summer and Winter Games into alternate even years. The objective was twofold: to increase revenue by freeing the call on sponsors from a single year, and to expand the global 'Olympic consciousness'. It is already apparent that the gain in income is backfiring, by shrinking the commercial market for individual world championships and thereby creating hostility.

He has had a way of dissolving problems by embracing them. Both Killanin and he have come under pressure from the United Nations Education, Science and Cultural Organization (UNESCO) for its involvement in the IOC. This has arisen because of the growing commercial success of the Olympic Games and UNESCO's consequent envy – 50 per cent of UNESCO's budget is said to be administration – and the fact that communist influence (now disintegrating) wished to convert the IOC from a private club into a 'democratic body' of one-country-one-vote. Samaranch in fact signed an agreement which effectively drew UNESCO's teeth. He was less successful in several unilateral moves to promote individuals, being obliged to withdraw in the face of criticism: in 1984 the attempt to have Vazquez Raña and Primo Nebiolo made *ex officio* IOC members – although Vazquez Raña was constitutionally elected a Mexican member in 1991, amid controversy – and in 1988 to extend an *ex gratia* invitation to Sebastian Coe to compete in Seoul when the double Olympic champion was not selected by the British Athletic Board. Such moments recall the statement he made soon after succeeding Killanin: 'One thing I have learned from an accumulation of experience is that every time I take a decision without thinking it through properly, it always turns out to be wrong.'

Yet there are not many people in the world for whom the President of the United States would uncomplainingly be kept waiting on the other end of a telephone. When George Bush placed a call from the White House to Salt Lake City on a Sunday morning, on the occasion of

Samaranch visiting the US candidate for the Winter Games in 1998, Bush was told that Samaranch was in church: would he like to call back in five minutes? No, Bush said, he'd hold on, because he didn't want to miss him. The Americans have come to admire Samaranch for his objectivity as much for his commercial instincts, none more so than Peter Ueberroth, president of the Organizing Committee for the Los Angeles Games. There were many disagreements as well as sympathies between two men of wilful personality, Ueberroth being spoken of as a potential US presidential candidate. He says of the other man:

'Samaranch has statesmanship. He is a consummate politician, who knows how to mix the carrot and the stick, and measures the two very well, while being unemotional about it. He's highly disciplined. He ought to receive at some time the Nobel Peace Prize, because sport has played a big role in the international dialogue. He's pragmatic, able to be flexible from a firm position. On drugs, for example, he knows some people in the Olympic Movement always cheat on doping, he fights to clean it up, but recognizes he can't stop all countries from participating. If he has a fault, I think it is that he doesn't really trust anyone. Either people agree with him all the time, and he suspects them because they are weak: or they disagree, and then he thinks they're contrary. During the preparations for LA, I'd not *obey* on this or that, because we had to stage the Games in a private fashion. It was a bit like London in 1948 – little money, using existing facilities, lots of volunteers. I hope he stays on and takes the IOC through their hundredth anniversary. It would be difficult to find someone the same before 2000.'

Luciano Barra, an Italian lawyer who is a member of the European Athletics Association, points to the oddity of Samaranch being so unlike many Latins. 'He is both President and chief executive of the company, so to speak, without being paid,' Barra says. 'He has the capacity to be President and remain democratic, and to be chief executive and know when to act. When he has a project, he does not promote it himself, but passes it to the relevant Commission, so that it is debated by members, sieved, and surfaces back to the executive board to be passed to the Session for a decision. As President, he could have abused his power, yet he does not behave as a Latin. Just look at the agenda for IOC Sessions: two days of listening to Commissions, to organizing committees – *that* is not the style of a Latin, that is why it is difficult to criticize him. The only thing outside the pattern was the change in cycle of the Winter Games, there wasn't enough consultation.'

Samaranch is proud of the contribution that the Commissions now make to the IOC's global efficiency. 'They really are working,' he says, 'creating the decisions. In the government of the IOC, the Session is the parliament, the executive board is the cabinet and the Commissions are special committees. You cannot govern the IOC with one Session a year.

Football and other sports hold them only every two years. We were able, for example, to hasten the solution to the South African situation by giving the executive board, at Birmingham in 1991, the power to decide, the same principle that had been adopted regarding the negotiations for North Korea between 1985 and 1988.'

Ashwini Kumar, an IOC member from New Delhi who for many years headed India's border security and advises Olympic organizing committees on this vital issue, particularly admires Samaranch for the way he confronts difficulties. 'If trouble is there, he brings it into the open,' Kumar says. 'In recognizing the importance of the Federations and the NOCs, and placing them equal with or even above the executive board, he has been far-sighted. Yet there is not a single view of him. There are views and views. How can I see you when I am kissing you? He has changed the Olympic Movement completely. When I was elected in 1973, I liked to believe it was still a select private club. Samaranch has changed the face of the IOC not only to make it dominant, but to be able realistically to face the year 2000. By abolishing sham-amateurism, he brought a new respectability. When Killanin succeeded Brundage, he inherited nothing but problems. He knew something had to be done, but what? The socialist countries were running away with everything that sport had to offer. The genius of Samaranch is that he has kept together the Olympic family and allowed others to feel that they were making decisions for the first time.'

The irony within Kumar's observation recalls the telling comment from Sonny de Sales, president of the Hong Kong Olympic Committee, and chairman of the Commonwealth Games Federation: that the immeasurable contribution of the socialist countries, never mind their motive, has been to bring sport to the *masses*. Consider, for example, the development of rowing in such countries as the Soviet Union and East Germany (that were), Romania and China. 'He has taken the movement towards the next century,' de Sales says. 'Firstly, he brought the IOC to the NOCs, *physically* visiting them. It is so important in international organizations for leaders to be seen, to hear first hand their ideas, to hear their complaints. Secondly, he has known when to identify with emerging forces, the Federations and NOCs. If the Games are to survive, they cannot just rely on glamour but have to adapt to social and economic trends. Samaranch has attempted to rationalize amateurism while retaining the virtues of sport.' Everything Samaranch has done to bring sport closer to the real world, Robert Helmick observes, has stemmed from his decision to move to Lausanne.

Leopoldo Rodes, who, by that strange manner of ungrateful Olympic cities, was rejected by the socialist local government of Barcelona following their election in 1986 as host for 1992, gives an insight into the unusual capacity of this private, almost withdrawn personality to acquire widespread popularity. 'When he was elected in 1966,' Rodes recalls, 'his closest friends said he would become President of the IOC, and this was *fourteen* years before it happened. In Catalonia, he is the most popular person of all. Polls have demonstrated this. I met him the year before he married Bíbis, with whom I'd grown up. I was aware of his ambition from the time I met him. In Spain, there are two distinct eras: Franco and post-Franco. Juan Antonio was never involved in any deep, ideological way. He always made a point of being seen as a sports professional. It was clear he was concerned with Catalan sport, yet it was impossible to work in sport *outside* the government. There were occasional references to his relationship with the Franco regime, but people took no notice. Francisco Fernandez Ordoñez, who was President of the Institute of National Industries in the Franco government, is now Minister of Foreign Affairs in the socialist government!

'In the mid-seventies Juan Antonio felt he was popular enough to become leader of a new political party, *Concordia Catalañia*, to which he gave the name. It was centre-right, half Franco and half younger middle-class. Its targets were the same as those of the UCD national party in Madrid, and it could have become a rival. UCD was worried. Adolpho Suarez, the first democratic Prime Minister after Franco, was the UCD leader, and I'm sure that he was afraid of Samaranch's potential, that he would prefer him with a job as Ambassador in Moscow. Suarez and Samaranch may have arrived at a political agreement, but Juan Antonio is a difficult man and could have demanded many things. Did he ask for, or did he accept, the appointment in Moscow? I suspect he asked! Yet it was his first appointment, he didn't speak English then, and his French was poor.

'Bibis has been the best partner Juan Antonio could have had: kind, honest, socially a good mixer, culturally educated, speaking English, French and German. When he became an IOC member she would have understood everything that was necessary for the climb to the presidency. When I had to contact all the members during the Barcelona bid, it was so apparent the extent to which she was involved. If Juan Antonio said to her, "We have to go to Tokyo in two days", she would go. Dinner for thirty? Okay! Always with a smile. Juan Antonio is not easily kind and warm. He *can* seem cold, with all but his best friends. He had no extended academic education. His dedication to the sporting world is such that he has no other hobby apart from stamp-collecting. He doesn't go to the theatre or cinema. Only two things interest him: politics and sport.

'With banking directorships, he's there as a figurehead. He's chairman of La Caixa, which two years ago merged with a Barcelona savings bank and it's now the largest. With all the knowledge he now has, I'm sure Juan Antonio wonders what he might have done with a university education. His motivation has been that he likes sport and likes power, though not for vanity. Appearing in newspapers does not especially please him. Power is an end in itself, he does not want it as an instrument. His manner is unaltered in twelve years. He has the same dozen friends he had before 1980, he likes to gather at weekends for lunch, go to the golf club before flying back to Lausanne, never seeking the company of dignitaries. He enjoys the simple life and he will go back to that when he retires.' His public life, in the opinion of Carlos Ferrer, a Barcelona banker and his fellow-IOC member, 'has been a masterpiece'.

According to Jean-Claude Ganga, IOC member for Congo and for twenty years leader of the anti-apartheid movement, there might have been no boycott of Montreal had Samaranch been President. 'Not until he arrived was the IOC wholly with us,' Ganga, who has been instrumental in South Africa's readmission last year, says. 'With Brundage, we were fighting all the time. Killanin was better, though I doubt if he was properly informed in 1976.' It epitomizes Samaranch's approach to problems that he should have had Ganga, one of the IOC's most dire opponents, elected as a member in 1986. As Walter Troger, secretary of the German NOC and also an IOC member, observes, Samaranch enlisted anyone who was competent, forcing them into action. Yet Wolf Lyberg, former Swedish NOC secretary and an eminent Olympic historian, reflects: 'You never see in public the picture of a powerful ruler. Samaranch is like a pianist in a hotel lounge, you are aware of him, but he is never intrusive. His diplomacy has been invaluable. He writes and thanks you for anything he receives, a combination of gratitude and persistence. Even when he has an enormous amount to do, he never appears under stress. I've never seen him visibly show regret, except when, in Seoul in 1988, he announced the name of Lillehammer as winner of the vote for the Winter Games in 1994. He was looking at the King of Sweden as he spoke, and I know that he had prepared for five minutes beforehand how to say "Ostersund" [the Swedish city he had expected to win]. The IOC used to be something you only spoke about once every four years. Now it has come alive.'

Samaranch's ascetic manner, seemingly scorning alcohol, smoking, and even food itself, is apt to give the impression of a non-sportsman. Yet after his early activities as a footballer were interrupted temporarily by a severe illness, he took to roller-hockey, at which he became expert, and he has won minor table-tennis tournaments. 'He loves his sport,' Kevan Gosper says, 'and does everything he can to attend events as though he were competing himself.' Leopoldo Rodes goes cross-country skiing with Samaranch and reports that his friend, with whom he started Langlauf ten years ago, is in excellent shape, having both stamina and endurance.

The fundamental principles of the Olympic Movement, stipulated in the Charter, are to promote the development of the physical and moral qualities which are the basis of sport, and to educate young people in a spirit of better understanding. There are many who wonder how these principles are compatible with the ever-increasing commercialism that is seen surrounding the Olympic Games. Samaranch reasons that when people around the world see the Olympic flag or the symbol of the Olympic rings, they think not only of the Olympic Games but of the youth of the world united in peace and sport. 'That is our motto and philosophy, and we are trying to do much more than stage a Games every two years,' he says. One of the shrewdest intellects being brought to bear upon the Olympic scene is that of Dr Jacques Rogge, an orthopaedic surgeon and the newly elected second IOC member from Belgium, an Olympic yachtsman and president of the Association of European Olympic Committees. Having spent part of his adolescence in Spain, and speaking the language – not to mention English, French and his native Flemish – he has a better understanding than many of Spanish psychology. 'There is something in Spain, an institution, the *grandezza*, a special type of nobility originating in the Middle Ages,' Rogge says. 'The King of Spain would appoint people, originally warriors, into the upper levels of the nobility. It carried a profound sense of honour, a high moral code, and these people were endowed with the responsibility of making Spain great. They were the hereditary grandees. Like monks, they were ascetic in their virtues, dedicated; they had "the *grandezza*". Here now is such a man: early to bed, a churchgoer, a moderate eater. He is ambitious, together with a kind of brutality, something similar to the Germans and Prussians. It is difficult to describe, yet you can almost instantly detect who he likes and who he dislikes. On the other hand, he's almost wholly without arrogance. When, in 1991, he was booed by the crowd in Athens at the Mediterranean Games, on account of Athens having been defeated the year before in their bid to stage the centenary Olympic Games, he merely observed, "It would be the same in my country in the same situation." There is about him a sense of destiny. Though shy, he senses he is a missionary.'

A cunning missionary. He uses the judo technique, Louis Guirandou-N'Diaye reflects. When you push, he pulls . . . and you are caught off-balance. It was not long after I talked with Rogge that King Juan Carlos made Samaranch an herditary Marqués.

Royal Decree, as published in the Official Spanish Bulletin, 31 December 1991:

The successful devotion of Juan Antonio Samaranch Torello to the promotion of sport and to an understanding between people in the distinguished public offices he has occupied has culminated in his brilliant achievements as President of the International Olympic Committee, by reason of which, in order to show him my Royal appreciation, I hereby confer upon Juan Antonio Samaranch Torello the title Marqués de Samaranch for himself and his successors, in accordance with the Spanish legislation governing nobility.

The Minister of Justice
Thomas de la Quadra-Salcedo
y Fernandez del Castillo

Juan Carlos R.

This was only the fifteenth time in seventeen years that the King had made such an appointment. As such, it must be the strongest refutation of those who seek to besmirch Samaranch's reputation with reference to his Franco period. As Rodes observes: 'During the time of Franco it was impossible to have any kind of public office or employment without the approval of the regime. It was that or nothing. Many of those prominent in the subsequent democratic era had been ministers or in high office under Franco: Suarez, the first prime minister, Fraga and Ordonez, the present minister of Galicia and the foreign secretary. But Samaranch had no ideological association with Franco, and I doubt if he ever read a political book in his life. What he did for sport in Spain was exceptional, and that would have been impossible without involvement with the government. He is the most popular of figures in Catalonia, and that is because he has always been pragmatic, and not a serious politician.'

Whatever the praise, whatever the criticism, Samaranch keeps his feet on the ground. 'I do not seek power for myself, only for the Olympic Movement' he says. 'Because the president of the IOC has power, the resentment and criticism are inevitable. I accept that. I try to do the best job I can, and the Olympic Movement must judge that. Of my position in Spain, I leave that to the judgement of the people of Spain. Everything about me is known. There are no secrets.'

2 Crocodiles

—

'I was depressed after the election. I felt so alone, felt that I couldn't cope with all the demands of the job, with the sizeable problems that I knew were there and had to be handled. It was a feeling that lasted maybe two weeks, during which it even crossed my mind how I might *withdraw*.' This is an unusually frank admission of uncertainty from someone who had just achieved the first phase of his life's ambition. Samaranch briefly felt overwhelmed by the realization of what lay ahead, never mind that the election had been so emphatically in his favour, with a clear majority over three rivals in the first round.

The other candidates were James Worrall of Canada, Willi Daume of West Germany and Marc Hodler of Switzerland. All had their support. Worrall, a big, genial man, carried the traditional backing of the Anglo-Saxon vote, though following the 20 autocratic years of Brundage, and what were perhaps unfairly seen as the indecisive years of Killanin, the position of the WASPS (white Anglo-Saxon Protestants) within the IOC had somewhat diminished. Daume, so instrumental in the technical success of the Olympic Games in Munich eight years before, had also been at the forefront of policy-activity with his thankless task of attempting to formulate a rational definition of amateurism under the eligibility code. Hodler, president of the International Ski Federation, and a Swiss lawyer of solid reliability, common sense and pragmatism, was a popular though reluctant runner. 'They're pushing me, but I'm not going to fight for it,' Hodler had said.

The subterranean swell of support for Samaranch had been steadily growing, so much so that Mzali of Tunisia and de Beaumont of France, who were both against the policy of continuing with the Games in Moscow, flew in and out solely for the vote, in loyalty to the 'unknown' Spaniard. After only one round, Samaranch had received 47 votes, Hodler 21, Daume 7 and Worrall 4.

Kumar, Daume and Lord Exeter – formerly Lord Burghley, who had won the 400 metres hurdles at the 1928 Games in Amsterdam, and failed as a vice-president when challenging Brundage's re-election – had tried to persuade Killanin to continue; but as Kumar says, Killanin had become jaundiced and had had enough. Killanin's lasting contribution on the election was his proposal, subsequently adopted, that a change of president should take place the year following the Games, so as not to over-burden the administration during what had become increasingly a year of frenzy. Killanin had also drafted, in July 1980, a letter to the president-elect, offering points of advice arising from his own experience:

perhaps the most relevant of which was an aside, regarding Commissions, that 'the best committees must have an uneven number of members, and *three* is too many'. It was a maxim that appealed to Samaranch in theory but not in practice. The main recommendations made by Killanin were:

> The establishment of a Commission to investigate the background of NOC decisions for non-participation, or boycott; the urgent need for the appointment of a financial director; the abolition of the Juridical Commission, the employment of professional lawyers when required; the continuation of a non-medical chairman of the Medical Commission; the importance of the chairmanship of the Press Commission, with a preference that this should not be left in the hands of the Director (Berlioux); serious review of the Solidarity Commission (allocation of funding to NOCs); the combining of Television and Press Commissions; the essential need for the IOC President to preside over the Tri-partite Commission; the inadvisability of a permanent site for the Olympic Games in Greece; the need for decentralization in the running of the IOC office, and attention to high staff turnover arising from the demanding standards required by the Director; stronger recognition for International Federations.

The final warning was that the new incumbent would find the post at times exceedingly lonely; though it is interesting to note the extent and the swiftness with which Samaranch would act on many of his predecessor's suggestions.

'I was not a rich man, but I was not poor. I had business interests that other people were handling and for which I was only required at a few meetings a year, so I could give 90 per cent of my time or more to the IOC,' Samaranch says. 'My first thought was to have an office in Madrid. Barcelona, my own city, is a fine place but less convenient. The Sports University in Madrid offered me an office, but I soon realized I *had* to live in Lausanne. That was the best decision I ever took. I have had the same bedroom in the Lausanne Palace Hotel since October 1980. I realized it was essential to the IOC to have only one office.' More to the point, Samaranch recognized that he had to be on hand day by day if he was to come to grips with the many problems that endangered the stability of the IOC; and not least that of a Director who behaved as though she were IOC President, and of a prominent president of an International Federation, Thomas Keller in rowing, who was attempting to prove that the IOC was inferior in international importance when compared with the continuous activity of International Federations. Neither of these individuals, nor indeed the rest of the sporting world, as yet appreciated the nature of the man who had just changed his overseas residence from Moscow to Lausanne. He might be small and quiet, but he was no lightweight.

Samaranch's first contact with the IOC had been in the 1940s, when he went to Montreux for a meeting of International Federations, and there met Otto Maier, who held the post then titled 'Chancellor' of the IOC: a posh name for Secretary-General and dogsbody, pursuing the ideology of de Coubertin in a small room over the top of his watch-mender's shop in Lausanne. Maier was helpful in giving Samaranch advice on the organization of the roller-skating world championships, due to take place in Barcelona in 1951. This was a sport originating in Britain, with Portugal, Spain and Italy also becoming strong. At this stage, roller-hockey and field hockey in Spain were a single federation, but subsequently split, Samaranch becoming roller-hockey president. By 1957, he had become vice-president of the Spanish NOC and was simultaneously developing his sports career with local government in Catalonia. He was head of the Spanish delegation for the Olympic Games in both Rome, 1960, and Tokyo, 1964.

'It was during the Games in Tokyo that I began to get to know many IOC members, and of course Brundage,' Samaranch recalls. 'A most important year for me was 1966. Madrid was bidding for the Games of 1972, the plan being for yachting and possibly also rowing and swimming to take place in Barcelona. I was helping Madrid, but there were many problems, and relations with Mayor Arias of Madrid were not good. He was to be the first prime minister after Franco for a few months, but at that time he was not in favour of the Games, and sent only a junior to Rome for the Session where the vote was to be taken. The front-runners were Munich and Madrid, and I think the determining factor was the absence of Arias, although the Germans worked much harder. Arising out of this bid, however, Brundage proposed me as an IOC member. The problem with *that* was that a country has a right to only one member unless it had staged a Games or was an important country. In 1966, therefore, Spain did not qualify, and there were objections to me in principle. Brundage negotiated privately, found that the decision would be close, and in the event got the proposal through without a vote. A few days later I asked why he had pushed so hard for me, and he said, "I think one day you will become President of the IOC." He was friendly with Spain, and often visited me and Bibis with his first wife.

'From then on, my career in the IOC moved quickly. Two years later I ran for the first time for the executive board, and lost, narrowly defeated by van Karnebeek of Holland. Nonetheless, Brundage appointed me head of protocol. Two years later I was elected to the executive board, was vice-president from '74 to '78, then retired under Charter regulations and was re-elected to the board in '79. It had all been relatively easy. There had been an important lesson for me at the Congress in Varna, the Bulgarian resort on the Black Sea, in 1973. [The Olympic Congress takes place intermittently at the discretion of the executive board. Varna was only the tenth, and the first since Berlin in 1930, largely owing to the antagonism of Brundage towards the rest of the Olympic movement and any public discussion about IOC affairs. The next Congress was scheduled for 1981 in Baden Baden, a key event in the formation of Samaranch's objectives, and there is now to be the twelfth in Paris in 1994 to mark the centenary of the formation of the IOC.] Brundage was an exceptional and idealistic man, but was running the IOC in an autocratic fashion. He was having constant confrontations with the Federations, led mainly by Keller, and also with the NOCs. Brundage was resolutely against the formation of an association of NOCs, the idea proposed by Giulio Onesti, of Italy. I realized that what was fundamentally important was not the IOC itself, but the Olympic Movement, the *total* concept. You cannot organize the Games without the partners: the sports and the competitors!

'Brundage was making many mistakes. When he got the IOC to suspend Karl Schranz, the Austrian skier, in 1972 for alleged professionalism, it was abundantly clear that if Schranz was guilty, then so was everyone else. They were all in the same position. This problem of eligibility, and all the others of commercialism and television rights, were just beginning to emerge in Brundage's time, though they had started to run the right way for the IOC, in the main, during the eight years of Killanin. His era was helpful, I have to admit, particularly the withdrawing of the word 'amateur' from the Charter at the Congress in Varna. Between '66 and '72, I was on the Press Commission, which I considered more important than Protocol, the development of linking the press with the IOC. I was not active, but listening and learning a lot, never in the front row. *That* was always the Director. When I was elected President, one IOC member came to me and said that I should get Berlioux elected as a member. I didn't reply.

'My political life in Spain had been developing in parallel with my sporting career. From '56 I was a member of the Municipal of Barcelona, elected to work in sport, and I created a new sports council in the *Deputacion de Barcelona*. With re-election, I was there until '68, and the year before that was elected as representative to the *Delegado Nacional de Desportes* in Madrid. From '73, I was President of the *Deputacion*, for two years under the Franco regime until his death in 1975 and for the first two years of the King's re-accession. Democratic life began in Spain in '75, and many people pushed me to form a new political party in Barcelona, the *Concordia Catalaña*. Adolpho Suarez soon succeeded Arias as leader of the Union Centro Democratico, the powerful governing party. There were discussions between Concordia and the UCD about an amalgamation, but I decided not to pursue this, and it was then that they proposed me as Ambassador in Moscow.

'I had been asked, discreetly, to "take care of the Prince (Juan Carlos)" back in the mid-Sixties. He accompanied me to the Mediterranean Games in Tunis in 1967, and on account of that I had some difficulties when I got home. Yet it was established in '69, at a meeting of the three hundred and fifty members of the Cortez [the ruling council under Franco, of which Samaranch was an elected member] that Juan Carlos would succeed Franco. Each member was asked his opinion individually by Franco, and only twenty or so said no. King Alphonse XIII had left Spain in '31 when the Republic was formed, living in Rome. When Franco won the Civil War in '39, he had stated that "Spain is a Kingdom without a king". Alphonse had died, and the first of his four sons had a bad relation with Franco, who decided to bypass him in favour of Juan Carlos. When this decision was taken, it was agreed that the studies of Juan Carlos, in the early Fifties, must be conducted in Spain at various military academies.

'Spain had evolved under Franco, who in my opinion did three sensible things. To stay out of the Second World War, resisting Hitler, which was not easy. To put the economy in the Sixties under the control of a group of educated, intelligent people, so that the change in Spain was not the problem it has been in eastern Europe; in Spain the working class was living quite well, with democratic employment laws, and we no longer had the rich-and-poor situation prior to the Civil War. And to choose Juan Carlos as his successor. The King represents the unity of Spain, even for the left-wing. The people now running Spain had nothing to do with Franco.

'My association with the King was close, though through sport. My wife had been at his wedding. He came often to Barcelona for the Davis Cup in the days of Manuel Santana and Gisbert.

'Diplomatic relations with the Soviet Union in 1977 had been reopened for the first time since 1917, and it was not easy to find the right person in such a delicate situation. Suarez and the King thought I was the right man, and also that it would be diplomatic to end the two-party situation in Barcelona. I was able to help the Soviet Union in many ways, not only as a bridge between Moscow and the IOC as a vice-president.

'It was a difficult period to be in Moscow, the two countries had been enemies for a very long time, yet by the time I left, relations were very good, with extensive exchanges in trade, cultural and sporting contacts, with Soviet trainers going to Spain. It was a valuable time for me. I knew that the IOC could and should be more important, but that while sport was going one way the Olympics was going another. How could it be right for athletes to take part in world championships but not, under eligibility rules, the Olympic Games? If the position had continued, the IOC would have collapsed. Maybe it was destiny for me to be in the right place at the right time. Until Brundage supported me, I don't think I had any chance of becoming President. I myself felt I was not on the same level as the IOC, as it was then, either socially or in their knowledge of sport. Yet when I arrived, I realized it was not as special as I had supposed. When I was elected President, I sensed the IOC *was* prepared to jump into the future, though I have been working with a team. That is a reality, not just a phrase.'

A highly valued friendship for more than forty years has been that with Andres Varela, a prominent journalist in Barcelona and former field hockey player. Their families had known each other for some while when they were still active players in their respective sports; and it was at a field hockey final in Geneva in 1952, by which time Samaranch was already president of roller-hockey in Spain, that Varela suggested that he ought to quit roller-hockey and concentrate on Olympic sport; that he had the time and money to do so, and had the right kind of personality. Samaranch protested: 'But we are world champions in roller-hockey!' Yes, Varela retorted, but that's a children's game, let's talk more seriously about it when we get home. It was he who persuaded Samaranch to make his shift in focus, recognizing that Samaranch was a leader rather than a player, with an ability to provide both practical knowledge and tactical leadership.

'I already knew a lot about the Olympic Movement,' Varela says, 'and realized that in my position as a journalist I could promote Samaranch's advance. He had, in particular, specific qualities that helped in the transposition from the Franco regime to democracy: exceptional patience, an ability to handle the most disagreeable problems, an elephantine memory. He studies problems close to the ground. He's an honourable, fair man, and from the start he always had good relations with the press. With such qualities he was bound to progress, and they quickly recognized this in the town hall. They saw that, with him, everyone counted. Because of his flexible nature, he could accept the political regime of the time. A significant year for him was 1955, when the second Mediterranean Games were scheduled for Barcelona, and the organizing chairman was sacked two months beforehand. The only possible replacement was Samaranch; and in eight weeks he turned a potential disaster into a success. Many IOC members who were there took note, including a delegate sent by Brundage. There *had* previously been two IOC members for Spain, stemming from de Coubertin's close relationship with Barcelona. In 1954, Baron de Guell, one of the two members who had been elected in 1922, committed suicide. Two years previously, his son-in-law, Pedro Ybarra, had also been elected, but never spoke a word at any IOC meeting. Brundage wanted to restore Spain's second membership. Lord Exeter, who didn't like Spain, opposed the proposal and demanded a secret ballot, the only time such a thing has ever happened [it remains unclear whether the vote was in fact taken]. At the end of the meeting in Rome at the Excelsior Hotel, I went to tell Samaranch of his election at his hotel on the opposite side of the Via Veneto, and it was one of the few times I have seen him emotional.

'There was a lot of jealousy in Spain about his advance in the Seventies, and he was sacked as national delegate for sport at the Ministry of Culture. He resigned, too, as president of the NOC, and for a time went back into business. Never previously had he earned so much! Politicians saw they were losing a good man, and I think that was why he was brought back in the Concordia Catalaña. He soon saw what a dirty game domestic politics is, that you had to forget about normal honesty, and that is why he pressed ahead with his ambition within the IOC. There had been some suggestion that he should oppose Killanin alongside de Beaumont in '72, but he sensed there was still a strong Anglo-Saxon tide that would be behind Killanin, and decided against it [the instinct for avoiding unnecessary defeats]. He realized he had South American, Mediterranean, and North African support, but also recognized that he needed the allegiance of the socialist countries. That was when he saw the best door towards this requirement was as an ambassador, and initially he thought that the best place might be Vienna. In Spain, there are two routes to such diplomatic posts, either through diplomatic school or direct nomination from a political career. When the government consulted the King in '77 concerning Moscow, Samaranch's was the name that emerged.'

If Samaranch was aware that his arrival in Lausanne was immediately going to precipitate difficulties in the relationship with Berlioux, he was shrewd enough to know that this was a battle that must be postponed, that for the first year or so he would need her administrative knowledge and experience to help him establish his own roots within the system. It was more urgent that he quickly establish relationships with IOC members, to make them feel that they were to be an increasingly important part of the framework. And to deal with the personable but threatening presence of the meddlesome Thomas Keller. The hostility of Keller towards the IOC went back to the Congress in Varna, and at the beginning of July, 1980, he had drawn a rebuke from Killanin for having sent, unilaterally, to all members of the Tri-partite Commission a letter suggesting that the themes for the Congress in 1981 should be rearranged on the following basis:

Day 1: The period 1973 to 1981, to be dealt with by the IOC. *Day 2:* Analysis of the Moscow Games, to be considered by the NOCs. *Day*

3: The *future* of the Olympic Games, to be dealt with by the International Federations[!]

Killanin rightly considered this document preposterous, and wrote to Keller reminding him that the Tri-partite Commission was a facet of the IOC, presided over by the President, and that the Congress was an IOC Congress, called by the IOC. Though snubbed, Keller would not be subdued. (He died three years ago.) It is difficult to judge precisely what were his motives; it might have been envy of IOC membership, a common enough phenomenon among those outside, for he had been a nominee for Swiss membership in the late 1960s, at a time when Raymond Gafner was preferred. Keller professed to believe that Federation presidents should remain outside the IOC in furtherance of the interests of their Federations. Killanin recalls: 'I tried hard to define Olympism in conjunction with Keller.' Although a member of the Tri-partite Commission, ostensibly working for harmony within the Olympic movement, Keller devoutly believed in the supremacy of the Federations, and his IOC antagonism mounted in direct proportion to the increasing expenditure by Samaranch through the expansion of Commissions, the involvement of more IOC members, and the payment, for the first time, of all IOC members' expenses. Fundamental to Samaranch's reasoning, apart from practicality, was the fact that if IOC members' expenses were being funded by NOCs or governments, then it was difficult for them to act independently.

Although intending to pull the ground from beneath Keller's feet, Samaranch would do so indirectly. Everything about his first year in office was marked by caution and exploration. One of his first moves was to send, four times a year, a personal signed letter to every member, keeping them up to date with events. 'What worked for him was his charm,' Alexandru Siperco recalls. 'He had had no great sporting achievement, little administrative prominence outside Spain, no one knew his capacity. At his election, he was given the benefit of the doubt, but once elected there was a huge change in his personality. He led the Congress in Baden Baden outstandingly, kept everything in hand, including Keller. Held the three arms of the movement together. That was the moment when he established himself.'

'My first trip from Lausanne as President', says Samaranch, 'was to Monte Carlo for a meeting of GAISF [the General Assembly of International Sports Federations]. Keller invited me. I'd regarded him as a problem way back, but to fight the IOC is not easy. He wanted more influence, was emphatic that the IOC should only deal with the Olympic Games. I told him that the IOC had some responsibility for the whole of sport. Face to face with me, he was very correct and friendly, and I knew well that for all his bluff he was not a particularly strong man, especially as he was not from one of the major Federations. We had the means to destroy him, and did so. Without the television money, the proportion for the Olympic Federations coming from the Games, GAISF was finished. Keller wanted the Summer and Winter Games' finances amalgamated and then shared. I realized the solution was to split the Olympic Federations, summer and winter, into two associations. These were created in '82-'83 and they had the right to deal with the IOC on television income. This left GAISF without power. When Keller realized he had lost the fight, he left GAISF. Subsequently, Dr Un Yong Kim from South Korea was elected, and GAISF grew closer to the IOC again. The Winter Games Federation was the first to be formed, under the chairmanship of Hodler, who was wholly co-operative. He was also wishing to protect winter sports. It was important for the IOC to win this battle.'

In the creation of the Association of Summer Olympic International Federations (ASOIF), Samaranch was aided by the ego of Primo Nebiolo, president of the athletics federation. At this stage Nebiolo was already president of FISU, the international university sports federation, in addition to athletics, and was eager to accept any personal promotion. In return for his election as president of ASOIF, Nebiolo decreed that athletics would forfeit its 20 per cent share of the portion of summer television income awarded to Federations – the remaining 80 per cent had been divided equally among the other Federations – so that now they would all have an equal amount, archery and athletics alike.

If the elevation of Nebiolo would create fresh tensions and problems, these for the moment lay ahead. The first of Samaranch's major controversies had been resolved with barely the sound of gunfire. I well remember going to Zurich to interview Keller, a charming and amiable host, and being gently assailed over luncheon with a profusion of accusations on how Samaranch was about to bankrupt the IOC by his expansion of expenditure. Sadly for him, Keller would not live to witness the time when the IOC would be achieving a gross income for the whole movement over a four-year period of $1.8 billion. As Alex Gilady, an Israeli-Anglo-American who is a senior executive of NBC Television and one of the most perceptive analysts of Olympic affairs, has observed, Samaranch knew that to make a dollar you often have to spend a dollar.

Power-broking is no different within the Olympic movement than from any other sphere of life, as Charles Palmer reflects. Palmer, a proficient judoist, subsequently president of the sport's International Federation and additionally at different times secretary-general of GAISF and chairman of the British Olympic Association, is a man of altruistic motives who, if less unintentionally abrasive, might have become an IOC member for Britain. In the 1970s he was deeply involved in the attempt to establish credibility for both NOCs and Federations, and for some years was hand in glove with Keller, but without the same antagonism towards the IOC.

'I first attended an IOC executive board meeting as president of judo in 1966,' Palmer recalls. 'I was horrified at how supine the Federations were, how well the IOC had it stitched up. The meetings were informal, and Exeter would always get Colonel Rudyard Russell from the International Boxing Federation in the Chair. I was busy trying to get judo into the Olympic Games, and it was infuriating the patronizing way Brundage dealt with IF presidents. It was that that led to the foundation of GAISF, initiated by Coulon, the French president of wrestling, and Keller in 1967. They created the name and the rules. So many Federations were wary of joining a super-Federation that might rise above them. Russell, who subordinated himself to the IOC, attempted to hijack the foundation meetings. At the same time Onesti was similarly irritated by Brundage's attitude towards the NOCs, and was trying to establish their association. Brundage was constantly changing categories of accreditation immediately prior to Games to suit the IOC. It was Coulon and Onesti who revived the idea of the Congress for 1973. One of the contentions for GAISF [which includes many Federations outside the Olympics] was television rights. Eventually the IOC came to their senses. I had often said, "Let's work with them, if there wasn't an IOC we'd have to invent them." Because the IFs were better organized than the NOCs, made better use of their television money, they were the greater threat to the IOC, and this led to the creation of the Tri-partite Commission, which did some useful work: not least in helping Killanin resist the "democratization" interference of UNESCO, and its un-subtle attempt to take over the Olympic Games! The initiator of that move was Marat Gramov, the Soviet Minister for Sport.

'Keller clearly didn't like Samaranch, and I think his attitude did a lot of harm to GAISF. I remember saying to him, if you want to fight, pick the right topic and the right territory. Samaranch had a problem in the divisive creation of ASOIF, choosing between two Italians as leader, the lofty Franco Carraro, a dynamic, young IOC member, and the streetfighter Nebiolo. The formation of the Winter Games body was relatively innocent. I think at that stage Samaranch believed he would be able to co-opt Nebiolo into the IOC. ASOIF, given the option, would probably have elected Keller as president, but he tended to be nervous about elections, and never even contested elections in the rowing federation unless by direct acclaim. My personal disappointment was the failure to gain admission for judo for the Games of '68. The IOC executive board had all agreed except for Exeter, who played a sharp card on the afternoon of the decision by stating that judo could no longer be discussed because the invitations for Mexico, in 1968, had already been posted that morning.'

The Congress at Baden Baden in 1981 had been a typically low-key yet major success for the new President. Reporting in *The Times* of London, Norman Fox had said: 'Samaranch is not a man for the *grand design*. He listens to other people, amalgamates ideas and then moves. Much of what he brought to Baden Baden for ratification seemed no more than tinkering with the words. But he was not only laying the foundation of a strong power base, but ensuring, contrary to popular belief, that the Olympic Movement will thrive for a few more years yet.'

A number of hurdles had been cleared. Not only had the Association of National Olympic Committees (ANOC) been formally recognized, but there had been the establishment of continental groupings of the NOCs, structures through which multiple Games in Africa, Asia and the Caribbean can be recognized as staging posts for the Olympic Games. Samaranch had hastened to accept the suggestion of an NOC inspection of potential Olympic candidate cities, and the report of Dick Palmer of Britain and Don Miller of the United States undoubtedly contributed to the IOC's controversial yet correct selection of Seoul for the Games in 1988. It was a subtle interim compromise on the eligibility issue to accept each sport's own definition. An athletes' Commission was created, with a prominent speech from Sebastian Coe, the 1,500 metres champion of the previous year, and substantial ground was made on the formalization of rights and marketing of the Olympic 'rings' emblem, a factor which within a few years would vastly increase Olympic revenue. By now, international status had been granted for the headquarters at Vidy in Lausanne, removing insecurity about tenancy.

There remained now the matter of a quid pro quo for Vazquez Raña, the president of ANOC and the man who behind the scenes had co-ordinated the election campaign of Samaranch: a Mexican millionaire who owned some seventy newspapers and also, at the time, UPI, the international press agency. 'I thought it was dangerous to have a trade union of NOCs,' Killanin reflects, 'and the possibility that you would get a tail-wagging dog. Samaranch knew that we did not want the tail to wag the dog, but he also recognized that a dog without a tail is not a dog.' In return for what he regarded as Raña's contribution to and importance within the Movement, Samaranch proposed to the executive board, at Delhi in 1983, the *ex officio* introduction of both Raña and Nebiolo into the IOC. The retired Killanin, although no longer an influence, disapproved also of this, for he was against the wearing of multiple hats. 'We never knew,' he recalls, 'who Lord Exeter was: IOC, BOA or IAAF? Nebiolo, of course, had been telling me for some time that he ought to be a member of the IOC.'

Samaranch persisted with his proposal up to the time of the Session immediately prior to the Winter Olympic Games of 1984 in Sarajevo, even though the executive board was cool. However, he came to detect that opposition extended to the floor of the house. Carraro, for example, and de Stefani, the current Italian members, were both rootedly against their compatriot and many were opposed to Raña. While many suspected that Raña and Nebiolo would harbour long-term ambitions for the IOC presidency, the opposition seemed to be not so much to the principle – that the presidents of ANOC and ASOIF should be *ex officio* members – as to the personality of the individuals. Faced with the opposition and the possibility of defeat, Samaranch backed off, even though aware that a frustrated Nebiolo would redouble his efforts to build the newly created world championships of athletics into a rival or even superior attraction to the Games. Frankly, I think that can never be possible, but Samaranch was all for unity. For the moment he would have to bide his time. He had to wait until the Session of 1991 in Birmingham, and the retirement of Dr Eduardo Hay, a Mexican IOC member, for the vacancy which Raña might fill. 'I dropped the proposal in 1984,' Samaranch recalls, 'because it was evident the Session was split, maybe 40 per cent against, and to proceed would not have been a good decision.'

Vazquez Raña, like Nebiolo, is the wearer of multiple hats. Besides being the repeatedly re-elected president of the Mexican Olympic Committee and the president of ANOC, he is also the president of the Pan American Sports Organization (PASO) and the guiding light of several stagings of the financially insecure Pan American Games; most notable of all perhaps the most recent in Havana, Cuba, in 1991, which were an outstanding success, thanks as much to his ceaseless advice as to the work of the Cubans.

The view of Samaranch, not unreasonably, is that in any global organization such as the Olympic Movement now is, it makes sense to have various prominent divisions – such as the athletics federation, ASOIF or ANOC – represented on the executive board. In any multinational business corporation it would be considered absurd if this were not so. Since, in the case of Vazquez Raña, no one could give him a single specific personal reason why he should not be elected, Samaranch was determined to proceed with his name as replacement for Dr Hay in 1991. In the preceding days at the Hyatt Hotel in Birmingham a ground swell of opposition, albeit unarticulated, began to grow, and there was a move to demand a secret ballot which requires the request of a quarter of the membership. When Vazquez Raña's name as candidate was announced, together with those of Dennis Oswald, president of the International Rowing Federation from Switzerland, Thomas Bach, the former West German fencing competitor, and Dr Jacques Rogge, there were requests from the floor to know whether Vazquez Raña had the support of his own country. Amid some confusion, Samaranch eventually called for a show of hands from those opposing Vazquez Raña. Between eight and nine were raised: six of the seven women members, DeFrantz (US), Glen-Haig (GB), Haggman (Finland), Letheren (Canada), Princess Liechtenstein, and The Princess Royal (GB), with Isava-Fonseca (Venezuela) abstaining as a member of the executive board; plus Prince Albert (Monaco), Wilson (New Zealand), and possibly Ramirez Vazquez (Mexico), whose hand was neither up nor down. Samaranch asked for those in favour, and once some twenty hands had gone up, he announced: 'Right. Elected.' It remains a matter of speculation whether or not the remaining fifty-odd members *assumed* Vazquez Raña was elected or deliberately abstained. Vazquez Raña, no doubt more annoyed than he would admit, believes he inadvertently contributed to the controversy at the time.

'I'd probably made a mistake two days before,' he says, 'when I was asked who I thought would win the Winter Games vote for 1998, and replied that I did not have a vote yet, but that if I did I would recognize the human problems of the Games' bidding process, that while Europe had three candidates there were about to be three consecutive Winter, Summer and Winter Games in Europe, that while the US bid might probably be the best, there'd been no Asian Olympic Games for twenty years and that Nagano of Japan deserved it. Some people thought I was intervening on behalf of Nagano. As president of ANOC, I would have regretted if the Games had not gone to Asia. As president of PASO, I was happy that the Olympic Games of '96 were awarded to Atlanta, and yet I campaign every day of my life for Olympism and I cannot believe still that the centenary Games did not go to Athens.

'So, a few people have communicated that they regret my election, and I'm left wondering why. Some friends say those people are jealous, that I might become President of the IOC. I was not seeking a superior function, I'm happy where I am. I couldn't do a better job than Samaranch, I've no ambition to replace him and my support of him is unconditional. This is not demagogy, and if I were to think him wrong on something I would try to convince him. My conflict with the IOC existed only with Berlioux, who resisted the formation of ANOC. I've always done what I can to support the furtherance of the Olympic Movement.'

One of the interesting aspects of this controversy is that the executive board, possibly by a five-four majority, opposed Samaranch's nomination of Vazquez Raña. One who certainly did was Isava-Fonseca, for it was she who co-ordinated the opposition of the other women. Her motivation is believed to be long-standing friction following events during the Pan American Games staged in Caracas, while other senior members of the executive board suggested that the decision would be seen as Samaranch's, that he would lose favour within the IOC, but that they would support him, having made clear their feelings. 'I considered Mario's position within the Olympic Movement was such that I could not refuse to put forward his name,' Samaranch says. 'He is a man of substantial importance.' Helmick, though he may have had a closer relationship than others with Mexico, believes the decision was objectively positive. 'The IOC is better off to include representatives from the powerful countries and organizations within the Movement, even where there may be some conflicts.'

Time will tell whether the inclusion of Vazquez Raña under the IOC roof will bring harmony for Samaranch. Seven years on, there is no doubt that the exclusion of Monique Berlioux, a Director of immense capability and dedication and with a thorough knowledge of the Olympic environment, has on balance been advantageous. Chris Brasher, the former steeplechase gold medallist and correspondent on the *Observer* in London, might describe her removal at the Session in Berlin in 1985 as an assassination, yet in a variety of ways she had helped to dig her own grave. A formidable and cultured woman of forceful character, a former Olympian, she had within the IOC created around herself a feeling of confident security which was ultimately to prove as illusory as that of Margaret Thatcher in Westminster. The two women had similar characteristics, including a belief in their own infallability and virtue, but for Berlioux there was the additional and fundamental disadvantage that she was not an elected member of the IOC but a paid employee. Her power had been accumulated through the absence of successive Presidents in Chicago and Dublin, with only occasional visits paid to Lausanne. Over a period of twenty years, Berlioux not only had her feet effectively under the President's table, but could and did lay her hand upon every doorknob, every appointment, every contract, every single decision that was made. IOC members would address letters to the President and receive a reply from the Director. So all-embracing was her influence that she tended to be dismissive of junior IOC members; so severe was her handling of the administrative staff at Vidy that there was a turnover of more than 25 per cent every year.

The staff will testify to the difficulty of the ambience in the office. She would ignore greetings; a room would fall silent when she opened the door. 'It was like a girls' public school in Britain, with the pupils scared of the headmistress,' one of her assistants recalls. 'If she didn't like you, you were doomed. We, the staff, were not supposed to speak to IOC members.' Another employee recalls that Berlioux boasted to staff that she had been able to control Killanin and that once she got Samaranch elected – unsuspectingly, she supported his campaign – she would control him too. She no doubt had a traditional feeling of French superiority, especially over a small Spaniard. It was to prove the most serious misjudgement she ever made. Yet even after Samaranch's arrival in Lausanne and the all too evident conflict – she with her own private telex, her own private telephone line – she remained reluctant to reduce the impact of her own authority. She refused to believe things could end the way they did, even though Samaranch began to take over from her piece by piece. She had *made* the IOC what it was, having adroitly leapt from the seat of press attaché to that of Director when it became vacant. Killanin had hinted before his election that it might be better to replace her, but had never acquired the authority or confidence to do so. Indeed, he *needed* her. 'Originally, she was in public relations,' Killanin recalls, 'and I had the feeling she was not the best possible Director-General, and indeed she was never actually appointed. She managed to get a double Director's salary out of Brundage, by continuing to handle press relations.' By the time of her forced resignation, she was one of the highest-paid sports administrators in the world, on a salary in today's terms of over £200,000 a year, and with an unexpired contract of three and a half years. 'A brilliant woman, who unfortunately was either at your throat or your feet,' one prominent IOC member said at the time of her dismissal. On the eve of her departure she appeared at a reception wearing round her neck an IOC member's medallion.

It is perhaps sufficient to quote that ultimate of aristocrats, the Grand Duke of Luxembourg: 'A very difficult woman.' Bibis was of the opinion that her husband should have taken the decision immediately on gaining office, but he was aware that, for all the inevitable friction, he would initially need to call upon Berlioux's experience. She resented Samaranch's increasing delegation of responsibility to other members, particularly the development of commercial marketing of the Olympic rings symbol by the International Sport and Leisure Marketing (ISL) company in Lucerne. The tensions between President and Director reached the point where Samaranch occasionally conducted discussions with important visitors, when the weather was fine, in the gardens of the Vidy headquarters, just as in Moscow for security he would often conduct conversations during a walk in the street. His room at the Palace Hotel, number 309, is said regularly to have been checked for bugging devices.

Dissatisfactions with the administration had mounted prior to 1985 with the appointment of Walter Troger as sports director, succeeding the deceased Arpad Csenadi of Hungary. Troger found that his work was being obstructed; he was one of those to whom Samaranch would talk in the gardens. 'I soon found out,' Troger recalls. 'She was efficient and knowledgeable, but she was a dictator. I told her that I accepted her position as Director but that she had to co-operate more with me.' There had been an initial attempt to question her conduct at an executive board meeting in 1983, but Samaranch was reluctant to precipitate a confrontation when he was already deep in negotiations to try to prevent the boycott of Los Angeles. He preferred to deal with one problem at a time, even though Troger was experiencing the same difficulties as Csenadi, Artur Takac and Harry Banks, the previous sports directors, Berlioux believing that all decisions had to be approved by her. It was decided by the board to force the issue in Berlin, and Troger was deputed to raise the matter in the course of normal discussion. IOC staff were asked to leave the room. When Troger and then Richard Pound started to say that they could not accept her interference, Berlioux lost her nerve and said: 'I cannot continue like this.'

Berthold Beitz of West Germany, Keba M'Baye, and Prince Mérode, the Belgian chairman of the Medical Commission, were assigned to arrange the settlement terms for her separation, which included legal protection for the non-disclosure of IOC affairs. This condition is said to have impeded Berlioux's publication of her memoirs. Kumar, who had been a member of the executive board from 1981 and was a vice-president in 1984-5 recalls: 'She would not accept that she was a servant of the IOC. Two years before, in Sarajevo, she was not even listening to Samaranch, and I had said that if a paid employee would not listen to the boss, they must go. But at that time she was defended by Siperco.' Yet even Siperco is of the opinion that she considered herself the second personality of the IOC, 'above the members'. Comte Jean de Beaumont of France, a retired senior member of the IOC, made the sentient observation: 'You couldn't have two crocodiles in the same pond, and Samaranch as the boss didn't want another one behind him. Until he arrived, she was the only man in the IOC.'

When Berlioux moved to Paris in 1985, to work in the office of Mayor Jacques Chirac, she tried to take some of the staff with her, but a number preferred to stay. While Pound, a lawyer, and Carrard were engaged with the legal protection of the IOC, many of the junior staff were aware that there would be a new mood and freedom once the present Director had departed. For example, Michele Verdier was promoted to the post of director of information, with full control of press relations and daily press conferences during Sessions and executive board meetings. Anne Beddow became director of NOC Relations, given extensive responsibility for making National Olympic Committees around the world feel that they were in direct touch with Lausanne. Howard Stupp took charge of the multiplicity of legal affairs, Michael Payne, from ISL Marketing, was appointed director of marketing, and Jacques Belgrand is now director of finance. Berlioux's role as Director was divided between Françoise Zweifel, who as Secretary-General deals with the administrative logistics, while from 1987 François Carrard has been Director-General: effectively the chief executive rôle which Berlioux had assumed for herself but now on the basis of daily reference to an in-house President. When Troger was elected IOC member, Gilbert Felli became sports director. Pursuing the principle of expansion and delegation, Samaranch now had a harmonious team working together in open communication. Jean-François Pahud is Director of Samaranch's pet project, the Olympic Museum, and Anselmo Lopez, a long-time Spanish colleague, continues as director of the Solidarity Fund in a separate office with a staff of four. The revolution had truly taken shape that day in Berlin.

Carrard had originally been retained as counsel by Berlioux when Henry Hsu, the member for Taiwan, had brought legal action over that country's exclusion, and in a four-day hearing, during which the IOC had run into considerable difficulty, the decision was eventually in their favour. The dispute continued until it was settled after Samaranch became President. 'Berlioux was unnecessarily aggressive at times,' Carrard reflects, 'though most of her ideas were sound. Although officially she resigned there were "secrecy of function" clauses to protect aspects of IOC business. Swiss law is brutal in its concept, and simple.' Carrard received the offer to become Director early in 1988, when Samaranch was resolving a ramification of Berlioux's departure. Samaranch's *chef de bureau*, Coupat, a man of considerable perception in Olympic affairs, had to an extent assumed he would be in a position to succeed Berlioux. Indeed he was a cousin of Berlioux's, but his loyalty during the first five years of Samaranch's presidency had been to the President. However, Samaranch had begun to feel that Coupat was orientating the information which was coming into the office, and upon which Samaranch was dependent, to a degree that was disadvantageous. Coupat, who had finely written the majority of Samaranch's important speeches, decided that there was no future for him and departed for the offices of the International Volleyball Federation down the road in Lausanne.

For Samaranch, the post-Berlin time was one of relief as well as development. He no longer felt restrained in the way he had previously. 'Monique Berlioux was hard-working, with an intelligent attitude,' Samaranch reflects, 'but she was not elected, she was appointed, yet day by day, before my arrival, she had been taking decisions on the running of the IOC. When I came to Lausanne as elected President, the collaboration was not easy. I had decided to ask for her resignation in 1983, but Siperco reasoned that she was necessary, that she could be given specific responsibilities. This worked for some months until we returned to the same problems. By then, I didn't want to create controversy immediately before Los Angeles, and yet I knew it was impossible to continue in the same way. By the time of Berlin, Troger was complaining to me many times, and I told him he had to put it before the executive board, though the complaints were not only from him. With Brundage and then Killanin, she really was the boss. The administration, however, is there to follow the decisions of the Session, the executive board and the President. I found in Lausanne I was being *observed* all the time – what I was doing, where I was going. Then, there was a single woman administrating, now there are several – seven new directors, who see themselves as an important part of the organization. It is essential to delegate and to give autonomy. The crisis boiled down to the simple fact that you can have only one leader. Among other things, it had emerged that Berlioux was not the best of negotiators. She had signed a contract for individual sport pictograms for all Olympic sports and for all host city organizing committees in 1976 that it took until 1990 to resolve. In 1987 we had lawyers demanding 67 million Swiss francs for a Swiss company on account of that contract in 1976.'

If male chauvinism might be alleged against the Spanish grandee over the dismissal of a powerful woman, the accusation bears no substance when one considers that, at the first opportunity in 1981, he had supervised the election of the first women members to the IOC after 85 years of male exclusivity. A privileged duo of Pirjo Haggman, the former 400 metre runner for Finland, and Flor Isava-Fonseca of Venezuela, were joined the next year by Mary Glen-Haig, four times an Olympic fencer for Britain. Princess Nora of Liechtenstein was elected in 1984, and in 1986 Anita DeFrantz, who had gained a rowing bronze medal in 1976 with an American eight and had vigorously opposed Jimmy Carter's boycott in 1980, became the first black woman member. Later came the Princess Royal, already president of the Equestrian Federation in succession to her father, the Duke of Edinburgh, and Carol Anne Letheren of Canada.

Killanin claims that the establishment of this important principle of equality was something he had regularly considered but which, in the absence of 'suitable' candidates, he had been reluctant to do, merely for the sake of electing token women. Among those considered by Killanin were Nadia Lekarska of Bulgaria, an elegant woman with a knowledge of the Olympic Movement and of sports equalled by few and attested by her numerous published works. She was the widow of an eminent Olympian, Bruhm Lekarski, a colleague in the 1924 equestrian event of Vladimir Stoychev, later a famous general in the Second World War during the liberation of the Balkans and of Yugoslavia. Lekarski and Stoychev had travelled for ten days by train with their horses from Sofia in order to compete in Paris and it was the existing membership of Stoychev that precluded the election of Madam Lekarska, sadly for all who were familiar with her wisdom and her charm. During the German occupation, with characteristic resourcefulness she supervised, in a tiny cottage in the mountains outside Sofia, the survival of some thirty souls, including children, on little more than the milk from a single collaborating cow and wild vegetation.

'Like none before,' Nadia says, 'Samaranch has enriched the IOC. Money counts today, and by this he has increased the authority of the IOC in many directions. The Solidarity Fund, for example, is useful, though,' – and she pauses thoughtfully – 'I feel it could be used more effectively. The arts are connected to Olympic sport, and that is not something marginal to me: museums and so forth. Samaranch has fought so hard to overcome the Cold War, with positive results. As for professionals, that's another matter. I hope it won't go too far. The election of women was an historic breakthrough. In eight decades no woman had ever been proposed. Had Killanin really wanted to do so? There had been nothing in the Charter that was a bar to women. I hope that the NOCs will follow up. General Stoychev [who died in his nineties three years ago] had not wanted to resign. There had been discussions about Bulgaria having two members, temporarily – if one died, then reverting to one. Samaranch talked about it with me, but it never came to anything. Holding the post is not a matter of personal satisfaction,' – the dignity is immovable – 'but if you have done a job it can be pleasing. I would have liked it not for the honour but for a closer contribution. I did not have ambition, though five times I have been an Olympic attaché at the Games. Normally, the Embassy in the country of the Games provides the attaché. The Bulgarian Olympic Committee has been very advanced.' Madam Lekarska remained until recently a respected member of the Programme Commission.

The failure to embrace Madam Lekarska is all the more regrettable because some of the first wave of women members have made less than a significant contribution. Eighteen months ago Flor Isava-Fonseca became the first woman member of the executive board, but Pirjo Haggman, who precedes her in seniority only by the alphabet, has been disappointingly inactive. The Princess Royal, though president of an International Federation and also of the British Olympic Association, positions which she fulfils with active and interested participation, is to a degree limited in her IOC involvement by her royal position. Although I have been favoured with three lengthy, informative and individualistic interviews with the Princess over the past eight years, it does not help the promotion of British involvement within the IOC that she is not available to media inquiries in the normal way. It will be interesting when Mary Glen-Haig reaches retiring age in 1993 if Sebastian Coe is chosen to succeed her at the relatively youthful age of 37, which would give him the opportunity to progress to high office. There exists in Britain, however, that deadening weight of envy which will lead to protests that he has not first spent twenty years in the administrative service of sport, never mind that he is our most famous Olympian of all time and a former vice-chairman of the Sports Council. There has been no frontline British involvement in the IOC since the death of Lord Exeter. Mary Glen-Haig was recommended by Sir Denis Follows in 1983: Samaranch flew specially to London, going directly to Follows's house, to discuss the matter, and returning home the same day. Lord Luke, when he retired in 1988, somewhat unconstitutionally manoeuvred his immediate replacement by the Princess Royal, foiling Charles Palmer, who until that moment believed that he might be a candidate and was close to tears at the news.Coe, however, will need to subjugate some business interests to sporting affairs to justify election.

It is difficult for the President to propose anyone who is heavily opposed in his or her own country, even though the principle is that the member independently represents the IOC in that country and not vice versa. Isava-Fonseca was indeed opposed by some in Venezuela, who sent their representatives with that purpose to Rome in 1982, but Samaranch persisted on the basis of private information that had been in her favour.

The Princess Royal, during my interviews with her, has given some pertinent views. 'The good news,' she reflected at the end of her first year of membership, 'is that more of the new members are from sport, either as competitors or as administrators. Trying to understand how the IOC works, at the moment it appears to me to be a one-man band. I am sure there are ways of involving members in the decision-making process, but it isn't encouraged as far as I can see. Because I don't have a political axe to grind, when given the opportunity to vote I tend to do so on what is applicable, which doesn't seem to apply to others as far as I can tell. In some respects, the executive system established by Samaranch works well, however. It cuts the time taken to come to decisions, though I get the impression decisions are taken at the Committee or executive stage. But there's not a lot of involvement from the floor. Partly because it was a very unwieldy structure, this [system] has speeded up the process and has done more, but with different people coming in with more background knowledge, the situation will have to loosen up a bit. I don't think I'm the right person to ask [on individual contribution]. Occasionally you may sound like a voice in the wilderness, but sometimes you discover there are more trees out there than you thought.'

Robert Helmick, the former president of the International Swimming Federation, was elected in 1985, and Anita DeFrantz a year later, both of them preferred to Peter Ueberroth, mastermind of Los Angeles, against what was believed to be Samaranch's private preference. There was, of course, substantial support for DeFrantz, a lawyer, from eastern Europe and Third World members. 'I have great hopes and optimism for helping to promote a movement which has been so much of my life,' she says. 'I think I have a feeling for the athletes in a way few of the older members are able to have, and of how sport works in the US. It is important for America to have a coherent voice in the IOC, which perhaps it has not always had in recent years.' There was a period, bizarrely, when the US Olympic Committee voted to exclude its then two IOC members, Roby and Roosevelt, from domestic administration.

DeFrantz's great-grandfather was the son of a French plantation owner in Virginia, whose Alsace origin donated the *tz* to her name. Her grandfather was prominent in the Pat Singleton Movement, which emancipated slaves from Virginia and led them to Kansas City in the mid-nineteenth century. He then moved to Indianapolis and became the executive director of the Black YMCA, while her mother and father have been prominent in the Community Action Against Poverty organization. In 1980, appalled by Carter's expedient ban on the American team, she took her formal protest to court, attempted to sue the government, and lost. Newspaper editorials, which four years later would praise Romania and China for going to Los Angeles, in 1980 condemned her for being unpatriotic.

Peter Ueberroth questions how seriously Samaranch wanted him as an IOC member. 'I think he could get anything he wanted. Could then, and at any time.' A member of the IOC staff, present at an executive board meeting, remembers the view thrown back at Samaranch by other members ... 'he's too commercial, too much of a shark'. The profit that Ueberroth had engineered at the Los Angeles Games rebounded against him. In 1985 there were three unofficial nominations besides Ueberroth, including Helmick and DeFrantz. Julian Roosevelt, then on the executive board, resisted Ueberroth. 'I'm not that disappointed,' Ueberroth says, pursuing a prosperous business career in Newport Beach. 'The reason is that there is very little that has happened in the Olympic Movement since then where I could have made a major difference. In sports they talk about "impact players". I've always tried to make an impact. The crises since '84 are such that I couldn't have been much help. To make impact, you have to be on the executive board, and I don't think IOC protocol would have allowed me to jump over Helmick if I'd been elected in '86 following the death of Roosevelt. Helmick was there already and I don't think I would have been supported. I'm old-fashioned on the amateur/professional status, yet I would have to go along with the group as a member of the board. If you serve, you should serve with loyalty. If not, get off. I was told by the US OC not to hire Anita DeFrantz, as a result of her behaviour over the boycott. I felt she was right, and a great lover of the Olympic Movement, so I immediately went out and hired her. If you read about what an IOC member is supposed to be, Anita exemplifies that.'

Originally, members nominated their own successors, and these nominations were usually accepted, a situation which led to family seats and was open to abuse. It may be that in ten or twenty years' time Samaranch will be accused of having democratized the membership too much. The transformation from the former days, when members tended to be remote aristocratic figures, to the ordinariness of many of today's members, some of whom are promoted professional administrators with sporting experience but lacking in breadth, vision, education and independence, may be seen as having swung the pendulum too far. It was certainly an improvement in 1964 to make it mandatory for members elected thereafter to retire at the age of 72 – later extended to 75 – but the unofficial departure from the requirement that all members must be able to speak either French or English, and the transparent affiliation of some members to government or state directive, are both to be regretted and can only help to weaken the IOC. It is most noticeable that some of the most significant comments at any Session regularly come in the closing speech of the senior member, the Grand Duke of Luxembourg, who, whether heeded or not, is able to put his finger on those issues of morality and principle which in earlier times had always been paramount in the special conduct of the IOC. Finding a balance between ideology and practicality is a task that is probably beyond the powers of even Samaranch.

To the charge that the IOC is becoming too ordinary, never mind that it is electing more ex-athletes and more prominent sports administrators, Samaranch replies: 'What is changing is our society, and we are following that. The IOC *must* change. If we remain as forty or fifty years ago, we will disappear. There are "ordinary" people, certainly, but what we are getting is the aristocracy of sport. Consider the Session at Birmingham last year: Vazquez Raña, president of ANOC and PASO, Thomas Bach, fencing gold medallist, Dennis Oswald, a rowing bronze medallist and federation president, Dr Jacques Rogge, four times Olympic yachtsman and president of European NOCs. These are the people we need. We have had very bad experience of some politicians, in power when elected, then subsequently totally without authority or position, and even in socially unstable positions. But we need people who understand sport, not business people. Society will not accept an IOC with dukes and generals.' This has not prevented Samaranch numbering, among his 54 elections up to 1991, two princes and two princesses along with eight communists, seven women, three Africans and four federation secretary-generals.

Admittedly, some of the members cause the President to shrug in despair at their permanent silence and inactivity, year in, year out, contributing nothing other than to the expenditure budget for travel and hotels. On the other hand, as he observes: 'If they were all active and always talking, life would be impossible!' When asked to comment on the contribution of certain members' during the past twelve years, he merely places thumb and forefinger together, signifying zero. It is for this reason that he welcomes the election of the four mentioned by him above, and also the election to the executive board of Pal Schmitt of Hungary, another gold medallist from fencing. 'Not a communist,' he adds with a glint.

'There are two aspects of Samaranch's policy I admire,' M'Baye says. 'He's made members feel responsible and involved in the progress and development of the organization, and shown the world that the IOC is socially and politically important as a contributor to peace. It is a major achievement. Regarding involvement: when Samaranch was elected, I had been there several years, and felt I wasn't used, that I was wasting my time. I came to Sessions, listened, and went away. So in '80, I wrote a letter of resignation and gave it to a colleague, not going myself to Moscow. Two days before the Session, Guirandou-N'Daiye telephoned me to say he was a candidate for vice-presidency and needed my support. Later I went to Samaranch to congratulate him, and he took me over to one side to say he was relying on me to help change the policy of the IOC, saying there was an important job to do in the role of world peace-making. I was surprised, and went to retrieve my letter of resignation, to keep it as a souvenir! I'm sure he did the same with other members, but he made it seem personal.

'Today, everyone who wants it, has something to do. He's open-minded, meets anyone who wants to see him. He leads, but changes his mind when he feels the majority has another opinion. The executive board is not a tool that he manipulates, and he abandons projects when he finds the board has a different view. For four or five years there has not been a single absentee from four or five meetings a year. That was unthinkable before. We are busy people, but we want to be there because we are not speaking into the wind. The IOC has a more important image, every year there is something important happening: a Games, a Session, a Congress, an election of a host city. The focus of the media has always been drawn to the IOC, and Samaranch has increased both the financial and moral stature. We are living in a world in which if you have no money you have no weight. Now the IOC can help everyone in sport. The President does not want always to be first. Of course he's ambitious, every good man is ambitious, or he is nothing. Yet I can assure anyone that he is not looking for the promotion of Samaranch but of the IOC.'

One or two recent cheap-skate, ill-informed books have sought to condemn Samaranch and the IOC; easy enough targets for the casual observer, with all the trappings of privacy, exclusivity and money. The IOC has many faults, to be sure, but the credentials of its president could not be defgended by a more exemplary figure than the retired Senegalese judge.

3 Moneybags

—

Gross revenue for the Olympic Movement over the four-year period 1989-92 is expected to be a phenomenal $1.84 billion. The residual income going to the IOC itself is a tiny percentage of that. By 1996, the income of the centenary Games in Atlanta *alone* is predicted to reach $1.16 billion, and that figure includes only the organizing committee's *share* of television rights, sponsoring and marketing programmes. While a sense of triumph runs through the IOC at the extent of the financial growth that has been achieved in sixteen years since Montreal, it is important to recall the words of Sir Denis Follows, expressed in 1983 on the publication of the *Howell Inquiry into Sponsorship*: 'It is the ethical content of the Olympics which makes them a thing apart. Without that, and with the new overt commercialism, the Games could become just another fixture in the sporting calendar.'

The concern of Follows should not be ignored, yet the underlying effect is that the greater the commercialism and the publicity surrounding the Games, the greater their perceived importance has become. Samaranch rightly claims that this immense income is providing the IOC, and the Olympic Movement, not so much with power as with independence. Kevan Gosper, vice-president and one his most loyal admirers, says: 'While his diplomacy has been a strength, the down-side is that he is highly pragmatic. I think he was fortunate to have had Ueberroth to set the pattern.' Michael Payne, who became IOC Marketing Director in 1988, says: 'It's agreeable, still, dealing with Samaranch privately, but the diplomacy has gone, on market matters. Now he is a hard, hands-on operator.' By one of those twists of coincidence, the contract for the start of the IOC's global marketing – entitled The Olympic Programme, or TOP – was signed with Horst Dassler, owner-founder of Adidas, and joint-owner with Dentsu, an advertising agency in Japan, of ISL Marketing, on the same day that 39 spectators died in the Heysel Stadium disaster of the European Cup final between Juventus and Liverpool. Berlioux, by all accounts, was furious: firstly because the decision was taken without her approval, and secondly because she claimed that marketing was not the IOC's role, though she signed the contract. In the event, Berlioux would be gone within less than two months.

The change in IOC fortunes had been remarkable. Prior to 1972, the organization was only surviving on money borrowed in advance on the strength of the television contract for Munich. By the time Killanin retired in 1980, the IOC had assets, including property, of some $2 million, though reserves of only $200,000: not much for an operation with a staff of over twenty. The first Games to have been televised were those in Berlin in 1936, with a limited audience, and much the same was true in London, 1948, Helsinki, 1952, and Melbourne, 1956. The first realistic commercial sale of rights was made for the Winter Games at Squaw Valley, in the USA, in 1960, at $50,000, with the Summer Games later that year in Rome earning $394,000, both deals done with the CBS network. One of the problems for the IOC was that, owing to a lack of awareness of potential, too much scope continued to be given in negotiations for television to the Games' organizing committees. It was only with the arrival of Samaranch that this came under control. 'During Killanin's time, the IOC was sailing gently along, marking time,' Lord Luke, a former director of Lloyds Bank International and of Bovril, recalls. A man of dry humour and considerable financial expertise, Lord Luke, who spent many years on the Finance Commission with de Beaumont, retired voluntarily in 1988 at the age of 83, to make way for The Princess Royal. 'The Olympic Movement was moving a bit, but not developing,' Luke says. 'Killanin had a lot of unreasonable problems to distract him: China, South Africa, two boycotts. Maybe it would be harsh to say he did little. When I was elected the year before the Helsinki Games, there were no committees or Commissions, and it was de Beaumont and I who wanted the Finance Commission. We realized this was increasingly necessary with the arrival of television money from 1960. Samaranch has proliferated Commissions in a remarkable way: a big improvement compared with Brundage, who thought he was God, and Killanin, who wasn't awfully good. Samaranch is a great listener. *And* clever in the way he spreads the load. De Beaumont, who was a banker, was very much in charge of the finance committee. I chipped in, wasn't too clever about it,' – typical British upper class self-effacement – 'but we had difficulty with Berlioux, who was very secretive, and people didn't like it, particularly Reggie Alexander of Kenya. We always believed it was Berlioux who got Alexander off the finance committee. I've liked Samaranch because he's so accessible, makes you feel *you're* the one. I know people go on about the IOC still being privileged, but I think you want some people who are not necessarily locked into sport, yet have position that is not political, such as de Beaumont, who was very neutral – people who live with dignity and have no political ambition.'

Zhenliang Hé, though bearing unavoidable political reflections as the member for the Chinese Peoples' Republic, is a man of dignity who, but for that political background, would be a popular candidate as leader of the Olympic Council of Asia. 'We cannot develop sport without financial backing,' Hé says. 'We have to take all possible available finance, though I am a little bit afraid that commercial aspects can dictate events. With all commercial support, you have to enter into agreement on the basis of mutual interests, though it is essential we maintain our autonomy in our own affairs, remembering the interest of competitors.' Hé's caution, notable when coming from a country in which sport is regarded to some extent as a political tool, reflects worldwide concern that Samaranch is riding a tiger that may get out of control.

Olympic marketing is not new. The official programme at Athens in 1896 for the inaugural Games carried advertising, including Kodak, a century later a TOP sponsor. Photographs in the film *Chariots of Fire* imply there was advertising in Paris in 1924 inside the stadium, with posters for Lipton's Tea. The Winter Games that year at St Moritz had 'official suppliers' of Ovomaltine. At Los Angeles in 1932, outdoor venues carried advertising for Texaco and others. Yet the exploitative trend was slow to take root. The $25 million which ABC paid Montreal for television rights did not even cover the cost of the host broadcaster centre. Los Angeles in 1984 had the first organizing committee to develop a structured marketing programme, only because the IOC's contract was not being covered by the city of Los Angeles, and a private committee *had* to meet their costs. The 1984 Games were so successful that they opened the way to future policy for the IOC, instantly seized upon by Samaranch and leading to the contract signed with ISL the following year.

Yet the Los Angeles sponsorship programme had been short-term strategy, ignoring the long-term interests of the Olympic Movement. Sponsors were sold worldwide rights, only to discover they could not use them without individual approval from the NOC in some countries, which had to be bought separately. Frustration led to some sponsors, such as Levi, handing back their rights. Exclusivity was breached, resulting for example in a dispute between Kodak and Fuji. In 1984, the Olympic Games' revenue was almost wholly derived from the sale of the television rights in the United States, and the fact that 95 per cent was coming from a single source, the relevant network, created vulnerability for the IOC in what could become a fluctuating market. Samaranch had already decided that alternative and additional sources of financing had to be found for future security, and that the IOC would have to exert more authority in the television negotiations.

As a result, the New Sources of Finance Commission was created, initially under the chairmanship of Guirandou-N'Daiye and subsequently Dick Pound, of Canada, who also took over negotiations for the television contract. Several developments followed. ISL presented the TOP concept to the Session in Delhi in 1983 and received a mandate to develop the programme. The Berlin Session in 1985 approved TOP's operation, with the final participation for the four years leading to Seoul including 154 NOCs, nine multi-national corporations and generating

$95 million. By 1988 the IOC was negotiating a percentage of local marketing programmes from Games' organizing committees – in return for general marketing support, contract management, et cetera – and also from ISL, with the percentage set at 3 per cent up to 1994 – Albertville, Barcelona and Lillehammer – and 5 per cent from Atlanta, 1996, onwards. The IOC marketing department, created to oversee and manage revenue programmes, estimates, as already stated, a $1.8 billion revenue for the '89-'92 period, almost three times that for the '81-'84 period leading to Sarajevo and Los Angeles. The TOP II programme included 167 NOCs, twelve corporations (including eight of the original nine), and generated $175 million.

Thus from the initiatives created eight years earlier, Olympic revenue had increased by 300 per cent, while dependence on US television had been reduced by two thirds. More important still, commercialization volume had been *reduced*, for there were fewer sponsors than in the early 1980s, these now paying substantially more for exclusivity and having a broader commitment to the Olympic Movement. At the Winter Games in Lake Placid in 1980 there had been some 300 sponsors individually paying insignificant amounts. Nine multinational sponsors for TOP I ('84–'88) generated as much money as 35 sponsors did for Los Angeles. The IOC had become the marketing model for all other sports organizations.

Within four years, 1984-88, the IOC had been able to build up its reserves to $5 million, even though itself taking only 8 per cent of the gross television revenue from worldwide rights and 3 per cent of the TOP programme. In the disposal of funds within the Movement, from 1988 every NOC was receiving a flat fee of $10,000, plus $300 for every competitor attending the Calgary and Seoul Games, from TOP alone. One of those countries perversely refusing to join the initial programme was Greece, who subsequently joined TOP II.

After much anxiety about the future stability of ISL Marketing following the premature death of Dassler in 1987, the TOP programme has continued on an even keel and seems to be secure at least far as the conclusion of TOP III in 1996. This is so in spite of a further upheaval in 1990, when Klaus Hempel and Jurgen Lenz, the two German executives of ISL, whose immense hard work in conjunction with such colleagues as Michael Payne (until he joined the IOC) and Andrew Craig had established the success of the marketing programme, decided to leave on points of administrative principle. This followed the sale of the other family company, Adidas, by Dassler's four sisters, to Bernard Tapie, the multi-millionaire owner of, among other ventures, Marseille's Olympique Football Club. Jean-Marie Weber is vice-chairman of ISL's parent holding company, Sporis AG. He had been Dassler's right-hand man, though little seen, since 1968.

'Horst was the pioneer in sports marketing,' Weber says. 'He set up the first company with Patrick Nally of Britain, as a subsidiary of Adidas in the mid-Seventies. Horst dealt with rights, sponsorship of sports clubs and national teams while Nally handled sales and daily business. They separated in '82, when Nally went off to handle the first world athletics championships in 1983. Horst created ISL together with the Dentsu agency, who had 49 per cent. Hempel and Lenz came together in '82/83, and while they conducted the daily business, signing contracts with NOCs, Horst and I were dealing with rights. We have an excellent team now, with Peter Sproggis looking after athletics and basketball interests, Steve Dixon taking care of soccer, and Andrew Craig handling the IOC in conjunction with Michael Payne. I switched from the Adidas family company after the sale to Tapie, when Hempel and Lenz decided to leave by mutual agreement. The TOP programme required a big investment from ISL and initially was a loss for us, but now we're re-appointed by the IOC for TOP III, and we don't at the moment see any major sponsors dropping out. Our role has broadened. We are not just concerned with sales, but in professionally advising sponsors to utilize their Olympic involvement. We are also now the agents for the IAAF, marketing their television rights. The problem I see lying ahead, however, is how much the more powerful NOCs will want to take from the pot. The Japanese Olympic Committee, for instance, are moving towards the USOC position [claiming a greater percentage on account of major multinational sponsors being Japanese]. It will not be easy.' Germany may be the same.

ISL have a staff of over 130 at offices in New York, London, Barcelona, Tokyo and Munich, in addition to its headquarters on the shore of Lake Lucerne. ISL are working in a specialized market in which they know that there are fewer than fifty companies in the world that could stand to benefit by involvement in the TOP programme.

The IOC is proud, as Samaranch is, that the Olympic Games remain, together with the Wimbledon Tennis Championships, the only major sporting event in the world that does not have advertising in the stadium. Indeed this represents a strong argument in defence of the IOC against the charge of commercialism. There is more to this, however, than ethics. Were advertising boards to be introduced within the stadiums, then there would be an immediate drop in revenue from both television and from top sponsors on account of the loss of exclusivity. There is no point in Philips, for instance, having the exclusivity of TOP involvement if Sony have advertisements displayed around the running track or on the canvas of the boxing ring floor. Although the world of football carries stadium advertising, the gross revenue of FIFA from its main event, the World Cup, is one-tenth of that of the TOP programme. If other people have done the hard work in making TOP a success, then much of the credit lies with Samaranch for recognizing the potential. Dick Pound of Canada was one of the many initial critics, saying that the involvement of some 160 NOCs around the world could never become viable. Samaranch's response was to say, 'Right, you're responsibe for *making* it work.'

Ueberroth and his committee may have grossed $126 million in 1984 compared with between $5m and $10m at Moscow four years earlier, yet the price, and the value, of sponsorship has rocketed under the panacea of exclusivity. The entry price for TOP II, unofficially, is believed to have been: Coca-Cola $30m, Visa International and Mars Inc. $22m, Eastman Kodak $21m, 3M $15m, Bausch and Lomb and US Postal Services around $12m. And that is only a start. It then costs two or three times as much again for the company to promote, through advertising, staff incentive schemes, hospitality programmes and the like, the involvement it has just purchased in the Olympic arena. What has been bought by the sums mentioned is only the right to use the Olympic rings in advertising and promotion *outside* the Olympic arena. As John Barr, a Kodak executive, has said: 'This is one we just had to win. The Olympic Games, like the World Cup, is a classic which gives us a world-wide marketing opportunity.' A consumer company such as Coca-Cola estimates that it simply cannot afford *not* to be seen to be involved in the Olympics, and associated with that intangible quality of Olympic romanticism. Yet fewer than half of all sponsors use their sponsorship successfully, in the estimate of Jim Crimmins, Director of Strategic Planning and Research at the US company DDB Needham Worldwide. 'If you don't build awareness before the Games, you are not going to get much value from them,' he says. The exploitation by Visa of the market has been classic. Visa upstaged American Express in commercials preceding the 1988 Games by claiming that 'the Olympics' only accepted Visa cards. Visa sales' volume increased an astonishing 18 per cent, way beyond the company's own projected figure of 12 per cent.

In 1987 a group of European sports journalists from some of the more well-known newspapers and magazines received an invitation through an agency in Belgium to accept an air ticket and to go and make a preview inspection of the facilities for the Winter Games in Calgary the following January. It seemed a nice idea. It subsequently became apparent that this was part of the promotion programme by 3M, of Minneapolis-St Paul, which had entered TOP I late in the day. When Dennis Conner regained the Americas Cup in Fremantle the year before, it had been in some measure thanks to the hull of *Stars and Stripes* having a drag-resistant synthetic surface, made by one of the world's largest manufacturing companies – of which few people have heard. Millions of those who would record some of the following year's events in Calgary and Seoul would do so on videotape made by the same manufacturer. Indeed, much of the world wraps up its Christmas presents with 3M's sticky tape, still contentedly unaware by whom it is made. The awareness problem was particularly acute in Europe, and that was why twenty of us were now setting off for a few idyllic autumn days on the picturesque and still snowless mountain slopes of Nakiska, west of Calgary. 3M has 50,000 different products, and was attempting to resolve its public anonymity by joining household brand names to the Olympic rings. Market research shows a remarkable consumer preference, well over 50 per cent, for merchandise carrying the Olympic symbol.

'We felt if we could get into the World Cup or the Olympics we could achieve impact on the consumer market,' Don Linehan, one of 3M's senior executives, says. 'ISL research revealed a public perception of superiority in Olympic-related goods. We got in late into TOP I. Our gross turnover is around $10 billion, but the competition had begun hitting us. We wanted to expand turnover on a worldwide scale, so we took a major step. I'd put the idea to the vice-president of our division, and ISL flew in Bill Breen from New York to discuss the project. Perhaps partially as a consequence of our involvement, 3M turnover has risen to $13.5 billion. Yet there are problems. As sponsorship has expanded – not only via TOP but specifically in America, with the programme of the US Olympic Committee [a separate operation following on from Los Angeles in 1984] – the value of the rings has diminished because of the clutter. There are mayby fifty companies in the US holding rights to the rings logo. For TOP sponsors this is bad news. We are paying a very high price for what we want, but we wonder whether ISL is doing enough to sustain and manage the image. We are worried by pressures in Atlanta for TOP III, with competition from the Atlanta organizing committee for prime-time space on American television. TOP II has been a comparatively smooth operation. Measurement of benefit is difficult. If we could establish even one per cent growth every year, then we'd go for involvement every time. But it's not an exact science. You look for awareness and "favourability", it's an image operation. If they come at us with a crazy price for TOP III, we'll go elsewhere with our money. ISL will probably offer a menu of services, as a disguised way of raising the price. Of course, part of the operation is protective. Kodak has 80 per cent of the US market, and were in a frenzy when Fuji grabbed the official rights for 1984. We need more attention on how TOP sponsors can be separated from the clutter.'

For twenty years, from 1960 to 1980, the goose laying the golden eggs for sport was television. This to a certain extent is still so, and the television market remains critical to the financing of sport; not only because of its own intrinsic value, but because it is the medium through which many of the sponsors promote their involvement. Yet from representing 95 per cent of the Olympic financial cake in 1980, television rights are now no more than 50 per cent. The other half, for the 1989–92 quadrennium, is derived from sponsorship, 38.6 per cent; ticketing, 5.4 per cent; coin souvenirs, 3.3 per cent; other licensing – cotton hats on the Costa Brava – 2.7 per cent. The pendulum has swung wildly in television negotiations. Undoubtedly, in the early years, on account of the ignorance of sports administration and the lack of professional advice, the television companies were buying exceptionally cheap air time when they acquired the rights; especially at indoor or small-court events such as boxing, snooker, or tennis, where only a few cameras and technicians were required to cover the event. The state of the market, however, has started to move in the opposite direction from the rights fee. CBS, having paid $243 million for the US rights at Albertville in France, was expected to have lost in excess of $50 million on the deal because of the declining viewing figures and advertising rates. If the US network market is experiencing undoubted decline, this is partially offset by the huge expansion of cable and pay-to-view television. Samaranch's objection to this section of the television medium, however, is that where a viewing customer has to buy the opportunity to see the Games, millions of children worldwide will be denied the opportunity to witness the most spectacular and emotional of all sporting events. The rights value outside the United States, on the other hand, had substantially increased – from $19 million paid by the European Broadcasting Union for Los Angeles to $30 million for Seoul, $90m for Barcelona and well over $200m for Atlanta – but only because the rights had long been underpriced previously.

Few in the medium of television have been more intimately involved during the period of Samaranch's presidency than Alex Gilady of the NBC network. NBC had obtained the rights for the Tokyo Games in 1964 and the Winter Games at Sapporo, also in Japan, in 1972, but in the unending struggle between the three major US networks they had subsequently been squeezed out of the Summer Games for sixteen years until regaining Moscow, a non-event in the US because of the boycott. ABC had leapt in at the deep end to grab the rights for Los Angeles at a price three times higher than Moscow's, partially of course on account of the synchronization with prime-time advertising by the Games being staged in America. Early in 1981, after repeated vain attempts and unanswered telex messages, Gilady obtained an interview with Berlioux to say that NBC wished to bid for the Summer Games of 1988. Berlioux informed him smartly that 'these would be in Nagoya', the Japanese city that was bidding against Seoul, the decision to be made in Baden Baden later that year. 'What should a boy from Israel telex to his bosses?' Gilady asks, self-mockingly. 'I caught the next plane to Nagoya, and never bothered to go another hour and a half to Korea.' The IOC duly voted for Seoul.

At this stage, none in the television world believed that anyone other than Berlioux was important. Samaranch was no more than a figurehead in the background, as far as they were concerned. Gilady began to sense that the situation might be changing, however, when he found himself caught fog-bound for hours at Belgrade, together with Samaranch, both on the way to the Session prior to the Sarajevo Winter Games early in 1984. Samaranch button-holed Gilady, and began to ask about NBC's intentions and loyalty. Eventually, they took an overnight train to Sarajevo, Samaranch telling Gilady to call him any time he needed information. Gilady was able to witness from close at hand the emergence of the rift between Samaranch and Berlioux in Sarajevo, temporarily camouflaged by Siperco. Previous dealing with the IOC by Gilady in the bid for the athletics world championships in 1983 had convinced him of Samaranch's emergence as the major force, but when it came to the point of bidding in 1984 for the Seoul contract he had difficulty in persuading his senior executives at NBC that Samaranch was the man with whom they must have preliminary discussions. Why bother, we already know Berlioux, was the reaction from Arthur Watson, president of NBC Sport. NBC had lost $35 million on Moscow, and were doubtful if they could now prise back the Summer Games from ABC. For strategic reasons, sensing the declining US television market, the IOC had decreed that the bid for the Calgary Winter Games in 1988 should be determined at the Sarajevo Session, *prior* to the screening of the Sarajevo Games and the success or otherwise of viewing figures in America. NBC were also going to bid for Calgary, but Watson and others were sceptical, in spite of assurance from Gilady, about the extent to which the bidding would be fair. In the opening round in Sarajevo, ABC and NBC both bid $300 million, then an exceptional figure, and more than three times what ABC had paid for Sarajevo and almost a third more than the Los Angeles figure, though now again tied to North American prime-time. Given a quarter of an hour by Dick Pound to come up with sealed second bids, NBC put in at $304m, ABC at $309m. ABC were furious, at the conclusion of negotiations at nearly one in the morning, at what they regarded as an auction, and were convinced they would lose $75 million on the rights they had just won. But Watson and his executives were convinced they would get straight dealing from Samaranch, and were determined to maintain their pursuit of the Seoul rights. (Berlioux, lax, had sold the rights for Los Angeles to ABC exclusively and *in perpetuity*: now rights revert to the IOC after one year.)

The irritation of ABC, and their president Roone Arledge – who refused to attend a luncheon the next day with Samaranch – was that they considered their purchase of the rights for Sarajevo and Los Angeles had somehow entitled them to a privileged deal for Calgary and Seoul. They did not like to find operating against them the same kind of market dealing from the IOC with which they were confronted by their own advertisers back home. This was a new IOC. Samaranch's 'hit man', the genial and slightly laconic Dick Pound, was proving himself adept at achieving the best market price on behalf of his master; or even better. Samaranch recognized in Pound, then a comparatively youthful 42, one of the main strengths of the IOC membership, and in the coming years the two of them, by mutual consent, would play a clever, soft cop/hard cop strategy within developing policies. 'Samaranch would ask me to try something out, to test the reaction, to stretch responses,' Pound says. 'He could always then retreat behind a defensive excuse that I was young and impulsive. I didn't mind, I could ride with that, and we were pursuing the same objectives.'

Pound would be less successful in the negotiations for Seoul some fifteen months later. By then the decline in the market was beginning to bite, ABC were beginning to realize the extent to which they had been forced to over-bid on Calgary, CBS were lukewarm, and NBC were determined not to make a mistake worse than ABC's. At the same time Samaranch, sensing that perhaps the deal done in Sarajevo for Calgary had been a 'sting', was concerned that American television should be allowed a profit margin for Seoul. A complication, as television candidates arrived for negotiations in Lausanne, was that the Seoul organizing committee, thanks to some misleading advice from Barry Frank, an adviser from Mark McCormack's International Management Group, had fantasy visions of a US rights fee in the region of $750 million. With competition times out of phase, even after collaborative adjustment from some of the Olympic sports federations, with American prime-time viewing, the South Korean figure was out of the question. There would be some painful talking, and some anxious telephone calls between Lausanne and Tae Woo Roh, president of the organizing committee – and later to be national President – back in Korea. It was said that the Koreans would accept nothing under $500 million.

US television ratings, measured in units of 840,000 homes, had reached 29 for the Decker-Budd race in 1984, but in Sarajevo – *after* the negotiations for Calgary had been concluded – they had been down to 18, following elimination of the US ice hockey team, eventually climbing to just over 20. The IOC were in no mood to kill the goose. The prime value of the sale of television rights is to the organizing committee of the Games. The division of the fee is 20 per cent set aside for technical installations, the remaining 80 per cent being split two thirds to the host nation, one third to the IOC, with the latter being divided a further three ways between Federations, NOCs, and the IOC. The IOC was thus left with 9 per cent of any deal.

In tortuous wrangling over many days, NBC finally won the bid at $300 million, less than had been paid for Calgary. That sum had been their initial offer, on which they would not shift. What they did, to appease the Koreans, was to offer substantial bonuses in a profit-sharing deal, should the market rise to take revenue beyond $450 million. It never did. When it came to negotiation for 1992, CBS initially proposed that a joint deal should be made for Albertville and Barcelona, but this was rejected out of hand. With the market now shrinking as much as Samaranch feared it might, CBS gained the Albertville rights for the Winter Games at $243m; and NBC, with their rivals again getting cold feet, retained the Summer Games in Barcelona at $401m.

These are the rights fees that have been paid over the past 32 years:

Winter Games

1960	Squaw Valley, USA	CBS	$50,000
1964	Innsbruck, Austria	ABC	$597,000
1968	Grenoble, France	ABC	$2.5m
1972	Sapporo, Japan	NBC	$6.4m
1976	Innsbruck, Austria	ABC	$10m
1980	Lake Placid, USA	ABC	$15.5m
1984	Sarajevo, Yugoslavia	ABC	$91.5m
1988	Calgary, Canada	ABC	$309m
1992	Albertville, France	CBS	$243m
1994	Lillehammer, Norway	CBS	$300m

Summer Games

1960	Rome, Italy	CBS	$394,000
1964	Tokyo, Japan	NBC	$1.5m
1968	Mexico City, Mexico	ABC	$4.5m
1972	Munich, West Germany	ABC	$7.5m
1976	Montreal, Canada	ABC	$25m
1980	Moscow, Soviet Union	NBC	$87m
1984	Los Angeles, USA	ABC	$225m
1988	Seoul, South Korea	NBC	$300m
1992	Barcelona, Spain	NBC	$401m

The ABC monopoly that had predominated, with a single break, from 1968 to 1984 was now at an end. The question today is whether, for instance, Ted Turner's CNN cable network will emerge as rights holder and/or host broadcaster for Atlanta in 1996. Removing the Games from open 'free' network television would not suit Samaranch's wishes, but a changing market may force the issue. It is coincidental that CNN is based in Atlanta, yet the tactic of using the Olympic Games as a sales-leader could bring Turner twice as much in new cable subscriptions, perhaps, as he would have to pay to gain the rights. CNN's coverage of the Gulf War, for instance, raised his cable subscriptions by some 20 per cent. It is Pound's opinion that Turner will be interested in one or other option, or both, and certainly Turner has been spending a lot of time in the past eighteen months in the company of those whose influence will count – Samaranch, Payne (President of the Atlanta organizing committee) and Pound – most notably during last year's Pan American Games in Havana.

The dangers to the ethics of the Olympic Games, voiced by Follows and others, remain. Being British, I tend to cite Follows, though this sense of responsibility towards the soul of sportsmanship is by no means the preserve of the British. When, at the athletics world championships in Tokyo in 1991, the French men's 4 x 100 metres relay team, world record-holders during the previous year, conducted themselves sourly on the medal podium when taking third place behind the USA, new record-breakers, and Great Britain, the French sports daily, *L'Equipe*, castigated its countrymen for their lack of grace. Ethical behaviour is indivisible, and the pressure from commercial forces unfairly corrupts the normal instincts of otherwise decent competitors. We do not know by how much those French sprinters suffered commercially by failing to maintain their world status. The sentiments regarding good behaviour in competition are no less evident in the United States than anywhere else; witness the irreproachable conduct of the majority of their golfers, runners, many of their professional baseball, football, and basketball players, witness the sentimentality of many of their spectators. For all the evidence to the contrary, I do not believe that the renowned American sporting principle – winning is all that matters – is true of all Americans. Corporate American business sponsorship would not be paying through the nose for Olympic association were there not millions of Americans who still perceive that there is something intangibly special about Olympic participation. The chauvinism of ABC television and its commentators at Los Angeles in 1984 may at times have been grotesque, and the same attitude may be evident in Atlanta in four years' time, yet I firmly believe in the fundamental goodness of all those who embark down one sporting path or another. When they are corrupted, it is by their failure to resist temptations that are placed in their way. I have been fortunate to experience this spontaneous decency in every continent. Restraining the forces of corrupting temptations from commercialism is the responsibility that should most keep Samaranch awake at night. It is no use the Olympic Movement having achieved a platform of financial independence if in the process the very purpose of sport, the reason why we play games – to help teach us the way we should live the rest of our lives – is being perverted *en route*.

The margins are so narrow, and the practices of commercial opportunism and exploitation are too infrequently challenged. The wretched irony is that those institutions which might have the moral intellect to challenge the commercial operators, generally do not have the finances to conduct such a challenge. That is why the conscience of the International Olympic Committee and its leaders, in particular its President, will be more than ever vital in its bearing upon the remaining years of this century. The challenge on morality, for example, offered by the Howell Inquiry in Britain ten years ago, lasted no more than a matter of months before it quietly evaporated. It was the stuff of academic argument, unlikely ever to find a foothold in the corridors where sporting power ebbs back and forth. Among the recommendations made by that inquiry were:

- Governing bodies and others negotiating sponsorship linked to television should assess the value to all interested parties of the events they are promoting.
- The government should refer to the Office of Fair Trading for examination the relation between the International Management Group and UK sport to establish whether monopoly exists.
- The IOC should involve all NOCs and International Federations in a fundamental dialogue about the future of the Olympics regarding eligibility and commercialism.
- The British Sports Council should supervise the principles of sponsorship for the application of proper ethical standards.
- GAISF must assess the financial involvement of Adidas with FIFA and the IOC.

This last recommendation was an impertinence which Dassler was swift to point out to me when I talked to him not long afterwards. 'An inquiry by GAISF?' he asked, incredulous. 'It was only our support which got *them* out of financial difficulty. How could *they* investigate us?' Here was the crux of the moral debate in the modern world. Everyone needs money to survive, and it is the Dasslers, the McCormacks, and the Turners – in other words those who operate the markets in the world of supply and demand among an anonymous public – who provide the means of survival. Dassler, I am convinced from my experiences of talking with him, was a moral man who loved sport, and invested, often unnecessarily, in the support of sport. The Soviet boycott of Los Angeles squandered a million dollars which Adidas had already given in equipment to eastern European countries, who would continue to expect patronage from Adidas for subsequent Games. Dassler, before his death, initiated massive support in areas where there was no commercial advantage: $50,000 to the African athletics championships, $300,000 to the African football championships. 'We've simply been too successful,' John Boulter, head of international relations for Adidas, France, has said. An Adidas investment in sport approaching $100m a year, in advertising, promotion, and public relations, is 5 per cent of their budget; yet sport is less than 30 per cent of their gross turnover, the remainder being in fashion leisure wear.

Dassler denied to me that Adidas had ever controlled competitors. 'Neither we nor ISL would ever handle athletes *and* events. Our role is to co-ordinate the interests of differing organizations. Following the Los Angeles Games, there was much bitterness because of rival sponsorship contracts by the organizing committee and the US Olympic Committee. Now we can achieve global uniformity for the Olympic Movement.' He questioned the alleged extent of his influence in the 1988 Games going to Seoul rather than Nagoya. 'I'm not interested in power,' he told me, 'only in pragmatic advantages. I could be much more in the limelight if I wished, but I avoid publicity. I love sport, which is my pleasure as well as my business.'

Sport, for Adidas, was and is a means of establishing and maintaining public awareness, not a matter of direct profit. It was sport's loss when Dassler died. It had been his even-handed influence, for example, with FIFA and Soviet sports officials, that enabled the Coca-Cola-sponsored FIFA youth championship to be hosted by Moscow. With transparent hypocrisy, the Soviet Union would subsequently protest, at an international athletics conference in Rome regarding relaxation of the eligibility code, that the door was being opened on commercialism. Nobody knew more about the workings of the Olympic world than Dassler, who kept a file on the election of every senior official throughout international sport; and when interviewed by the Howell Inquiry, Dassler had stated candidly: 'We are ready to make this information available to all who ask for it.' Some of those who criticize the operation of companies such as Adidas and ISL might do a better job if they were as well informed in their own affairs as was Dassler.

Samaranch, at the time, dismissed the Howell Inquiry almost out of hand, for no interviews had been staged which might have given a proper insight into IOC affairs. 'I can understand the concern,' he said, 'but *we* are just as concerned, and it was surprising that these recommendations should be made without formally consulting us.' More recently he said: 'Dassler was an important man, very helpful to sport throughout the world, especially to the Third World, to whom he supplied much material. He was a good friend to the Olympic Movement throughout Asia and Africa, but to say he had a strong influence within the IOC is simply not true. You could count the IOC members over whom he had influence on the fingers of one hand.'

Dick Palmer, secretary-general of the British Olympic Association, is an administrator whose experience is respected around the world, and it is unsurprising that Atlanta should hire him as adviser. Samaranch at one time wished him to take charge of the Solidarity Fund. Palmer is in no doubt about the virtues of either Dassler or the TOP programme. 'The BOA was on its knees at one time, financially,' Palmer recalls, 'surviving thanks to donations from the Trades Union Congress and support from the private sector gained by George Nicholson's Olympic Appeal campaign. It was Dassler's vision that persuaded Samaranch to start the TOP programme, enabling Olympic organizing committees to enter every country to co-ordinate global benefits. What the programme did was to raise the profile of the Olympic rings. Now, instead of living from one Games to the next, the BOA can be a contributor to the sports movement, a force in sports politics. Yet in 1973, a British government White Paper on sport did not once mention the BOA. Thanks to the development of the TOP programme, the BOA can now appoint better staff on a broader front to carry out essential functions in medicine, psychology and education.'

Criticized alongside Dassler, by many besides the Howell Inquiry, is Mark McCormack, with his extensive global network of agents and negotiators. While I am sure that McCormack sees his multi-million dollar operation as an illuminator and benefactor to the world of sport – never mind to himself – his style and principles are more difficult to defend on an ethical basis. His deals unequivocally seek to exploit simultaneously all aspects of the market: performers, sponsorship, television and the competitions themselves. Such amalgamations of interest inevitably cannot be beneficial to all parties, whatever the range of benefits that IMG may bring to its many clients. What McCormack has done for the Wimbledon Championships, for example, formerly one of the most traditional and conservative events in a similar manner to the Olympic Games, is inestimable, yet he now has a hand in almost every facet of that tournament. He negotiated the contract with NBC, and simultaneously represents the BBC commentors, John Barrett and the former champion Virginia Wade. In 1968, at the time of initial discussions between IMG and the All-England Club, the tournament's profits were under $70,000. They have now risen to in excess of $13 million. That is one thing. As yet, IMG has little influence over the shape of the Wimbledon competition, other than to have pressed, through television, for the common practice of 'rest' periods, even after the first game in a match of no more than half a dozen strokes, for the benefit of commercials. But at the US Open Championships at Flushing Meadow, another of the four Grand Slam events, the behaviour of CBS Television in the manipulation of the schedule, and rescheduling at no notice, of individual matches is nothing short of scandalous. When protesting last year about such an incident, Martina Navratilova, who is hardly an unimportant figure in the game – and admittedly has more than her fair share of the advantages from the commercialisation of her sport – was abruptly told by CBS officials to 'shut up'.

The sports performers represented by IMG are predominantly from golf and tennis, quite different in their nature and requirements from many Olympic sports, though the manipulation of the televising of athletics is often unacceptable. A contrived re-run in London of the confrontation in Los Angeles between Mary Decker and Zola Budd, in which Decker had controversially fallen during the 1984 women's 3,000 metres final, was a showbusiness operation with grotesquely disproportionate rewards for the runners and of no genuine athletic standing whatever. Such manipulations are becoming increasingly common, though it would be unfair to say that IMG has a hand in all of them. The danger, however, is there; most noticeably in the arrangement of appearance money, opposition and distances in the IAAF Grand Prix. It is almost inevitable that within a few years such manipulation may extend to world championship events, with the probability that before the end of the century there will be prize money for running in the IAAF world championships, now to be biennial.

When I put the question of the possibility of prize money or appearance money in the Olympic Games to Samaranch last year, he replied: 'I cannot see it happening in my time, but in the future, who knows?' Where then would be de Coubertin's hallowed principle of the honour of taking part? Where will that then leave those honourable competitors from small, unheralded countries upon whose participation the traditions and reputation of the Olympic Games have always until now rested? It is one thing for Carl Lewis or Mike Powell magnificently to attempt to break world records, and subsequently benefit from the commercial advantage that such achievement brings. Olympic champions for much of the past century have subsequently profited from their accomplishments under the pure white flag of the Olympic rings. Where will they, and the Olympic Games, stand if they should be competing on the day not for glory but for $50,000? I question whether McCormack, or the successors of him and Samaranch, would still see anything objectionable in this.

McCormack has long sought to gain IMG's involvement inside the Olympic arena. There are obvious potential anomalies should an agent be controlling too many facets of a single event. Experience shows, too, that IMG pays disproportionate attention to its more famous sporting clients. Tessa Sanderson, the former British Olympic javelin gold medallist, has observed that IMG did little for her, concentrating on their more famous names. For the moment, IMG operates in handling licensing for organizing committees such as Albertville this year and Lillehammer in 1994. Their involvement, sitting at the same table, is already creating severe embarrassment for ISL. IMG offered their services for this year's

Games in Barcelona, but the Spanish organizing committee preferred to use Saatchi and Saatchi. Discussions took place last year between IMG and William Payne of Atlanta, and that relationship may yet come to fruition.

The one benefit of commercialism which as yet cannot be doubted is the opportunity created for the Solidarity Fund to offer assistance to emerging and under-funded NOCs around the world. The Fund was launched following the yield from the Munich Games of 1972. By 1984, NOCs were receiving worldwide over $400,000 for administration and coaching courses. By 1988 this had risen to $3 million, and by this year it is expected to pass $20m. For that, sport is obliged to be grateful to the likes of Horst Dassler and Mark McCormack.

4 Reality

—

Field-Marshal Viscount Montgomery, whose mind had been sharpened under gunfire, expressed the view, prior to the Olympic Games in 1960, that the Olympic Games should be a contest between the best competitors in the world, whether or not they were amateurs. The Second World War had been a watershed in social history: the old order would never be the same again. Quite apart from the fact, say, that women had suddenly found themselves being treated, out of necessity, as equals, the eyes of the uneducated working class in the western world had been opened to show that many areas of life previously regarded as inaccessible could now be attained through effort and perseverance. Everything, from government to education to culture was experiencing metamorphosis. Everything, that is, except for the International Olympic Committee under the direction of Avery Brundage, ideologist or bigot, depending upon your point of view.

At the Session of 1957 in Sofia – following the Melbourne Games the previous year, overshadowed by the Hungarian uprising and Soviet suppression and by the Suez crisis, with only 38 members travelling to Melbourne – the IOC turned its mind toward the question of amateurism. In America, and elsewhere in the mood of enlightened social conscience that had followed the war, there was concern about the principle, and definition, of 'broken-time' payment to athletes taking time off work to prepare for major sporting events. Many felt that they deserved, when representing their country, some reimbursement for lost wages, and the principle was viewed with sympathy by realistic NOCs. Reality, however, was not a quality to be found within the ranks of the traditional, hidebound IOC. In a half-hearted attempt to address the problem in Sofia, the following revised conditions were drawn up under Rule 26 on Eligibility:

The competitors would *not* be regarded as amateur if they participated for money, or goods easily converted into money, or prizes, exceeding $40 (then £14); coached for payment (excluding schoolmasters); received financial benefit to help them compete; received unauthorized expenses; declared an intention to become professional following the Games; ceased work for training for more than thirty continuous days.

These principles, never mind how patently inoperable the last three might be, were in tune with the view expressed, for example, before the Melbourne Games by the Duke of Edinburgh: that Britain did not want to send a team of 'temporary civil servants'. That sounded nice in the drawing-rooms of Britain and the chandelier-hung mansions of Belleview Avenue, Newport, Rhode Island, but was not much help to honourable working men such as Don Thompson, who was to win the 50 kilometres (31 miles) road walk at the Games in Rome. The alleged nobility of the Games was being upheld by ageing idealists from an era that was no more, those such as Avery Brundage, Lord Exeter, Rudolphe Seeldreyers of Belgium, and others. Quite apart from the question of amateurism and broken-time, how was it possible to enforce the matter of an amateur's *intention*? The history of the Olympic Games had been littered with the names of boxers, swimmers and figure skaters who had converted their Olympic success into material reward in subsequent years. Some of the best-remembered Olympians of my youth were Johnny Weissmuller and Sonja Heine, as famous on celluloid as in the Olympic arena. Jesse Owens, the most legendary of all, had been forced by circumstance to demean himself by running professionally in stunts against racehorses. The grandiose opinions of the high priests of the IOC were and continued to be out of touch with the real world. In my adolescence, when my sporting bible was the written accounts of the Games of Paris, Los Angeles, Berlin and London, one of the respected figures of British athletics administration was Harold Abrahams, the 100 metres gold medallist in Paris. None could have been more resolute in the retention of amateurism. Yet, even as a boy, it did strike me as a shade inconsistent that Abrahams should substantially enhance his income as a lawyer by his regular work as athletics writer and broadcaster while challenging any illegally charged ten pence for a competitor's bus fare.

When Otto Maier, the IOC Chancellor, resigned in 1964, to devote more time to his own affairs, he stated: 'The whole concept of amateurism has changed so completely, during the eighteen years I have been Chancellor, that there must be some changes made in Olympic ideas of what constitutes an amateur today. The Olympic Movement must face up to the fact that the amateur of today is a vastly different person to the amateur of past years.' Maier added that he was tired of political wrangling, of being obliged day after day to attempt to deal with quarrels about two Chinas, two Koreas, and two Germanies. 'How can sportsmen be called upon to make decisions about situations which have no foundation in sport?' he asked. The controversy of South Africa, he said, made the job impossible.

The incomparable Paavo Nurmi, winner of nine gold medals in the 1920s, had been declared professional prior to the Los Angeles Games of 1932 by the International Amateur Athletic Federation upon the prompting of the IOC. He was later reinstated by Finland for domestic competition, and it was Nurmi, the national hero, who had borne the flame into the stadium at the opening of the Helsinki Games. His statue stands outside the stadium. Pragmatism was rife in Scandinavia long before the small Spaniard would import it to Lausanne. When Brundage belatedly established an Eligibility Commission in 1969, worried about talk of payments to alpine skiers, it was symptomatic that the member he asked to be Chairman, Hugh Weir of Australia, was then 75 years old. Weir's friends would say that he brought the experience of half a century's administration to the post: critics would merely observe that his education began in the nineteenth century and it would be reflected in his sympathies.

Avery Brundage became progressively more neurotic about the perceived evils of the Winter Games. Between those of Grenoble, 1968, and Sapporo, 1972, he told James Coote of the *Daily Telegraph* of London: 'Alpine skiing was not introduced until 1936. There is a great deal of exaggerated comment on this subject. Of our 125 National Olympic Committees, at least half have no interest whatsoever in winter sports. Half of the other half have no mountains. Baron de Coubertin was against them for that reason – they were a limited sport. The Olympic Games cover more than twenty sports and all are subject to the same rules. You cannot have special conditions for that alpine circus now going on in the mountains.'

It was not only skiers who had Brundage in a lather. He was grinding his teeth over the suspicion that some athletes at the Mexico City Games had received remuneration for wearing particular running spikes. 'This will be stopped before the next Games,' he fulminated. 'The IAAF are taking steps to have neutral equipment at all times. An all-white running shoe, for instance.' Brundage fervently believed that because the entry form for the Olympic Games had to carry an assurance on eligibility from the competitor, and from his or her national Federation and NOC, it was not possible for three people all to be lying. Sadly, that alone demonstrated how far out of date was this ideologist.

It was not only the issue of amateurism that Brundage failed to understand through the five Olympiads during which he maintained his abuse of professional sport. I believe that, to a degree, he did not understand sport itself, the many varying motivations which drive individuals to strive for excellence either as amateurs or professionals. It is possible for the amateur to be motivated by the prospect of glory in various forms, and for the professional to be motivated by pride, honour and satisfaction more than by money. Brundage had many misunderstandings, evident in his repetitive speeches: that the amateur played only for recreation and fun, the professional only for entertainment; that amateur sport was for the participants and professional sport for the spectators [whence, therefore, the television fee for Rome, 1960?]; sport that was not amateur was not sport at all; amateurs gave, professionals only took. This fanaticism induced Brundage, at the solemn opening ceremony of the Sapporo Games, 1972, to astonish the audience in his address from the rostrum with a tirade against the Winter Games, wishing an end to them before 1976. It was more obvious than ever that he had over-stayed his time.

Philip Krumm, compatriot of Brundage and former President of the US Olympic Committee, had made the revolutionary suggestion, in conversation, that the Games ought to admit professionals to produce competition of the best against the best. A quarter of a century later, Sepp Blatter, the secretary-general of FIFA, who was involved in the long-running debate on the eligibility of Olympic footballers, once said to me: 'As long as commerce does not influence the spirit, form, place, and result of sport, we cannot prevent its development.' *There* is the real issue. The old ideology was less a matter of the privileged middle and upper classes of the western world being financially free of material need, but of the *manner* in which they played. From where I stand, if everybody in the Olympic Games is true to sportsmanship, it is irrelevant whether or not they are paid.

Amateurism, by definition, is a voluntary condition, a state of mind. You cannot *command* someone to be an amateur. My education took place in the most amateur-minded of conventional environments, at an English so-called public school – one of those out of which grew in the mid-nineteenth century the game of association football – and Cambridge University, where, on a tree in a public park in the 1850s, were pinned the first formal laws of the game as it now is. I played for Cambridge at Wembley Stadium against Oxford, for England Amateur XIs, and with a British Olympic squad training for the Games in Melbourne, missing the trip because the squad was reduced by two for economy. My belief in amateurism was absolute, because that was how I enjoyed playing, the way Brundage would have wished. But it did not close my mind to the circumstances of other people. My family had no money, my school fees being paid by a benevolent aunt, and I well understood those colleagues in the provincial Eastbourne team for whom I often played in the Corinthian League – milkmen, postmen and joiners – who welcomed five pounds' 'additional' travelling expenses. The moment we took the field we were all *players*, and some of the most enjoyable games of football I ever played in were the Boxing Day local derbies against neighbouring Worthing in front of crowds of several thousand. More emotional still were the many matches for Pegasus, that combined club of Oxford and Cambridge, which immediately prior to my joining them had twice won the Amateur Cup – later abolished when the Football Association advisedly dropped the definition – in front of 100,000 crowds at Wembley. Playing for Pegasus was a crusade, was the last fling of front-rank old-fashioned amateurism at an international level, certainly in Britain, maybe in the world. But I knew, and so did my colleagues, even while we were playing, that what we represented was an attitude that, for sheer economic necessity, could not survive in top competition. The demise of Pegasus in the mid-Sixties arrived because the new intake of undergraduates could no longer resist the pull of illegal incentives from other clubs, in an age when it was becoming increasingly difficult for an impecunious student to find the price of a meal in a restaurant as opposed to a café. I spent my summer vacations selling toys, and working as an office clerk to pay my debts incurred playing as an amateur for Cambridge University. Let no one tell me I do not understand amateurism.

Lord Exeter and his like, who conditioned for close on fifty years the thinking of the IOC, understood amateurism but failed to understand the world. A couple of years ago I was invited to give an address at the Summer Session of the International Olympic Academy at ancient Olympia, on the theme of professionalism within the Olympic Games. My premise was simple. Anyone taking part in the Olympic Games, now and at almost any time since the First World War, who wished to have a chance of winning a gold medal, is required for some weeks, months, and even a year or more beforehand, to train or practise full-time. Anyone who does so must be financed by some source or other. They may enjoy inherited money, or rich parents, or a supportive college, a sympathetic employer, a benevolent NOC, a helpful government, a voluntary sponsor, or they may even be professional and paid for performing. By devoting themselves full-time to the pursuit of their sport, they are all by my definition professional. Yet professional is not necessarily, as Brundage thought, a dirty word. I have met or watched thousands of honourable professionals and some pretty rotten amateurs. One of those deliberately trod on my foot in full flight, tore my ligaments and put me out of the game for a year. Some amateur! As I have said, what matters most about the Olympic Games, and indeed any sporting tournament, is the spirit in which it is played. Among the truest amateurs in spirit I ever knew – though on reflection there have been many – have been Norman Creek, who played for the legendary Corinthians and was team manager of the British Olympic Squad; my late colleague Geoffrey Green of *The Times*, another Corinthian and said to be the best centre-half of his day, amateur or professional; John Landy, that peerless one-mile world record-holder of Australia; Rafael Osuna, the Mexican tennis player; Gary Sobers, the West Indian cricketer; and Stanley Matthews, the doyen of professional footballers during an unparalleled 33-year career.

By the time the Princess Royal was elected to the IOC in 1988, the transformation in the eligibility code was effectively complete, yet her attitude is revealing, especially when compared to that of her father, Prince Philip, whom she succeeded as president of the International Equestrian Federation. When I asked her in 1984 for her view of appearing side by side with professionals in the Olympic Games, she said: 'I was happy enough [in 1976]. My expectations were rather different, and it was a bonus. In addition to those who want to be professional, there are many who gain in their careers on the side, if successful, as teachers or coaches, and why not? Many are temperamentally unsuited to stay in competitive professional sport, which is a hard game! . . . Can the Olympics embrace both? I think it would be very difficult to have an Olympics with any division. They say there is no such thing as an Olympic amateur. That's partially correct, because I think everybody has to be professional with a small "p" in their attitude to get to that level, and to have the freedom to do the training which is necessary. Sponsorship does make it easier. I hope I would not have been regarded as professional in my approach, although I was thorough in keeping up my standards. More than that I don't think I was professional. I did do other things at the same time.'

Following the admission of full professionals in 1988, the Princess observed: 'The Games have huge value and potential to professionals and to those who want to make a career of sport, and a medal will enormously enhance their earning ability. Whether that's right or wrong I'm not sure, certainly it would be wrong to have a direct reward for winning. Obviously in the old days there was no scope for earning money and it was forbidden, but nowadays with greater leisure time activities, this is one of the world's growing industries, where sport is available to more and more people, and a proportion of those want to do very well. I wouldn't argue that this is not a reasonable ambition . . . The growth in professionalism represents the growth in popularity of a sport which makes it possible to become an earner. The degree of popularity allows more people to be employed to entertain. In that sense it's inevitable [the degree of professionalism in the Games], though not everyone wants to compete at that sort of level. It's been necessary to be professional, in attitude and application, for a long time now to be a potential medallist. It's paramount. There's a hell of a lot of effort in being successful in any international sport, you don't do that on a casual basis. There are those who have jobs who say they could not compete full-time, and others who say a job is too distracting. Fortunately, there are both attitudes, as long as administrators continue to accept this.'

With Killanin succeeding Brundage in 1972, the IOC belatedly began to knock some sense into their eligibility code. Much against Brundage's wishes, the first Congress in 43 years was planned for 1973 in Varna, and it was here that Killanin, in that genial and conciliatory way that was to characterize his eight years as President, supervised the revision of restraints upon the amateur. The word itself was removed from the Charter. A code was established which, though it was not to last long, was to the satisfaction of all 26 International Federations; to the extent that not a single allegation of professionalism reared its head at either of the Games in 1976 at Innsbruck or Montreal. 'Amateurs' would now equivocally include specially trained state-sponsored amateurs, military personnel co-opted in the same fashion, and athletic 'scholars' at educational institutions; none of them previously recognized by Brundage. The new code still specified that competitors must never have received any financial reward or benefit, and must abide by the rules of the respective IF, even if those rules were more rigid than those of the IOC; must never have been a professional or professional coach in any sport (schoolmasters excepted); must never compete in championships open to professionals; must not be used for remunerative advertising unless payment was to the Federation or NOC, must not write or broadcast for payment, nor do so in any form during the period of the Games. The duration of training was now to be at the discretion of IFs, and therefore became effectively a dead issue. Broken-time payment was to be permitted, 'in case of necessity', though in no case was payment to exceed the sum which the competitor would have earned in the same period. If the compensation was not paid by the employer, it might be paid by the National Federation or NOC. When these proposals were ratified at the 1974 Session in Vienna, the *Daily Mail* of London reported: 'Olympic Games amateurism died here last night, killed by the acclaimed guardians of sport, the International Olympic Committee.' Amateurism might be dying, but not hypocrisy.

Die-hards within the IOC saw the revision as a manoeuvre to shift the responsibility from the IOC to the Federations, who had now united under the newly-formed GAISF, the first secretary-general being Oscar State of Britain, secretary of the weightlifting federation, who believed that the Federations had the right to decide for themselves what constituted amateurism. The table tennis federation, which would have to wait another fourteen years for admission, had long before resolved this by dispensing with any definition, and having merely 'players'. Though Killanin may not have sensed it at the time, in producing a temporary and partial solution to one IOC controversy, he had supervised unwittingly the creation of another. Thomas Keller would now begin to co-ordinate the rivalry to the IOC on the new platform of the General Assembly of International Sports Federations.

The seeds of a further controversy had also been sown. While competitors were not to carry advertising material on their person, including sponsors' names on start numbers, the names of ski resorts might be carried. It was intended, naively, to protect competitors from carrying advertising which might be offensive to them. By the time we arrived at the IAAF World Cup in Barcelona in 1989, aggressive officials were pinning, without consent, sponsors' names on the chests of competitors immediately before they went to the podium for the medal ceremony. It is this sort of abuse upon which Samaranch and all IF Presidents must ruthlessly stamp. As a rider to the Session in Vienna, it is worth noting that Alexandru Siperco expressed during the debate the same point I have made: 'Amateurism is a state of mind.'

In 1976 there had been rumours of illegal payments to skiers at Innsbruck, but in the absence of evidence the IOC turned a blind eye. By 1978, Willi Daume of West Germany had become chairman of the Eligibility Commission and found himself confronted by an irregularity of FIFA. At its Congress prior to the World Cup finals in Argentina, FIFA had decided that, for the Olympic tournament of 1984 – arrangements for the qualifying tournament for 1980 being already approved and underway – previous World Cup players of Europe and South America, the strongholds of professional football, would be excluded from eligibility. The intention of this was to prevent the Soviet Union and other eastern European countries from utilizing the same players in both the Olympic Games and the World Cup. In other continents all players would remain eligible. The regulation would clearly penalize such European nations as Luxembourg, Iceland, Norway and Denmark, where there were no professional teams, not to mention Cyprus, Malta and Monaco. Protests by Daume and the IOC proved in vain. Football is the one sport with the strength to remain immune from IOC pressure, and I cannot see when this is likely to change. Although the football tournament consistently provides the largest number of spectators by a single sport in any Olympic Games – 107,000 attended the final at the Pasadena Rose Bowl in 1984 – João Havelange, FIFA's president, if pushed to conform to IOC uniformity of regulations, would be happy to withdraw.

While football is the one sport that does not need the Olympic Games, it is equally true that the Olympic Games could well survive without football; this might not be true of 1992, when Spain, clearly, would have felt deprived had they been denied it, and it was perhaps for this reason that Samaranch agreed that the IOC would yet again yield to FIFA's inconsistency in order not to jeopardize the Barcelona tournament. Having maintained their principle of excluding previous World Cup players in 1988, FIFA introduced their own unilateral regulation for 1992 that eligibility for all countries would be for players under 23. As a restraint upon what had been, until 1990–91 and the dissolution of many of the communist regimes, the socialist bloc, the FIFA code would be only partially effective, because it has always been policy in the socialist countries to utilize the Olympic tournament as a proving ground to give experience to younger players who would be subsequently included for the World Cup. The abolition of any amateur-professional distinction for the football tournament, on the other hand, was long overdue, because Italy, Spain, Germany and others had long been fielding lesser professionals in their Olympic squads. This was true of the Italian team humiliatingly beaten by Costa Rica in Los Angeles in 1984. There is a further reason why it is impossible for FIFA to agree to an open tournament without age restriction; it is that the qualifying tournament for the continental championships of Europe, Africa and South America is taking place simultaneously with the Olympic qualifying tournament, and it would be impossible for the best players of these countries to play in both tournaments.

While Daume was battling with FIFA, a shift in policy in athletics was taking place that was to be of paramount importance to the intentions of Samaranch when he succeeded Killanin after the Games in Moscow. Epitomized by the rivalry in those Games between Sebastian Coe and Steve Ovett – 21 million people in Britain alone stopped to watch the late afternoon 1,500 metres final showdown – the appeal of athletics to professional promotors was reaching such proportions, with attendant television and sponsorship enthusiasm, that the IAAF was obliged to regularize amateur-professional anomalies. Leading athletes had been receiving under-the-counter payment for as long as anyone could remember, indeed way back to the period between the two world wars. The practice was so firmly established that wise athletes such as Coe had been privately declaring their income, illegal under sporting regulations, so as not to be in breach of civil law should the practice come into the open and the tax authorities attempt to take retrospective action. The IAAF therefore established, at their Congresses in 1981 and 1982, the latter immediately prior to the European Championships in Athens, the principle of Trust Funds. Monies received could be paid into such funds during the athlete's career, but were not to be 'cashed' until the athlete retired from the sport. Subsidies could be withdrawn for training, medical and travel purposes in connection with performance, the operation to be supervised by the respective national federations, who, in return, would receive a percentage as a service fee. Much of the legal planning of this policy was devised by Robert Stinson, a solicitor and former hurdling colleague of mine at Cambridge, and now the honorary treasurer of the IAAF. This rationalization of athletics was to be an invaluable springboard as Samaranch moved towards similar freedom of thought in all Olympic sport and an acceptance of professionalism within Olympic ranks. A surviving oddity is the word 'Amateur' in the title of the IAAF. 'The modernization of the IAAF's policy gave a lead to other Federations and an example to which Samaranch could point at the Congress in Baden Baden in 1981,' John Holt, former secretary-general of the IAAF, recalls. 'Samaranch was discussing the situation with us, before our Athens Congress in '82, and saying that he would like to see the pattern clarified by other Federations.'

At the IOC Session that took place jointly at Baden Baden in 1981, the by-law to Rule 26 was amended to state: 'Each IF is responsible for the wording of the eligibility code relating to its sport.' Guidelines to the eligibility code were based on the principle that 'an athlete's health must not suffer nor must he or she be placed at a social or material disadvantage as a result of preparation for and participation in the Olympic Games and international sports competitions.' It was, however, still illegal at this stage to be a registered professional; to be involved in advertising other than under the supervision of IFs, NOCs or National Federations who must receive respective payments; to carry advertising material on clothing during Olympic and related events other than trademarks as agreed by the IOC with IFs.

The only eligibility issue at the Session of 1982 in Rome was to confirm to FIFA that the regulations in Los Angeles, in 1984, would be the same as in force in Moscow, in 1980. At New Delhi in 1983, the individual eligibility codes of all Federations were approved other than those of ice hockey and football. Kevan Gosper expressed concern that the Olympic Movement had seemed preoccupied with restrictions for top competitors, and risked removing necessary incentives for young people, who would consider it too difficult to compete against athletes of near-professional status. Gosper stressed the historic tendency for public and government support for the national Olympic teams to be forthcoming largely on account of the amateur character of the Olympic Movement, and that care should be taken to see that this support was not lost. João Havelange observed that, with the word 'amateur' having been removed from the Charter ten years ago, the same should now be done with the word 'professional', to be replaced by a definition of the 'Olympic athlete' by each Federation. By the time of the first Session in 1984 at Sarajevo – there is a session prior to each Games, Winter and Summer – the problems of neither ice hockey nor football had been satisfactorily resolved. Ice hockey was a particular thorn, because the Federation permitted the readmittance for participation of a professional after three years of ceasing a professional career.

In the Sarajevo Games, Carey Wilson, who used to poach goals as nimbly as Marco Van Basten on the football field, feinted his way past what was left of the crumbling defence of tradition when he scored three times to help Canada inflict a surprise 4–2 defeat on their arch rivals, the United States. This not only caused heart failure within the control room of ABC Television – with its $91.5 million investment in the US market – but embarrassment for Daume and the IOC. Wilson had played contract professional hockey in Finland. The Ice Hockey

Federation specifically excluded from Olympic eligibility professionals of the North American League, but not others. For them, professionals in the World Hockey League in Europe did not exist. Wilson, John Harrington and Philip Verchota, of the American team, most certainly did exist, the latter pair having played as professionals in Switzerland and Finland. Rick Cunningham of Canada, playing as a naturalized Austrian in the 4–3 defeat by Finland, had appeared 323 times in WHL matches. Daume, Berlioux, and Samaranch, under cross-examination at a press conference, could give no satisfactory answer. The controversy was fuelled by the fact that Canadian national heroes such as Gretzky and Lemieux, who had starred only a week before in the Canada Cup victory over the Soviet Union, were ineligible because of their NHL affiliation. Adding to the spice in Sarajevo was the torment of Vladislav Tretiak: not knowing whether to accept a $1 million contract in the NHL after the Games, or to return to teach young Russians how to play ice hockey. Tretiak had won gold medals in 1972 and 1976, and only a silver at Lake Placid in 1980, when the Americans had achieved their shock victory to much acclaim from the expedient President Carter.

The Soviet team was not now permitted to celebrate any victory, forbidden from drinking until after the funeral of President Andropov, who had suddenly died at the commencement of the Games. Here was another blow for Samaranch: while Andropov lived, though unwell, there had been hope that the Soviet Union might still participate in Los Angeles that summer. His successor, Chernenko, was of the old hardline Soviet school. Samaranch spent much of the Sarajevo Games, in public, ducking controversy. Asked whether he was happy with the ice hockey situation he replied: 'Yes and no.' He went on to repeat the maxim that players of different social/political systems should be given equal opportunities and that the IOC would be reconsidering the ice hockey question after the Games. He insisted the current agreement 'would be respected'. Few were happy. Nor were they when, at the final press conference, he was asked to explain why it was that Carl Lewis, Coe and Ovett could freely advertise under the control of their national Federations and remain eligible, while Stenmark of Sweden, doing the same in alpine skiing, could not. Samaranch passed the question to Marc Hodler, president of the Ski Federation, for explanation, and Hodler could not provide it. Samaranch was in mid-stream with his revolution, up to his armpits, and still struggling to get to the far bank.

Meanwhile, the Yugoslavs in Sarajevo embodied the Olympic spirit as much or more than at any Games I had encountered. By their individual and collective generosity, their patience, humour and courtesy, they made the Winter Games of 1984 a pleasure for competitors and press, not to say spectators, even allowing for the limited facilities in catering and accommodation which are part of the non-capitalist environment. From the organizing committee down to the humblest coat room attendant, taking wet coats and working sixteen hours a day for little or no pay, the Yugoslavs had worked in the belief of an ideology that was continuing to have a rough ride. The centre-forward of FC Hamburg, Schatzschneider, who succeeded Hrubesch, the 1982 centre-forward for West Germany in the World Cup final, was busy preparing himself for the Games in Los Angeles. Almost all the members of West Germany's Olympic team would be professionals in the Bundesliga, and eligible because they had *not* played in the World Cup.

The LA Games, however, would in many ways prove as enjoyable as Sarajevo, in spite of the awfulness of ABC's hysterical coverage. It is too facile to say that the now un-reined gallop of commercialism was the prime motivation of the competitors. Of course Carl Lewis gained enormous material benefit from his four gold medals, but he would have competed just as feverently to emulate his legendary compatriot Owens had the commercial factor not been present. It is no longer possible to prevent the corruption of ideals and images which can follow the acquisition of Olympic fame. The emphasis on the financial aspects of Lewis's career was more a product of contemporary society than of the Olympics. The Games could survive the commercialism. The music of the jackpot reaches fewer than one per cent of the competitors. The majority know from before the start that they have not even a slim hope of becoming affluent celebrities. Without such people as Elenora Mendonca of Brazil, who came 44th and last in the women's marathon, the Games do not exist.

More fundamentally, such are the standards of today's championships that exceptional success can only come with a gift of rare ability nurtured by years of anonymous preparation. There are no short cuts to the victor's rostrum. The LA Games proved that sport among a nation that started playing for fun, moved onward in search of excellence and only latterly had become trapped by the jingoism of national pride, was still thriving.

Samaranch, looking back on the Games at their conclusion, reflected to me: 'De Coubertin's philosophy existed at the beginning of the century. We are now near the end of the century. We have to move with the times. We shall review the Games of Sarajevo and LA, talk with everyone, including the Eligibility and Athletes Commissions. We don't want to discriminate against any group of competitors, so long as they are under the jurisdiction of the International Federation, and we are opening the doors wider and wider. We have our present discussions on tennis, and I think we will have an outstanding tournament in Seoul. Of course it is possible for Sebastian Coe to make a lot of money. I am happy for him. What makes him Olympian is not the money he earns away from the Olympics, but how he deports himself. He's sporting to his opponents, speaks out for what he believes, and gives time for developing the interest of others, as with his work for the Athletes Commission and for the Sports Council in Britain.'

The process of reintroducing tennis, a demonstration sport in Los Angeles, where Mecir and Graf were the winners, was proving the most traumatic of any of the negotiations on eligibility. By painful degrees, Samaranch was convincing his colleagues that the Olympic Games, by definition, had to include the best competitors. Even such veterans as the nonagenarian General Stoychev of Bulgaria was now committed to the principle. During Sofia's bid for the Winter Games of 1992 – awarded in 1986 to Albertville, in France – Stoychev had said to me: 'As a cavalry officer, my career was almost wholly involved with horses, prior to the Second World War. Almost every hour of my working life I was involved with horses. How could I, as an Olympic equestrian rider, be said to be amateur? How can a gymnast, who has to repeat certain exercises many thousands of times to achieve perfection, still be called an amateur?'

At the IOC Session in 1985 in Berlin, the debate on amateurism continued; it was here that Willi Daume, the Chairman, delivered a report which in character and content is a testimony to the sincerity of those in the IOC who care about the future of the Olympic Movement. A former basketball player, Daume, at the age of 72, with his rotund figure, flushed face and limping gait on account of knees suffering the arthritic legacy of years of jumping, might be considered at a casual glance to be one of those IOC members whose years had surpassed his wisdom. Not so. In the course of his ten-page address, he said profoundly:

'The never-ending development of practical standards in high performance sport has cast aside all the former rules. Whether we like it or not, the fact remains that Olympic sports have developed far beyond reality. Even worse, far beyond justice and equality. . . . The Olympics have become an integral part of big business due to the astonishing development of income from television rights. The crucial point is ultimately how this money is used. If, in general, it is made available to the poor and needy, the advantages would outweigh the risks. But that is not my subject. . . . We must consider not only justice and equality, but also power: Olympic power, that is to be the best among the best. Power plays a role in all social relations, not only in politics and government. Power and justice are opposite poles and power is usually stronger. In contemporary ideology, justice is conceived as "equal rights for everybody". But this means the obligation to create equal chances and fairness. . . . Simone Weil, the French philosopher, deploring the fact that power was replacing the underlying purpose of justice, has said: "Justice is fleeing from the camp of the winners." It was impossible even with the anachronistic notion of the so-called amateur of former decades, to create a genuine ideal, even if this was claimed time and again in official speeches. Everybody knew that manipulation established a different situation from what we admitted to the outside world . . . We [the Commission] do not feel that so-called "open Games" are the desirable or inevitable objective. Ethical postulates vary too greatly to allow such a model. Without noticing it, perhaps we have given all countries the common wish to overcome the nineteenth-century concept of classes. This rejection of class concepts constitutes a tremendous success for the Olympic peace movement far greater than any success in sport . . . It is the athlete who always comes first in our consideration. Other areas of life and human activity, such as art and science, have never had such problems [as we]. If a young person restricts himself in his personality and is obliged to do so by rules alien to his life, if he is put at a disadvantage or discriminated against, how can he become an ideal for others? . . .

'It has been demanded that the IOC should be exclusively responsible for compiling mandatory eligibility rules for all disciplines of sport. That would be absolute madness. Such demands simply spell out intolerance, and it would mean the end of the Olympic Games. We could never organize the Games against the wishes of the International Federations . . . An obligation requiring athletes to have a job or undergo professional training while pursuing a career in top performance sport could not be set forth in definite rules either in the West or East; in particular not by the IOC alone . . . Only in this way can we counteract the influence of international agencies and the way in which they make our athletes dependent. Current conditions in this respect are catastrophic, not only in the classical expression of sports such as football, ice hockey, cycling, boxing and tennis . . . The eligibility rules must be enforceable worldwide, only possible by co-operation with the Federations. This is why the Charter allows payments resulting from participation in accordance with the rules of the respective Federations . . . The IAAF no longer allows athletes to be provided by agencies for individual events . . .

'The objective of the International Tennis Federation is to open the Olympic tennis tournament to all players who belong to a National Federation and this shall have nothing to do with a player's income, whether enormous or not. The ITF wishes to observe the Charter in that neither appearance nor prize money shall be paid and that tennis should be fully subject to Olympic conditions . . . Virtually all the tennis players are managed by agents, and these . . . undermine general practice, a scandalous state of affairs. Since we acknowledge the ITF as an Olympic Federation, we must offer our support.'

It is significant that in the eligibility discussions during the Sessions of 1985, 1986 and 1987, the latter the most critical of all in relation to the introduction of tennis, Samaranch spoke hardly at all. If the debate on one of the most far-reaching changes in the history of the Olympic Games was to be resolved in the way he wished, then it had to come about through the democratic process of discussion among the members, and not as a result of remonstration from him. When I talked over the issue with Daume at his NOC president's office in Olympia Park in Munich, under the shadow of the still-innovative 1972 stadium, he may have been bloodied but was unbowed. 'I have known Juan Antonio for more than twenty-five years and have co-operated closely with him in different fields,' Daume recalled. 'He was a natural choice in 1980. Since then, the IOC has undergone a transformation as under no president ever before. An heir to de Coubertin's legacy, Samaranch recognized that the IOC could not afford to abide rigorously by traditions, but had to move with the times. A number of older members were unhappy with this policy, but it was the only way ahead. I was delighted when he supported my views on liberalization of the regulations on amateur status. Previously, the IOC had permitted any kind of support for athletes provided by the state, but had prohibited any financial assistance from other quarters, especially in the world of business. There was no such thing as equal opportunities any longer, except through lies and deception. Everyone knew the machinations and the funding going on behind the scenes. This situation had reached a point at which it was untenable, and for this reason the IOC changed its philosophy by raising its ban on financial support for athletes, allowing assistance in the same way as young artists or young scientists are sponsored for compensation for their work and the sacrifices they have to make. The idea was not to create differing social statuses within the individual social orders and ideologies; the aim was to make it possible for all competitors, or more precisely the best competitors in the world, to take part in the Olympic Games. This development was, and is, highly significant for the future of the Olympic Games, and it culminated in the inclusion not just of football and tennis, but also the best professional players in these disciplines, in the Olympics.

'In promoting this development, Samaranch showed far-sightedness. He had a sense for true sport and fair play. Furthermore, he had diplomatic skill and a sense of how to turn these ideas into majority votes. These qualities were enhanced by a predilection for Spanish *grandezza* and an urge to promote the Olympic ideal throughout the world. Yet he has been not just a diplomat, but a successful businessman. The growth of television allowed him to make the IOC a wealthy organization. It is now important that the funds are put to good use, and that poorer countries in particular, receive the assistance they need.

'At the Olympic Games in Munich [Daume was chairman of the organizing committee] I met Brundage at the airport and took him straight to the Village. He went around throwing out from competitors' rooms the airline bags of Lufthansa and British Airways, exclaiming, "Not allowed!" There were two Germanies: everything was allowed that the GDR did, but what free enterprise did in a free country [West Germany] was forbidden! What was the difference between the two Germanies in sporting purity? It was a system of lies. And, as I have said, what is the difference between the young sportsman, or young artist or young scientist? If you are a top-grade athlete you cannot have a full-time job. Are athletes less important to society than artists? The requirement for competitors changes with the times. Nurmi was an exception in the Thirties. Then, swimming and basketball were totally amateur. The system then was still the best for the highest standard in America. The full recognition of tennis was a most important step. In my opinion such a marvellous sport as tennis must be in the Games, otherwise the Games do not represent the best sports in the world. It was Killanin who made me chair the Commission. At that time I was not so interested, but he persuaded me of the need for change. We have experienced the problem of history. At the original, ancient Games, they didn't know the word amateur, they were all professionals. The olive wreath reward is a nonsense. At the ancient Games, they were paid. Why should the competitors of today voluntarily put themselves at the service of an ideology which makes a virtue of sacrifice and poverty?'

The Session in 1987 at Istanbul will come to be seen as historic. During the debate on eligibility, no fewer than 31 members contributed from the floor, a record for such occasions. Almost the first to speak was Gunther Heinze, a former Stalinist from the GDR (who resigned by mutual agreement following the amalgamation of the two Germanies). The decision to adjust the rules in order to accept tennis was, he said, 'divergent'. Fifth to speak was Anita DeFrantz, and it was perhaps her contribution more than any which reached to the heart of the matter. The bronze medallist appealed to the members in the name of athletes who aspired to the highest attainable level in sport. In the case of tennis, she said, it was necessary to become a professional in order to reach the top. The best tennis players should be given the opportunity to share in the Olympic Movement and the celebration of the Olympic Games. She was quickly supported by Nikos Filaretos of Greece, on the basis of it being experimental. The veteran Wajid Ali of Pakistan, sixth most senior of the IOC, much respected but of the old school, predictably said it was incompatible. Gunnar Ericsson of Sweden thought the IOC should support the ITF and its integrity. Dr Kim of South Korea reminded the meeting that tennis had been one of the first Olympic sports. Masaji Kiyokawa of Japan, another of the old school, was not in favour because the ITF was not the only governing body of the game. General Holst-Sorensen of Denmark emphasized that the IOC had already decided to accept the *sport* and that the task was to define the rule of eligibility, and he saw little difference between the proposal for tennis and the situation relating to other sports. Raja Singh of India, second most senior member, said the IOC should not espouse hypocrisy and that competitors in other sports received financial rewards. Maurice Herzog, French hero of Annapurna in 1950 when he lost all his fingers on the successful climb, underlined the Olympic ideal dictating that the best should win, and it was not for the IOC to analyse competitors' motivation. Lamine Keita of Mali wondered whether professional tennis players would accept Olympic regulations of village life. Franco Carraro commended DeFrantz for her comment, the more meritorious from someone dedicated to a sport in which little if any money can be earned. Carlos Ferrer of Spain had spoken to Chris Evert, who had declared that she would value a gold medal more than any victory in a major tournament. Alexandru Siperco of Romania, fourth in seniority, reminded the members that nowhere in the words of de Coubertin was there an indication that he supported an immutable concept of amateurism, and it was only right that a contemporary competitor should be able to make a living from his sport. Willi Daume stressed that the real threat to principle did not come from the competitors, but from the contractual dependence of sport on television.

The meeting approved the tennis tournament as proposed.

Professional tennis players, some of whom found difficulty in even sharing the same court with an opponent, would now be expected to share a bedroom in the same way as any competitor in the Olympic Village in Seoul. 11 May 1987 was the day the Olympic Movement finally acknowledged the truth which it had sought to camouflage for thirty years or more: that the Games had to be opened up. Istanbul, for five thousand years a cultural crossroads, had seen capitalist western logic break the pantomime ideological rules of the socialist east. Daume was asked by an American journalist at the press conference afterwards whether the IOC contained more members sympathetic to the old Brundage fanatical amateurism, or to Samaranch's contemporary pragmatism. The ageing Olympian, a basketball player in Hitler's Olympics, was clear-cut in his answer. 'The commercial danger of the Olympics is not from the athletes, whether they are receiving $10 or $50,000 in their normal sporting career. The danger is losing the independence of the Federations to television, promoters and agents.'

Samaranch, not for the first time, had employed cunning. On a morning without coffee break, he had inserted the eligibility issue as the last item before lunch, and thereby avoided a formal vote among hungry members, though there was sufficient support across the floor to convince the members to accept the experiment. 'Without Samaranch, the move would never have succeeded,' Philippe Chatrier, the ITF president, who would be elected to the IOC three years later, said to me. 'Some of the members would accept a player who was earning $100,000 a year, but no more! I'd said to Samaranch: we've been excluded for sixty-four years since the Paris Games; either everyone comes back or no one. I didn't have total support within the game, because the British and Americans didn't want the Olympic Games competing with them. Samaranch was ready to compromise on the eligibility of players, and the determination on this was more mine than his. I didn't want to live again through the compromise that existed before Open tennis, so I said to Samaranch that if he wasn't ready for us, we would rather wait for Barcelona in 1992, or even 1996. I was ready for a delay.

'At the Session in Istanbul, Samaranch used all his skill in handling the meeting, having all the opposition speak first. Princess Anne was against it, and de Beaumont. It was a debate of over two hours, and everyone was longing for lunch. At the conclusion Samaranch said: "So. We are agreed that tennis is accepted!" Afterwards, he said to me that it was the best meeting of his whole life. Prior to Istanbul, he had flown from Geneva especially to meet me in Paris. I went to Charles de Gaulle airport, and at the end of our talk he said: "You have convinced me", and flew home.' The IOC felt the decision was justified, in part, when, at the tournament in Seoul the following year, the Argentinian flag in the opening ceremony was carried by Gabriela Sabatini.

The return of tennis to the Games had two immediate effects. Powerful sporting nations such as the Soviet Union and China substantially raised their interest in the game, and the pressure rose on football to enter full teams of World Cup status or none at all. The move towards the return of tennis had been sparked by a conversation in the Lenin Stadium, Moscow, during a Davis Cup tie in 1973, when a Soviet official talking to Chatrier had criticized the ITF for not doing more to help the spread of the game. Did Chatrier not realize, the Soviet asked, that 80 per cent of governments would give no grant to a sport that was not in the Olympic Games? Four years later, when Chatrier became president of the ITF, he made the return of tennis one of his priorities. By 1989 there was to be a Grand Prix event in Peking. The Soviet Union, instead of sending their players to the 1988 US Open, spent three weeks acclimatizing them in Tokyo for the tournament in Seoul.

Chatrier says: 'The effect of our return on the development of the game on Africa and Asia will be rapid. Many countries want to expand,

and that should be the first consideration of an International Federation, not just the fostering of established competitions.' He is dismissive of those who say – and there are many – that tennis does not need the Olympics. 'From whose standpoint do they talk?' he asks. The top performers may not need it, but he had been adamant that tennis would only return on an all or nothing basis. How could you exclude Edberg, say, from the Olympics, when Carl Lewis was running in an athletics Grand Prix for $20,000 a second? For those wanting to make a moral debate of the issue, the argument favours tennis. While the majority of top competitors in the Olympic Games probably have their financial career hanging on the result – Boris Onyschenko cheated in the modern pentathlon's fencing event in 1976 because victory would give him the top Soviet coaching appointment – tennis players are, conversely, sacrificing substantial income to play for the honour of being in the Games. Stefan Edberg said in Seoul: 'I'm here because playing in Los Angeles was a really nice experience. It's like playing for your country in the Davis Cup, and that means something to me. It's only once every four years, and I see nothing wrong with it. I enjoy not having to be so tense, defending points, and I like staying with my colleagues in the Village, and going to see other sports, like the men's 200 metres in swimming yesterday. That's something I could never normally do. This isn't Wimbledon, certainly, but maybe in future it will be something more.'

The difference between Wimbledon and Seoul was that the small tennis countries such as Canada, Peru, Nigeria, Finland, South Korea, the Ivory Coast, Greece, Algeria, and Indonesia had entrants. Kitty Godfree, holder of a record five Olympic medals, flew to Seoul as sprightly as ever in her late eighties. 'Of course tennis should be in the Games,' she said. 'I cannot see what is the objection.' For the 1992 tournament, Samaranch did not want an obligation for Olympic qualification to be participation in the Davis and Federation Cups, but Chatrier told him: 'We should not change the rules to suit two women [Monica Seles and Martina Navratilova].' Samaranch told him it was his tournament, he could do what he wanted. Chatrier reflects: 'He's the best President we've had since de Coubertin. Brundage never had the same battles to fight.'

Comte Jean de Beaumont might have had his doubts about the admission of full professionals, yet has been supportive of Samaranch throughout his twelve years as President. Now retired as an honorary life member, he told me during an interview at the offices of his bank in the Bourse: 'I met de Coubertin long ago, in 1928 when I was a young fellow. He was not exactly the dogmatic ideologist he is represented as being. The world is changing very quickly sometimes, so quickly it's difficult to follow. Like all people, I'm getting older and sometimes getting afraid of the acceleration and change within the Olympic Movement. I don't say you can't change, but I believe it has to follow the soul of sport. If the soul is not quite so pure as it used to be in my young days, when we used to play for fun, I admit I'm a little astonished to see people practising for money. I don't say it's wrong. As you know from reading the Bible, when you are sitting on the steps of the temple, sometimes you can see cracks in the walls, merchants on the steps. This can make the temple collapse. But, as I know well, my friend Samaranch is diplomatic, a clever man, he's trying to give the Olympic Movement the greatest strength it ever had.

'Is money interfering too much? That's what we have to ask, because money, wherever it goes, always spoils things. Money is necessary to help sport, but sport must not help money. Money can be useful to build stadiums and fields, but when sport starts to make money for people, that's not good business. Money brings betting, and betting brings violence. The two things we have to fear are doping and violence. When I was a young man, we had been living in a golden era. Now gold has taken us over. We must not lose sense of direction in the Movement. De Coubertin understood the world at his time. What would he say today? He said the best competitors must come to the Games – though he never said the best women! The Games without women would be like a military barracks.

'I was the one who began the Association of European Olympic Committees, and was the first president. I admire the way the British are running their sport, the way the British Olympic Association find money without their government, and I take my hat off to them. Would that we could in France.

'All my colleagues have given full support to Samaranch because he is the fellow who has given the world a feeling that the IOC matters, that it is valuable to youth, that we can influence the world's leaders – Bush, Yeltsin, Major, Mitterrand, Mubarak and de Klerk. That is important. We are, right now, and everyone should understand it, talking about peace, about enjoyment of life, about sport . . . and, unfortunately, a little too much about money. Brundage tried to stop the current tide of events and forgot that life is changing. The flow of the stream of life is stronger than the rule of institutions.

'I admire Samaranch, though sometimes he's walking on the edge of a precipice. He is clever, but he should be aware of the danger of the fall. The Olympic Movement has been brought down previously, not by quarrels but by misunderstandings. The ancient Games collapsed. Now, the Games are bigger, more popular than ever because of the media. I would not take a bet to say how long they are going to last, knowing they have previously failed and been recreated. It is the task of men of goodwill now to hold on to the ideal, and to try to forget sometimes about the power of money. We have people who try to copy us, such as the Goodwill Games. I voted against having the Olympics every two years, a big mistake in my opinion. I don't want to scatter the name "Olympic" too many times in the newspapers, because that devalues it. The idea to bring the youth of the world together every two years, this was made for money, because Federations thought they could find more this way.'

Like de Beaumont, Zhenliang Hé of China had reservations about full professionals, as did Vitaly Smirnov of Russia. 'Elite athletes have to spend many, many hours every day,' Hé observes, 'otherwise they can never achieve a high level of success. Everyone has to live, so it's right to allow the athlete the opportunity to gain financial support. But I'm against those who make sport an exclusive business, I am not in favour of athletes who have contracts with agents as opposed to Federations.' Smirnov said to me: 'In the Soviet Union we accepted that contract professionals might play against us in 1972, though I'm not very much in favour of the professional world. We did learn that acceptance of them did not damage our own prestige. It would have been impossible to have a leader such as Samaranch twenty years ago.'

Ivan Slavkov, of Bulgaria, is sanguine about professionalism. 'It was necessary for Samaranch to introduce it; as in music or culture, it was unavoidable,' he reflects, 'but in the long term it does present a threat to the Olympic spirit. The Goodwill Games, television-orientated, concentrate on quick sports, and conceivably it could kill the Olympic Games.' Boris Stankovic, secretary-general of the basketball federation, saw no alternative. 'We needed a new spectacle, the chance to show the *best* basketball in the Olympic Games,' he says. 'Samaranch has been revolutionary, yet in some countries we had a situation in which the players were being paid by their National Federations, Spain and Italy more than most. We know that in eastern Europe there were bonuses for medals, while the United States was paying under the table. We *had* to finish all that. Samaranch has encouraged all Federations to think the same way. At our basketball congress in 1986, the majority were still against acceptance of professionalism, America as well as Russia, but we changed things by 1989.'

The views of the amateur-professional debate were perhaps different in Africa from the conventional standpoints, both for and against, elsewhere. Louis Guirandou-N'Daiye, from the Ivory Coast, a past vice-president, reflects: 'In Africa, we were in neither group. We felt that ultimately it was easier to say, simply, that the Olympic games needed the best athletes, and now that we have them they are still bound, in various ways, by our Charter, so that between the opening and closing ceremonies they comply with the Olympic spirit. I was part of the delegation in 1984 that returned the gold medal of Jim Thorpe, from 1912, to his family [Thorpe had been disqualified subsequently for a trivial breach of the amateur rules, and was reinstated posthumously in 1982, though only as a joint first]. A few dollars did not mean you were professional. I deeply agreed with the action we took. It is very difficult for the IOC to put itself in a position of accusing individuals.'

5 Boycott

—

'The boycott by African countries of the Olympic Games of 1976 in Montreal could have been avoided,' Jean-Claude Ganga, the member for Congo, suggests, 'if the Canadian government had been more aware beforehand that it might happen. At the time I arrived in Montreal, there was a meeting taking place in Mauritius, a week before the Games, of African heads of state. I went straight to see the Commissioner of the Games, M. Rousseau, the former Ambassador in Yaoundé, Cameroon, whom I knew, and told him he should take a plane to Mauritius immediately, and that if the meeting was over before he got there, he should contact the Organization of African Unity, in order to get the measure of African concern [about the forthcoming New Zealand rugby tour of South Africa]. When Abraham Ordia of Nigeria (President of the Supreme Council of Sport in Africa) and I confronted IOC members in Montreal, the general reaction was that "rugby is not an Olympic sport". I approached Lance Cross [Sir Lance Cross of New Zealand, who died in 1989] and said to him that if he would do his bit, actively to try to prevent New Zealand from continuing with the tour, as a demonstration of the IOC's attitude against apartheid, I would do what I could with the OAU, to persuade them that African countries should participate in the Games. We were to meet again the next day. During the next twenty-four hours, I received the green light from the OAU, if a postponement of the tour would be discussed, but the next day Cross did not show up at our rendezvous. [Killanin's view remains that Ganga was not a key figure and that he himself though available, was not consulted.]

'Madame Berlioux knew what I was doing, but I was unable to get to see Killanin. I think Trudeau, the Canadian premier, could have contacted New Zealand about the tour, but he did nothing. A year later, Trudeau was the first to propose the agreement, reached at Gleneagles, regarding international attitude towards sport in South Africa.' Samaranch has the impression, shared by others, that Ganga and Ordia failed to meet Killanin because Berlioux unwisely insulated the President from the urgency of the situation. 'Killanin should have sensed the danger,' Samaranch recalls. 'That Africa, more than Trudeau's refusal to admit the Taiwan team to Canada, was the greater threat.'

Political interference with the Games was hardly new, though it had never been as serious as it became in 1976. Minor arguments had disrupted Paris in 1900 and London in 1908; many countries had recommended the removal of the Games from Berlin in 1936 because of Nazi policies; several had withdrawn from Melbourne in 1956, in protest against the Soviet crushing of the uprising in Hungary; Indonesia and North Korea had withdrawn from Tokyo in 1964, because of China's invitation to competitions in Jakarta; and there had been threats of an African boycott at Munich in 1972, were Rhodesia not excluded from those Games. That last event should have been sufficient warning to Killanin of the danger four years later. It was all very well for sporting ideologists to proclaim that politics should not interfere with sport, yet the reaction of such ideologists was itself often political: as when some European nations suggested a withdrawal from Mexico in 1968, following the massacre of several hundred students by the Mexican army during a demonstration immediately prior to the opening of the Games. After Rhodesia had been forced out in 1972, Brundage had further antagonized African opinion by his grotesquely inappropriate references to African behaviour in the middle of his address at the memorial service for Israeli competitors murdered by Arab terrorists. That incident had been another blight upon the fragile status of the Olympic Games, the more so on account of wretched incompetence by the Germans in attempting to dispose of the crisis within 24 hours, and the added blunder of the announcement at midnight that the hostages had been rescued when in fact they were already all dead.

The decision in 1972 to withdraw the invitation to Rhodesia, narrowly taken two days before the opening ceremony, was merely an extension of the campaign against South Africa, begun by Ordia at the 1960 Games in Rome, and leading to the exclusion of South Africa in 1964 and 1968 and their removal from IOC membership at the 1970 Session in Amsterdam. Two months after the Montreal Games, the IOC executive board met the International Federations of Olympic sports to debate the withdrawal of 26 NOCs. No retrospective action was taken against NOCs, and only Charles Palmer, of the judo federation, supported a policy of suspension: of Canada from international sport, for the refusal to admit Taiwan, and also of the boycotting Africans.

Caught in the vice of political opportunism, the IOC and its associated organizations made several self-defensive pronouncements during the next two or three years, none of them adding up to much more than dignified posturing. The President of the IOC, when attempting to take a moral stance, rated somewhat lower in political estimation than did the Vatican in the infamous rebuke by Kruschev, when advised of its condemnation: 'And how many divisions has the Pope?' At a meeting of the IOC executive board with ANOC in Abidjan, Ivory Coast, in 1977, Canada and others proposed that countries withdrawing from a Games should be suspended from the next Games, and be required to refund expenses incurred by the host country. Ordia, addressing the meeting, said that the African boycott was based on humanitarian and moral grounds, and not on political considerations. Similar expressions on suspension were voiced at a meeting later the same year in Lausanne; though by now, under Killanin's conciliatory hand, the mood had shifted from hard-line action to friendly discussion. The Tri-partite Commission would debate the issue – interminably – and there was alarm among some IOC members about the influence upon the Tri-partite Commission of UNESCO. At the end of the meeting in Lusanne, Killanin stated: 'I know some people were expecting us to go on the attack, but we have preferred a constructive position.' Shortly afterwards there was a meeting in London of European Ministers of Sport, at which Dennis Howell of Britain opposed any UNESCO involvement and suggested that the IOC must govern its own regulations.

While the Olympic Movement was still attempting to organize its thoughts on 1976, the Soviet Union gave sudden cause in 1979 to clarify the mind with their military intervention, 'by invitation', in Afghanistan. As the nations gathered at Lake Placid, up-state New York, for the Session preceding the Winter Games of 1980, sport was once more heading for crisis. President Carter was already proposing a worldwide boycott of the Summer Games in Moscow, in conjunction with a suggestion that the Games should be removed from Moscow and staged elsewhere. The failure by political leaders such as Carter and Margaret Thatcher even to begin to understand the dimensions of the organization required to stage a Games for 160 countries, and 10,000 competitors, was evident in their naïve belief that the site of the Games could be altered as simply as switching an orchestral concert from one hall to another. When Thatcher despatched Lord Carrington, her Foreign Secretary, to Lausanne to make this proposal, offering a paltry £50m as inducement, while at the same time making not the smallest attempt to halt conventional holiday tourism to the Soviet Union, or commercial contracts for Britain to construct industrial pipelines on Soviet territory, many people in Britain began to detect the hollow expediency of Thatcher's support for Carter.

In his opening address to the Session, Killanin said that it was one of the most important meetings ever held since 1894. He stressed the technicalities of the IOC's position: that the Games had been awarded, respectively, to Lake Placid and Moscow at Vienna in 1974, that agreements were signed according to the Charter, and that these must be honoured. Political problems of the world were not, he said, the responsibility of sporting bodies. 'I have never denied nor ignored the intrusion of politics into the Olympic Movement, and I believe it to be in all our interests that these intrusions must be resisted . . . We can only pray that the leaders of opposing factions can come together to resolve these differences, in order to avoid another holocaust. I have continued to attack the chauvinism of certain aspects of the Olympic Games and sport in general. We have not been helped by those who, for instance, produce tables of medal results on a national basis, contrary to our rules, which state: "The Games are a contest between individuals and not between countries" . . . We live in a world where there are totalitarian regimes on the left and the right. Are there any countries which can claim fully to respect human rights, and not to practise discrimination of some kind? . . . I now call on Secretary of State Cyrus Vance to formally open the 82nd Session of the International Olympic Committee.'

In an extreme breach of protocol, Vance immediately launched into an attack on the Summer Games in Moscow: 'As we meet here tonight, the world faces a serious threat to peace which raises an issue of fundamental importance to the Olympic Movement . . . the ancient Games were held in the city-state of Elis in Greece. They marked a "truce of the gods". During this truce, warfare against or by the host city-state was forbidden. In the view of my government it would be a violation of this fundamental Olympic principle to conduct or attend Olympic Games in a nation which is currently engaging in an oppressive war and has refused to comply with the world community's demand to halt its aggression. This is not a question of whether a national team should be barred from competing on political grounds. It is whether the Games should be held in a country which is itself committing a serious breach of the international peace . . . It is impossible to separate this decision from its political consequences. To hold the Olympics in any nation that is warring on another is to lend the Olympic mantle to that nation's actions. We already see the nation selected as host of the Summer Games describing its selection as recognition of the "correctness of our foreign policy . . . and enormous services in the struggle for peace" . . . Responsibility for this matter should not be shifted to the athletes. That would only force them to carry a burden which properly belongs to the leaders of the Olympic Movement. None of us wants our athletes to suffer, but neither should we let them be exposed.'

It could not have been clearer that President Carter was hell-bent on the destruction of the Moscow Olympics. Vance's attack on the IOC was greeted in near silence by a stunned assembly; though they might have expected it, following the demand the previous day to the executive board by Robert Kane, the president of the US Olympic Committee, that the Games in Moscow be moved, postponed or cancelled. As IOC members re-gathered in twos and threes outside the conference hall afterwards, many were already wondering about not merely the prospect of the Games in Moscow but of those in Los Angeles four years later. Killanin, sensing that he was in a powerless position, maintained a dignified position during the Games in Lake Placid – notable for maladministration and transport failures in a village conspicuously too small for the event – taking a defensive position behind the statutes of the Charter: that the Moscow organizing committee had carried out all the requirements of their agreement, that to move the Games was both illegal and impossible, and that the decision on whether or not to accept the invitation to attend in Moscow rested solely with National Olympic Committees and each individual competitor. He hoped that all those interested in the Games of 1980, and of the future, would not now allow events to be dictated by politics that were outside the control of the IOC.

Vitaly Smirnov, then a youthful 45 and the driving force of the Moscow organizing committee, together with its chairman Novikov, recalls: 'Following Vance's political attack, the Moscow Games delegation at Lake Placid decided that we should leave. It was, incidentally, this incident which persuaded Samaranch that, at the opening ceremony of a Session, the President should speak last instead of first. Many IOC members told us they did not share the American sentiment expressed by Vance, and there were those who refused to attend the reception given by the Americans afterwards. Many people came to me to express support for Moscow from whom I would not have expected it: General Holst-Sorenson from Denmark, serving with the NATO air force, made a firm statement in support of Moscow, and subsequently had difficulties at home on account of this. The same with Wajid Ali [from right-wing Pakistan]: people for whom it was not easy to make such views public, but who wanted them to be recorded. From that moment, I really understood that whether we are from the east or from the west, what we care about is the Olympic Games. It was a big lesson for me.'

For Samaranch, head of Protocol and standing in the wings, it was an intimidating foretaste of the kind of crisis that awaited a President of the IOC. 'Vazquez Raña arrived in Lake Placid direct from an executive board meeting of ANOC in Mexico City,' Samaranch recalls. 'They had resolved to support the IOC, and it was with this message that he arrived for the Session, yet he told me he had been unable to gain access to Killanin. Apparently, Berlioux had instructed secretaries to block off all non-IOC personnel, and all requests for access to the President must be made through her.' Not that, frankly, Vazquez Raña's message of goodwill would have made a scrap of difference to the American attitude, but it would have been comforting to the members as they sat there obliged to listen to the hectoring of Vance.

The drift towards the boycott of Moscow, between February and July, would be protracted, painful and inevitable. Killanin flew back and forth between Dublin, Washington and Moscow, to no effect on the main combatants, whose positions would be unalterable; but was able, inch by inch, day by day, to achieve some solidarity among the rest of the world in support of the Olympic principle. Important allies, in the sporting sense, such as Germany and Japan would be lost, but the loyalty of Britain, led by the chairman of the BOA, Sir Dennis Follows, was a critical reinforcement of Killanin's cause. Follows stood firm in spite of continued intimidation by the Conservative government and demands from the Prime Minister. In the public debate in Britain the stance of the government increasingly came to be seen as opportunistic, and, although the argument failed, the same accusation was being levelled against President Carter in America by Anita DeFrantz and others. Killanin, booking flights on Concorde with Berlioux under the name of Michael Morris – his more humble journalist by-line in earlier days – and her married name, Madame Groussard, drew the conclusion that Carter was a weak President under the influence of powerful advisers such as Lloyd Cutler; it was Cutler who determined who should be in the room at the White House for the meeting between sporting and political presidents, with all its overtones of the Mad Hatter's Tea Party, neither really comprehending the other.

Day by day further important losses were being suffered, such as the withdrawal of Canada, in spite of the efforts by Pound and Worrall. Australia stayed in, by one vote. There would be enough competing nations in Moscow – some of them, such as Britain, under the neutral Olympic flag – to save the face of not only the organizing hosts but, more important, the Olympic Movement. Kevan Gosper, a 4 x 400 metres relay silver medallist at Melbourne, has lived down his decision at the time to support the boycott, being elected to the executive board in 1987, ten years after joining the IOC. 'I think Killanin was too easy going,' Gosper says, 'and we were lucky to survive his presidency. I went off on the wrong line, and argued for the postponement of Moscow, that it should be delayed, and I soon realized there was a lack of reality in that approach. A strong president might have pulled me up on that view. Killanin was insufficiently active with Carter and Brezhnev, and took three months before he met them, following the emergence of the crisis at the end of 1979, during which damage limitation was the requirement.'

The damage might, indeed, have been worse; and for such a gentle soul as Killanin, bred in that pacific era of British gentry between the wars, university contempory of Burgess and Maclean, to have survived as well as he did the torrents of political manoeuvring was as much as might have been expected of him. The man about to succeed him was of a different mettle. 'Samaranch felt a responsibility towards the success of the Games in Moscow,' Smirnov says. 'He felt involved. He was not just an outsider living in our city, and had begun to understand the Soviet mentality. He could have made a good political career.' There are those who say, indeed, that Samaranch as IOC President has been too much a political leader, too little a sporting ideologist, in the traditional sense of that expression. Those who admire and respect his achievements would argue that his skill has lain in understanding the relationship between the metamorphosis of human perceptions of morality and the history of mankind.

Samaranch would have to pick up the pieces where Killanin left off; and he, too, would discover, in his first four years, that the might of the world's most powerful nations was way beyond his influence. Yet he would demonstrate, by a diligent attention to detail, background and planning, that it was indeed possible effectively to lean upon, assist and even to mould the attitudes of some politicians whose power is less extreme and therefore less intoxicating. From the day he received the key to the HQ at Vidy from Killanin in Moscow, Samaranch lived with the scarcely veiled prospect of retaliatory action by the Soviet Union and its allies against the Games in Los Angeles four years later, even though with Andropov succeeding Brezhnev there had begun to be the prospect of an end to the Cold War.

'Brezhnev died in 1982, just before the military parade of 7 November,' Samaranch recalls. 'Andropov came to power, and that was the beginning of *perestroika*. Gorbachev was his heir. I had the word, unofficially, that the Soviet Union would be in Los Angeles. Andropov realized that to be there and to win more medals than the Americans was a marvellous opportunity to be exploited for political prestige, and not to be missed. Yet Andropov always had the resistance of Gromyko, the strong man of foreign affairs within the Soviet Communist Party, and in some ways the real boss. I had met Andropov during my time as Ambassador, when he was head of the KGB, yet when he became President there was a breath of fresh air coming in. On the day of the closing ceremony in Moscow, I'd had dinner with Brezhnev, Killanin and Andropov and their wives, and I'd gained then a sense of Andropov's broadmindedness. It was therefore a great blow, to us, when Andropov died, just at the time of the Winter Games in Sarajevo in early 1984. He was succeeded not by Gorbachev but by Chernenko, from the old guard. Chernenko was sick, and was dominated by Gromyko, who hated the US.

'Gromyko was a most interesting man, who had been in the front row for nearly fifty years. He'd been there, immediately behind Churchill, Roosevelt, and Stalin in 1945 at Yalta, as Deputy Foreign Minister, and afterwards was Ambassador in Washington and then at the United Nations. I could never discover precisely why he disliked the Americans. With this man it was impossible to get on friendly relations.

'If Andropov had survived, I think we would have been OK in 1984, but he was in hospital for much of the previous year, and his death did not come as a surprise. What was immediately apparent, with the arrival of Chernenko, was the change in attitude of the IOC's two Soviet members, Andrianov and Smirnov. You could feel their new uncertainty.

'No one in the Soviet Foreign Ministry could do anything to cross Gromyko, and there was then still a total control on information within the Soviet Union. At Sarajevo, I went on a tour of the broadcasting centre, and said to the Russian technicians that I was sorry to hear about the death of their leader. They didn't even know. The situation now would be that Marat Gramov, with the two IOC members and others, would have to provide reports to Gromyko on the suitability or not of the Soviet Union attending the Games in Los Angeles. With such a regime, people would always send in a report that they knew would be approved! With the appearance in America that spring of banners and T-shirts saying "Kill-a-Commie" there was bound to be Soviet concern. Castro stated that if the Soviet Union pulled out, Cuba would not attend as a matter of solidarity, but I was not too worried about him.'

The Soviet approach to their non-appearance in Los Angeles would be built upon a platform of alleged lack of security. Whether this was calculated or spontaneous is difficult to judge. The announcement of their non-appearance occurred, by coincidence, on the day that the Olympic flame from Greece arrived in New York, while Samaranch was present with Peter Ueberroth at La Guardia Airport. José Sotelo, a Spaniard and one of Samaranch's trusted aides who co-ordinates daily worldwide press information, called La Guardia from Lausanne to say that there was a meeting of the Soviet NOC that day and that their withdrawal was imminent.

'The difference between Samaranch and Killanin,' Dick Pound says, 'is that the moment the Soviet withdrawal happened, Samaranch was on his way around the world, not just to see Chernenko and Reagan, but many other leaders, in the attempt to hold the Games together. There was not much he could do about the attitude of the US State Department towards the Soviet Union, which was equally tumescent, saying, "Nobody's going to push us around", but Samaranch knew that there were relatively few who would accept the Soviet claim of lack of safety if he worked hard enough and quickly enough on damage limitation. As for the Soviets themselves, he knew when he went to Moscow to see Chernenko, and was put in a guest house with a third-rate chauffeur, that he was dead in the water on that one.' Alain Coupat, his *chef de bureau* at the time, reflects that the low-key reception in Moscow was a sore disappointment. 'Samaranch felt from his former position of Ambassador that he had the ear of the Kremlin and all socialist peoples,' Coupat says. 'One of his deepest disillusions was that he was unable to meet Chernenko then. He tried every channel to obtain this meeting. He met Kosygin at a reception, but that was not the same. However, he was able to see all the other communist leaders, Honecker, Ceaucescu and the rest, travelling non-stop throughout the spring and summer, and he was hoping to the very last moment that the GDR might still come, until they too were forced by Moscow to pull out.'

The two dominating successes for Samaranch were the decisions by China and Romania to attend, China for the first time in fifty years. 'I'd been assured by Zhenliang Hé, our member in Beijing, that there would be no problem with China, not least because their relations at the time with Russia were not particularly good. Vazquez Raña and Primo Nebiolo went with me to Moscow, and we were not optimistic about the visit. I sensed that Russia's decision was absolute, and that the official excuse remained the question of security. We failed to meet either Chernenko or Gromyko, and it was emphasized that the decision had been taken not by the NOC but by the government. The efforts by Alexandru Siperco were a huge service to the Olympic Movement, the extent to which he was able to help convince Ceaucescu to be there. The moment when Romania marched into the stadium in Los Angeles was one of the highlights of my time as President. Siperco was on the executive board for a long time and a man of important responsibilities, not least in his links with UNESCO, and now he is one of those helping to formulate the shape of our Congress in '94. I was never sure whether his influence on Ceaucescu was direct or indirect. Once, when I went into a room to talk with Ceaucescu, Siperco was left outside. Alexandru is, or was, a Communist, but on the more routine line. Now he has changed, like many others.

'People have criticized my awarding of the Olympic Order to Ceaucescu, yet that had nothing to do with any recognition of his domestic governing of the country, but the important action of breaking the boycott by the communist countries, which was something of paramount importance to the future of the Olympic Games. I had attended *all* the annual meetings of Ministers of the communist countries, whether in Cuba, North Korea or Mongolia. In the spring of '84, the meeting was in Prague, and all of them spoke against participation in Los Angeles, except for the Sports Minister of Romania, who stated bravely: "We have decided to take part in Los Angeles."

'When I met President Reagan together with Ueberroth, Peter suggested to him that he should invite Chernenko to join him in the main tribune at the official opening of the Games in LA, as a conciliatory gesture, but Secretary Schulz vetoed the proposal. I did not have the impression that Reagan was a hard worker, it seemed to me he was passing the responsibility to other people. He was nowhere near as diligent as Bush. The idea of inviting Chernenko was revolutionary for the time, four years before the first summit meeting with Gorbachev, and I suppose it was too much at the time for the White House to contemplate.'

It is difficult for people in western cultures fully to comprehend the

with other sporting bodies, there may be a swing of votes for the interests of Africa and Asia, and whatever some people may think about keeping the Games in one place, competitors like them to move about. The best competitors may not notice, they've travelled so much, but lower down the scale those who simply appreciate taking part also appreciate seeing different countries. It would be difficult to pick any country with a lily-white record, totally free of political interests or whatever boycotts are likely to be about. There are advantages in spreading the Games. They did much for Japan and Mexico. If they could stop being quite such a burden, there is a lot to be said for taking them around the world. Individual countries put in a tremendous effort, as Sarajevo did, and it gives them facilities for an international future.'

Once more, however, the Olympic family would depart from a Games for a bout of soul-searching, looking at means whereby, at the fourth consecutive attempt, a major boycott might be avoided. Samaranch, shrewdly, had resisted high-riding emotional calls for action during the Session prior to the LA Games, and had proposed an Extraordinary Session for December of that year, requesting members in the meantime to submit their various suggestions and steps that might be taken.

Recommendations flowed in. Comte Jean de Beaumont, of France, proposed the withdrawal of recognition of boycotting countries for the next two Games and, ipso facto, respective IOC members, with simultaneously the agreement by IFs that they would cease to accept judges and referees from NOCs which were no longer recognized. Nor would a country at war be eligible to stage the Games, although the NOC of such a country might compete elsewhere. José Beracasa, honorary member for Venezuela, went further: suspension from the next *three* Games and fine of $2 per head of the population. Turgut Atakol, of Turkey, more moderately proposed the suspension of Olympic Solidarity Aid for a certain period of time and the prohibition of other sports events in countries which withdraw participation. João Havelange, echoing de Beaumont, called for the suspension of NOC officials, and of officials and referees by IFs, of countries that withdrew, and the ineligibility of IOC members from such countries for the executive board or for Commissions for a period of eight years. Judge Keba M'Baye characteristically produced some legal thoughts: that no NOC may withdraw on the grounds that conditions for participation have not been fulfilled by the organizing committee, because this is the responsibility of the IOC alone; and that if an NOC should do so, it is claiming a right which it does not possess, and therefore violates the Charter. It is not a matter of imposing a sanction, since the NOC has taken the initiative by leaving the Olympic family, an act which places it outside it.

Dick Pound proposed the following: 1) the athletes of a boycotting country may compete at the next Games but without their national flag, without identifiable uniform and with the Olympic hymn instead of national anthem should they win; 2) if any country should not participate in two successive Games, or in two of any three, or in any Games and engage in efforts to influence others to act in a similar manner, then the suspension of the NOC until after the next Games, loss of Solidarity Funds, no election of IOC members for four years after the lifting of the suspension, readmission of the NOC to be at the discretion of the executive board.

I hope I do not sound too much a cynical journalist in observing that, almost needless to say, no such proposals would be put into practice, other than the exclusion of NOC representatives from the current Games.

The staging of the Extraordinary Session did promote, however, the sending of a letter of more than two thousand words to the IOC President by the two Soviet members, Andrianov and Smirnov. This letter, absurdly, attempted to discredit totally the Games which had just taken place and which, with hindsight, would be seen to have saved, possibly more than any other factor, the future of the Games: an event which, when awarded, no other city had wished to stage because of financial risk – indeed not even Los Angeles, for the organizing committee had been private – yet had succeeded in making a substantial profit. The profit was not evil; even if it was unsatisfactory, and widely criticized, in that the exclusive beneficiary was the United States. The letter of the two Russian members condemned the Games for making a profit, for being private, and simultaneously for, on the one hand, having no contact with the government and, on the other, for the government not having given guarantees. From there the letter descended into trivia such as the inconvenient placing in the main stadium of the seats for IOC members; aeroplanes advertising beer overhead; and the chauvinism of ABC Television. The letter concluded, having protested about breaches of the Charter, with the demand that the IOC must maintain close contact with the UN and UNESCO, and NOCs with their governments, all of this *equally* contrary to the Charter.

Andrianov and Smirnov arrived in Lausanne for the Extraordinary Session looking exceedingly uncomfortable for having penned a letter, under duress from their seniors, which achieved no more than to make them look foolish. Constantin Andrianov, elected in 1951, is now dead. Smirnov, reflecting wryly upon the political environment which had obliged the pair of them to go through the motions of protest so laughably, says: 'The Games in LA produced great agitation in Moscow, which resulted in the letter. Andrianov had a Stalinist breeding, in which there were good guys and bad guys, yet in his way he was something really special, a man from whom you could learn so much. There *were* bad phrases in the letter, criticizing Killanin for "selling" the Games to LA. There was so much conditioning from Stalin's time. Many athletes from the Thirties and Forties went to prison for "failures". In 1952, when the Soviet Union lost to Yugoslavia in the early stages of the football, Stalin had a furious row with Tito, and when we finished on equal medals with the USA, the celebration reception for the entire Soviet team was cancelled. There are some members of that 1952 team who have still not received their Merited Master of Sport Award, which is always given to Olympic champions. Throughout the pre-war era the Olympic Games had always been considered *bourgeois*.'

In his address to the Extraordinary Session, Samaranch, continuing with a policy of avoiding punitive measures, and believing that the prevention of boycotts in the future lay more in the creation of improved relations than in the threat of stringent regulations, had said: 'The serious problems which appeared several weeks before the recent Games provided us once more with the opportunity to demonstrate our unity and our faith in the future. The very large and unquestionable success of the Games of the XXIII Olympiad in Los Angeles is something of which we may quite justly feel proud. We have shown once again in difficult conditions that the Olympic Movement will follow its own path . . . We did not wish to react in the heat of the moment in Los Angeles, but preferred the calm and neutrality of our "homeland". We have come here with the sole aim of learning a lesson from our experiences . . . There is no stipulation in the Charter which compels National Olympic Committees to compete . . . It is our duty to remind them that they were created by Pierre de Coubertin in order to facilitate and prepare participation of their athletes in the Olympic Games . . . The refusal to participate . . . is a failure to comply with the fundamental duty of each NOC . . . This means that they are forbidding their athletes to complete against their world rivals in a prestigious competition which only takes place once every four years . . . Such action is willingly to put oneself apart from a number of decisions and meetings, to exclude oneself from various bodies, to risk having participation in governing bodies put into question. The sanction in all these cases is immediate and probably irredeemable.'

Here Samaranch introduced M'Baye's logic. 'When it is pretended that one's decisions stem from the study of the Charter, I must recall that the IOC's role is to insure the interpretation of the Charter, and no one may assume this right without contravening the rules of our Movement . . . The IOC members themselves guarantee the function and spirit of independence by faithfully respecting the commitments which they accepted upon their election. It is only by means of this primordial and vital condition, only if the IOC members do not forget their obligations, that we can hope to conserve this pride and uniqueness

. . . And the very nature of the approaches which are made to us from various sides are reassuring, seem to me to indicate a sprightliness of mind, alert enough to reassure us of the good health of our Movement.'

All of which, it could be said, was a polite way of saying: 'Don't let's be too hasty.' The resolution that would be declared at the end of the Session was that it is the duty of NOCs to ensure their athletes compete; that athletes should not be punished by boycotts and then further penalized by additional exclusions; that true motivation of boycotts will be identified, and the NOC representatives of such countries excluded from the (current) Games; that the sole authority of the conduct of the Games and maintenance of the Charter is the IOC; and that the IOC, IFs and NOCs fully support the next Games in Calgary and Seoul.

As is so often the case, Samaranch was ahead of the game. By the time of this meeting in December, four and a half months after the Games in LA, Samaranch had clear indication that offending nations recognized the futility of boycotts, conceding that the main victims were the countries that stayed away; and that, whatever the formal diplomatic relationships, every nation that mattered intended to be present in South Korea four years later. In reaching such conclusions, Samaranch was greatly assisted by the counter-intelligence of Siperco of Romania, the Asian experience of Ashwini Kumar, and the legal alertness of Dick Pound.

'The Session had given the executive board full powers regarding 1988 and all negotiations with South Korea,' Samaranch says. 'This was important, giving the board and myself freedom to deal with the controversy precipitated by North Korea. A lot of feeling and emotion had emerged during the Session, and there were thirty-seven speeches from the floor – one of them, by Carraro of Italy, in very poor taste, for which he received an official communiqué. There were many who wanted to be tough with the defectors in Los Angeles, but now they realized the need for caution. Although I knew there were immense anxieties lying ahead for the Games in Seoul, I now felt optimistic.'

6 Turning Point

When Michael Killanin was elected to the IOC in 1952, he was not a man of means, never mind his title. Attending the Olympic Games in Helsinki that year, he made good use of the available seasonal bus pass. 'Not a bad principle, when you come to think about it,' he reflects today. The practice of private cars standing by on permanent call for members only started in Munich twenty years later, when BMW beat their motor rivals for the public relations prestige of providing the service. 'When I attended Olympic Games before I was President,' Killanin says, 'I would have to go as part of the Irish quota of officials. For the Games in Melbourne, I went as a director of Aspro! Their headquarters were in Melbourne. I would not otherwise have gone, even as the chairman of the Olympic Committee for Ireland, to which I had been elected in 1950. We sent only twelve to Melbourne, including a single official, and we came back with one gold medal, Ron Delaney's in the 1,500 metres, one silver, and three bronze.'

The Games in 1984 proved to be a turning-point in Olympic history: necessity, as the old adage goes, being the mother of invention. A privately run event, these Games had to operate in the black, and did so with such spectacular success that they would help create the start of a new era in the Olympic Movement. Now there was going to be money flowing in future for everyone: too much so, perhaps, as Robert Helmick, later to become president of the US Olympic Committee, would learn to his cost. When Los Angeles challenged Moscow in Vienna in 1974 for the Games in 1980, their bid had the appeal of being low-cost; a trend that many felt desirable following the expensive constructions in Munich and the alarm that was growing at uncontrolled spending by Montreal for 1976. Los Angeles failed in Vienna, however, because a majority of members, some against their better instincts, considered the Soviet Union carried such a reputation of successs within the Olympic Movement that, irrespective of any political doubts, it was not ethical to reject the application of Moscow. Tom Bradley, the Mayor of Los Angeles, was encouraged by Killanin to bid again. He did so, and when the time came in Athens four years later to decide, Los Angeles was the only city bidding. Tehran had withdrawn. Elsewhere, potential candidates had been frightened away by the debts heaped upon the citizens of Montreal.

And there was a snag in the new bid by Los Angeles. Committed by the vote of the city's population not to put at risk one dollar of public money, Los Angeles was now seeking a contract that in many instances ignored the Charter. The most serious of these was over the requirement for the contract to be between the bidding city and, jointly, the IOC and the respective National Olympic Committee, the latter accepting financial responsibility. Bradley's committee adamantly rejected such a deal, and the Athens Session ended with no contract signed. Ultimately, the solution devised by Robert Kane and Don Miller, president and secretary-general of the USOC respectively, was that the Games would be awarded to Los Angeles, which would then consign them to a private organizing committee. In the absence of alternatives, the IOC had been obliged to accept this breach in its Charter. What now happened was that, to guarantee its commercial safety, the private committee established a chain of commercial sponsorships; and these would create the pattern that henceforth precipitated a dramatic upturn in the finances of the Olympic Movement.

What was to ignite controversy more than anything in the perceived commercialism of Ueberroth's Games was a proposal concerning the torch that traditionally lights the flame in the stadium at every opening ceremony. Contrary to general opinion, this tradition has no ancient historic or mythological derivation from the mountains of western Greece, but was the suggestion, in 1928, of Theodore Lewald, an IOC member for Germany, prior to the Games in Amsterdam. It had been his proposal that the flame be lit in Olympia and carried thence to the host city, though it was not until Berlin in 1936 that the ceremony of lighting the torch from the rays of the sun at Olympia was carried out. It was, therefore, singularly inappropriate for the Greeks to have mounted a high horse of principle over Ueberroth's intention to stage a *sponsored* torch run, considering that the Greeks themselves had for 48 years been charging the IOC a substantial fee for providing the facilities at Olympia. Ueberroth's plan was to raise $3,000 a kilometre from every volunteer runner, and this proved to be an inspirational concept in small-town America. More than four thousand sponsors were to donate $12m, which would all go directly to YMCA clubs and charities without deductions. The organizing committee were contributing $200 for every runner's torch – which the runner was to keep – and obligatory running kit, which was entirely without advertising and the exploitation against which Greece needlessly protested. More than half the population was turning out in little towns and villages for a unique sight of the flame as it meandered its way across America, producing an Olympic consciousness and pride, many of the runners being handicapped. Ueberroth was correctly optimistic that it would become a permanent feature of future Games.

'You've got to remember the backdrop of our Games,' Ueberroth reflects. 'Some 83 per cent of the people of Los Angeles voted against the Games. We had four years of antagonism in the press, and we knew we needed to change public opinion. You can't have an Olympic Games in a country that doesn't want to have it. So we did a lot of work with youth groups in southern California, for instance. I considered that if we could get thousands of kids involved, they would sway local public opinion. The idea of the torch was that if it went through cities and towns, those people carrying the flame and donating the money would build up a huge caring attitude, would make the public more friendly, and make competitors more caring.'

At the time when we spoke at Ueberroth's offices at Newport Beach, the world was eight hours away from the deadline for a UN Allied invasion of Kuwait for the removal of Saddam Hussein. 'You need positives to balance the tide of events,' Ueberroth continued. 'Even within our own committee there were people against the idea of the flame, and there were administrative negatives: that we would need fifty thousand parade permits across the country, that some torch carriers *might* get seriously burned: there were a hundred reasons against. We carefully explained to the IOC that it was not a commercialization of the flame, and that the way to create the run was by making it a charity event for children. What better motive than $3,000 given to the local community? It turned out to be successful beyond expectation. More than forty-four million Americans came to the roadside to watch the flame go by. In fact it was a financial loser for us, with the cost of the equipment. We arranged for AT&T (the telephone company) to sponsor the administration because they were one of the few organizations with retired people available in every city across the States. I was optimistic we'd convince the Greeks, if only because it didn't make sense to oppose it,and that they would finally see the light. The opposition was a political conspiracy that failed. At one time we planned to keep the flame permanently alight from the Winter Games in Sarajevo, but they [the Yugoslavs] couldn't stand the political heat from the Greeks and put the flame out. We had to devise another solution for bringing the flame from Greece, secretly, which Samaranch helped us to scheme, in case the Greeks refused to co-operate. It couldn't be done publicly. One of his skills, if he thought you were right, was to advise you privately. We filmed the lighting of the alternative flame at Olympia with a group of students, so that it couldn't be said we had not obtained it from the traditional source, but few people know to this day which flame it was that arrived in New York for the start of the run.'

The two Greek members of the IOC, Nissiotis and Filaratos, had protested to the executive board about the sponsored run. Berlioux had made it clear, at the time of the Winter Games in Sarajevo, that the concept of torch and flame belonged to the IOC and not to the Greeks. For the first kilometre the flame was to be carried by Gina Hemphill, a granddaughter of Jesse Owens, personally sponsored by Peter Ueberroth.

'Samaranch may be short of stature physically,' Anita DeFrantz observes, 'but he cast a long shadow across the Games of 1984, his influence was so extensive, even in very small ways. He came to the University of Southern California's Olympic Village, where I was the head administrator. I'd been put there by Peter particularly to look after all the Africans and I had wanted the challenge of the larger village. When Samaranch arrived, he didn't want to drive in a buggy, but to walk everywhere, and I remember my staff being impressed. On the day we'd heard about the boycott, a pall had fallen over the staff, just as if they'd lost a relative. Samaranch had realized during his dealings with the organizing committee that, as President, you had to be active, had to be *seen* as the leader, rather than Monique [Berlioux]. Early on, if there was an obstruction, we'd tried to keep both of them happy, aware that they might have a different set of needs. In the early days, Peter was aware that though Samaranch was President, it was still Monique who knew where the buttons were, but by degrees Samaranch began to change that perception.'

As Ueberroth and his committee, jointly led by Harry Usher, put together their financially foolproof Games, Ueberroth persistently cited de Coubertin's comment from 1909, following the Games in London: 'The Olympics must be more dignified, more discreet, more intimate, and less expensive.' The dynamic, smooth-tongued American also liked to quote Churchill: 'Some see private enterprise as a predatory target to be shot, others as a cow to be milked, but few are those who see it as a sturdy horse pulling the wagon.' I still have the paperweight with that inscription on my desk from my first visit to talk with Ueberroth at the porta-cabin headquarters at Culver City, early in 1983. By degrees, Ueberroth's message of efficiency, in the staging of an inexpensive Games, was reaching the community.

Bill Toomey, the 1968 decathlon champion, married to the 1964 long-jump winner Mary Rand, was emphatic that Los Angeles would bring respect back into the Games. Toomey lived an hour's drive from the Memorial Coliseum stadium, built for the Games of 1932 and now renovated, down the eight-lane Santa Ana freeway in opulent Laguna Hills. 'The Olympics should be a competition for sportsmen,' Toomey said, 'not an architectural festival for frustrated late-adolescents. I think the organizing committee is a pretty moral group of efficient guys, who've done the serious bit extremely well.'

The 45-year-old Ueberroth, a water polo trialist for the Games of 1956, was irritated by stories that his committee was playing bandit. 'There is no *message* to the world from this committee,' he insisted. 'Munich wanted to show that it represented the new industrial, free-and-friendly nation. Montreal spent two billion dollars to prove it was not stepchild to the United States. Moscow wanted to demonstrate that it was the most notable socialist state, that its ideology had worldwide acceptance. We haven't any message, except let's have a nice Games.'

He had previously built from scratch the second-largest travel company in America. His administrative ace had been to reduce the number of sponsors, thereby creating exclusivity and higher fees – a principle to be steeply developed by the IOC thereafter. With no local or federal subsidy, no lottery (illegal), he had found the $470m to fund the Games, a fraction of what was spent in Montreal and Moscow. The money had come from television ($250m), sponsorship ($115m), ticketing ($85m), equipment contributors ($14), trading licences ($13m). A predicted 10 per cent surplus would be divided, under IOC rules, between the USOC, the Education Department of Southern California, and the national sports governing bodies. The organizing committee's many hundred staff was paid by interest accruing from up-front television, sponsorship, and ticket money. Low pay, long hours, and guaranteed termination of contract comprised Ueberroth's only offer to his huge, multiracial, and visibly happy staff. His slogan for supporters of the LA Games was: 'Pay now, live later.'

So successful was Ueberroth's budgeting that the surplus would prove to be many times greater than expected, leading to worldwide criticism rather than gratitude, on account of the money being retained within America. Part of the reason for the financial success was the initial deduction, from the up-front US television rights fee of $200m from ABC, of more than $90m for 'service facilities'. Equally important was the economy of using predominantly existing facilities; this meant that the Games were stretched over 100 miles (from canoeing and rowing at the natural Lake Casitas in the north, three-day eventing in San Diego County to the south, football at the Pasadena Rose Bowl to the north-east, as well as on the east coast). The only two new stadia, both sponsored, were for swimming (McDonald's, $3.6m) and cycling (Southland Food, $3.12m). Atlantic Richfield renovated the Coliseum, with its famous peristyle arched end, and also built six training tracks. The Games would produce an economic investment in southern California of many millions of dollars: a slice of that, it must be said, from over-charging the press for telephones. Those who believed that there might never be another Games after Los Angeles, that the XXIII Olympics to be opened by President Reagan would be so bedevilled by boycott, excessive finance, shameless nationalism, acknowledged professionalism, rampant and undetected drug-taking, security against terrorism, immovable traffic, and insufferable smog that no one would want any more of it, were to be proved spectacularly wrong.

Writing in *Olympic Review* shortly before the Games, Ueberroth admitted that it might be difficult for some to believe that an event traditionally as expensive as the Olympic Games could be staged without direct cost to the citizens of the host city. He stressed that there was a distinct principle. 'We would like to state unequivocally,' he wrote, 'that while we will have a Games that benefits from commerce, we will not have by any means a commercial Games. Sponsoring the 1984 Games is not a matter of money alone. We require of our sponsors what has traditionally been asked of Olympic athletes: dedication to sports.' How ironic that the man who was busy rendering the Olympic Movement such sterling service would within the year be rejected as a potential member of the IOC for being, it was said, too smart and therefore too dangerous.

During the four years between Moscow and Los Angeles, Ueberroth had the opportunity to observe the balance of power between Samaranch and Berlioux. 'I thought the relationship started very well,' he recalls. 'I remember in Moscow having dinner, the day he was elected, Berlioux and her aide and my wife and I, in her suite, and Mrs Samaranch coming to say thank-you. Berlioux had supported him in the election, wholly and fully, and was clearly pleased he'd been elected. Then his determination became apparent, and she couldn't understand it. Their objectives were primarily the same. Both were dedicated to and had a love affair with the Olympic Movement. There was an initial period when we had to have two channels of communications, one to Berlioux, and one to Samaranch. Then we began to realize that Samaranch was very clearly the leader. For us in LA, Monique had gone through some real battles. She had got Killanin to insist to the world that the Games would still go to LA even after the boycott of Moscow. After our Games, Berlioux and Samaranch seemed to continue to get on well together, because the record attendance had been something of a triumph for him. I got some credit, but he deserved it too and so did she – they'd kept the ship on course. Afterwards, she remained the person to deal with, in *her* opinion. This had been our experience in 1979, negotiating on television and so on. As Samaranch spent more and more time in Lausanne, of course he began to put in his own people, but right up to our Games, with two-thirds of the decisions Berlioux was there. We thought a lot of her, even if we didn't get along with her all the time. When there were difficulties between us and Berlioux, Samaranch would decide one way or the other. I guess the word statesmanship jumps out at you. We were just one of the many parts of the Olympic Movement that he had to balance. We had to put on a Games not using much money, and I think the Olympics are *still* the least commercialized major sporting event in the world, especially when you put them alongside our Super Bowl or World Series baseball.'

In his address to the Session prior to the Games, Samaranch would say: 'If I've learned one thing in my life, it is that only through human contact can our differences be overcome and dialogue opened. Perhaps that is what our world today lacks the most.' By his own efforts, travelling the world ceaselessly to meet National Olympic Committees and to the outer limits of the International Federations, Samaranch was attempting to achieve that contact. If he made a contribution towards the coherence of the Games in Los Angeles, his efforts on behalf of Seoul over the next four years would be even more significant. But for the moment, he would share the sense of achievement exhibited by the crowd at the Coliseum, where a huge cheer greeted the appearance of the Chinese during the march past in the opening ceremony. 'Our seat had been restored during Killanin's time, at the executive board meeting at Nagoya in 1979, when it was resolved to submit the decision to a postal vote, which was in our favour,' Zhenliang Hé recalls. 'We took part in Lake Placid but withdrew from Moscow, so our participation in Los Angeles was for the first time in fifty-two years, our first full appearance after our restoration. In 1932, I think we had one athlete in the 100 metres. Now, we won fifteen gold medals. Not only we, but many people were happy about that. Security in Los Angeles was not a factor that bothered us. The Chinese people feel very different from eastern Europe. We know what we were forty years ago, and what we have achieved in that time. I do not deny that there are people in mainland China who would prefer to live under another political/economic system. We *could* have fifty million wealthy people, but we would then probably have one billion poor.' The Soviets, East Germans and the rest would lick their self-inflicted wounds at home and wish they were there.

The United States might carry the conscience of the modern western world but now, with a Hollywood zap which acclaimed friendliness more than vulgarity, Los Angeles welcomed 142 nations with an open-heartedness that so genuinely meant 'Have a nice day'. The three-hour opening ceremony display was often stunningly spectacular, yet never boastful: an exposition of the remarkable kaleidoscope of ethnic races and cultures which have made America great. It was a pageant in which the overriding theme was of a community with a zest for life and progress, which no smug European should scorn: from the immigrant settlers with their wagons, the negroes emerging from subservience, through to the twentieth-century extravaganza of music, dance and technology. The older world, bred on history and tradition, could not remain unmoved when assailed by 750 trumpets, drums and trombones of the All-American Marching Band playing Prima's 'Sing, Sing, Sing' with uninhibited exultation. It was, above all, a ceremony memorable for its sense of social justice. When the jet planes had finished their sky-writing, and the 84 grand pianos had paid a tribute to Gershwin; when the thousands of gymnasts had unleashed the youthful energy which is the voice of the nation; when the bands had played and the 142 teams had paraded, with echoing cheers for the communists from Romania and China; when the crowd, after no more than a five-second countdown practice, had unknowingly suddenly produced a canopy of international flags with 90,000 individually-held coloured sheets, which upstaged the carefully rehearsed Russian display in Moscow four years before; when the huge American team had made its disordered, extrovert entry, and the American President had humanly fluffed the order of his 18-word formal opening speech, there came the moment which two and a half billion television viewers awaited. The lighting of the flame.

Half a century earlier, Jesse Owens, a poor cotton-family black, had been obliged to enter stadiums by the side door, even after he had become, in Berlin, the greatest Olympian of this century so far. Now, into a hushed Coliseum with the sun's sinking rays illuminating the Olympic flag and the golden letters at the eastern end of the stadium, 'Games of the XXIII Olympiad', ran Owens's granddaughter Gina Hemphill. Bearing the torch which had wound its way around 10,000 miles of America, she lapped the track once, side-stepping competitors with cameras, to pass the torch to Rafer Johnson, the decathlon champion of 1960, who climbed a Busby Berkeley 99-step staircase beneath the stadium arches to light the symbolic flame. Owens would have been a proud man. He would have believed, as I do, that the flame can still carry its intended meaning of the unity of man. And when Ed Moses, another black Olympic champion, also forgot his lines when taking the athletes' oath, it reminded Americans that we are all ultimately humble.

TASS, the Soviet news agency, described the ceremony as 'an obvious political spectacle', but that was just Moscow sour grapes.

What Ueberroth had done was to embrace tens of thousands of volunteers to make these Games memorable. The Botswana team, for example, lived as guests in private homes because they could not afford more than a fortnight in the Village. Should you have needed an emergency eye operation, or broken your ankle, you were attended, free, by volunteer surgeons in the expensively equipped medical complex of the University College of Los Angeles, which was probably the best appointed Olympic Village there has ever been. The training facilities for track and field, in rolling, relaxing grassland, and for gymnastics, were superb. A huge weight-training gymnasium, a positive torture-chamber of elaborate modern gadgetry, was superior to anything I had previously seen, and testimony to the unparalleled finances of American university sport. As Samaranch had said at the Session, sport *does* unite people. 'If it was suddenly necessary for governments to repay all those people who have freely and generously given their time to sport, very few states would be in a position to do so.'

While the volunteers were working long days, sometimes ten or twelve hours, for no more reward than a sandwich and an iced Coke, and the opportunity to meet different people from, to them, remote places such as Turkey, Mauritius or Uganda, Samaranch's executive board was adjusting to a daily routine that had never been experienced before: the first meeting of the day at 7.30 with the LA organizing committee plus one representative each from the NOCs, IFs and the Athletes Commission, together with written reports from the previous evening, on each sport, of anything important or untoward such as aspects of security. 'Those meetings could last two hours,' recollects Walter Tröger, then the sports director, 'and might be followed by an inspection as well to investigate anything that was incorrect. The running of the Games is much more difficult now than ever before, with all the aspects relating to sponsors and the media. At previous Games, these things had been neglected. Samaranch needed people to whom he could talk freely. Behind closed doors, he wanted to be told of *any* deficiency. Other than at the Games, he would rarely let a small meeting run more than half an hour, but he would always *listen*. He might not react directly to what you had said, but you knew it was being considered seriously. He intensified the activity of the executive board, and it's inevitable that whenever you create work, more work arrives. A good example of that is the expansion of the staff on the Solidarity Fund under Anselmo Lopez.

'There are so many things Samaranch has created. The Sport for All promotion, with clinics, especially in eastern Europe, and in 1986 the first Sport for All Congress in Frankfurt. Sport for the Disabled. The new Commissions, including the Evaluation Commission for bidding cities. The new museum. Olympic philately. The strengthening of the legal department, because of the looseness of some of the earlier contracts.' Dick Palmer, several times a member of Evaluation Commissions and on the executive board of ANOC, adds: 'LA was a bitter-sweet experience for Samaranch. He hadn't been able to overcome the political poison of Moscow, but LA was such a phenomenal commercial success, it changed the nature of the Olympic Movement.'

Determined economizing of facilities by Ueberroth made for some discomforts. While the main press centre was superbly equipped, the special bus service which many were obliged to use consisted of ancient bone-shakers with wooden seats and no air conditioning and normally inflicted only upon uncomplaining schoolchildren; I rented a car, for flexibility, and in two and a half weeks travelled 1,500 miles without going outside the Olympic circuit.

Samaranch defends the policy of economy and does not consider, in the light of the eventual profit, that the organizing committee had been misleading. 'I don't think so,' he says, 'because it had always been stressed that the organization was private, and that there would be restrictive, decentralized budgets for each individual sport. Near to the opening of the Games, the sports were told that they could spend more, but by then it was too late, though it had been unclear until quite late exactly how many countries and competitors there would be. The organizing committee were not very fair with the IOC, telling us towards the end that maybe they would have a surplus of *some* millions. By degrees, it became apparent that the figure was steadily increasing, even though for the first time we were paying the travelling expenses for four athletes and two officials per team. It was excellent that there *was* a profit, because this meant there were a number of candidates bidding for the forthcoming Games, but with hindsight it was not good for the relationship to have been protesting such poverty all the time. The USOC tried to make it sound better by offering an aid programme for the Third World, but this was to have lasted only for two years. The IOC can never demand part of the surplus, because you can be sure that there will then never *be* a surplus.'

If the Games had been heading for unimagined profits, so too, potentially were some of the competitors. The professionals, though not yet in all sports, were there to stay, their rise inexorable. It was not professionalism that needed to be halted, but the attendant phenomenon that accompanied it, performance-enhancing drugs exploited not only by competitors but in many instances by cheating coaches and doctors. It tends to be forgotten that Ben Johnson won the 100 metres bronze medal in 1984. For the great competitors, who devoted themselves full-time to the pursuit of excellence, to have a share of the rewards now available, through the vast television audiences they attracted and the sponsorship that went hand in hand with them, was no more than reasonable. 'I always felt,' Lord Killanin says, 'that if Seb Coe or Said Aouita could fill a stadium, they should have some sort of cut.'

In 1984 Robert Helmick was president of the international swimming federation, FINA. It was the following year that he would be elected president of USOC and a member of the IOC, positions that would be rudely bumped in 1991 by his admission of the acceptance of extensive legal consultancy fees within the framework of Olympic administration and carrying an apparent conflict of interest. Helmick defends the 10 per cent share of the US television rights fee which is granted to USOC. 'That percentage we receive,' Helmick said at the time of the Pan American Games in Havana in 1991, 'should not be allowed totally to alienate us. I think the rest of the world does *need* the Americans. We've struggled for long enough, to get enough money for our team, with people laughing at us when we got beaten by communist opposition. But since 1984, we're successfully marketing, and people from Europe suddenly come in and want to market our patch. We secured the Olympic Movement with the LA Games, yet that 10 per cent of television still bugs people. There is not one American from the world of Madison Avenue in ISL Marketing to advise the IOC on the division between spheres of interest. I think it's a sad state of affairs when a major country, with an NOC thoroughly supportive – bar 1980 on account of the US government – has a battle over marketing that overshadows other relations. People negotiate with us [the American market] then tell the world we're greedy. Samaranch has said that if USOC pulled out of the TOP programme, it would collapse. So I think people are entitled to look after us.'

There is some logic in Helmick's comments, though some of this is lost by the necessity of his resignation as president of USOC in September 1991, following the exposure of extensive consultancy fees on Olympic issues. Money corrupts; even by inference, when there is no question of illegality and only the possibility of ethical confusion. I am sure that in 1984 those technicians and commentators of ABC Television who made its coverage of the Games in Los Angeles so unacceptable – Samaranch lodged an official complaint – had no conception of the distortion they were creating. They will have even have considered, in their enthusiasm, that they were doing a fine job. Roone Arledge, president of ABC Sports and News, writing in *Olympic Review* prior to the Games, had said: 'The role of television is, first and foremost, to document the Olympic Games, to present them just as they are. One of the best aspects of this is that there is more than just the competition. There is a feeling of harmony among nations and athletes, and a spirit that one senses not only at the Olympic venues but also throughout the entire Olympic city. To those who have never attended an Olympics, this is impossible to describe. Yet all who have been to the Games, surely understand what I mean. Our presence [in LA] will be comprehensive and our presence will be dignified.'

Unfortunately, almost every aspect of what Arledge wrote here was to be corrupted by his presenters. Joe Gurgan of the *Los Angeles Times*, contemplating the unending celebration of America's 174 medals and the prospect of a five-day national tribute tour, reflected: 'Another week to teach our children the wrong lesson, not only about the nature of the Olympic Games, but the essence of sports.' Gurgan went on to relate a tale of a US ice hockey player who became a part-time teacher in order to train with his Olympic squad, and was mocked by the pupils because he had no large limousine like the professional baseball and football stars.

The sorrow of the Games in Los Angeles was that, through television, they would only have served to make the average American arrogant towards rival sporting competitors. de Coubertin's premise of the honour of taking part was, and is, still very much alive, but no one would have known this in 1984 from watching or listening to the objectionable and extreme chauvinism of ABC Television. Through the banal words of the trite Jim McKay, the ignorant Kathleen Sullivan, the naïve Jim

Lampley, the tedious Howard Cosell, and the self-parodying Ted Dawson, domestic television managed to nullify the internationalism of Ueberroth's organizing committee. American viewers were hardly aware that there were foreign competitors; even when, annoyingly, they won. The men's marathon, like every event, was superbly filmed, for instance; yet while Lopes, Treacy and Spedding, the three inexperienced converts from successful track careers, ran away from de Castella and the hard men of Africa and Japan, the commentators dwelt endlessly on the ailing American, Salazar, out of touch a minute or so behind the leaders. In the climax before the closing ceremony, Lopes's gold medal for the most symbolic of the Olympic events was upstaged by equestrian showjumping . . . because there the US was first and second.

We must admire so much of what was achieved in Los Angeles in 1984, and may expect a similar degree of competence, and no doubt of commercialism, at Atlanta in 1996. It is to be hoped, however, that by then American television will have discovered that there are other competitors out there, on the other side of the Atlantic and Pacific, who occasionally are as good as them, and sometimes better.

7 Travels

—

'Surprisingly,' Vitaly Smirnov recalls, 'Samaranch became familiar very quickly with Russian customs, with people from a range of different circles, from politics, art, sport, and all the time keeping in contact, between his appointment as Ambassador in 1977 and 1980, with the Moscow organizing committee. In those three years he did more as an ambassador than others did in many years. His habit of travelling as President of the IOC began, you could say, in Russia: travelling all over a country that covers one-sixth of the world's surface.'

In 1985, Samaranch was to make a complicated journey through central Africa, visiting twelve countries in eleven days. Reuters, the international news agency, had been invited to send a journalist to accompany him, but at the last minute withdrew, and the spare seat on a small charter jet due to depart from Geneva in mid-October was offered to me. Those making the trip, besides Samaranch and his assistant, Coupat, were Louis Guirandou-N'Daiye, member for Ivory Coast and at that time a vice-president; Anani Matthia, member for Togo, and president of the African Association of Olympic Committees (ANOCA); Jean-Claude Ganga, president of the Supreme Council for Sport in Africa and the following year to be elected member for Congo; Amadou Lamine Ba, from Senegal, secretary-general of the Supreme Council based in Cameroon; Lamine Diack of Senegal, vice-president of the International Athletic Federation; and Samuel Kamau, president of the Kenyan Olympic Committee (who has subsequently died in a motor accident).

Nouakchott, Mauritania

Following only a brief stop in Dakar, Senegal, we touched down in this most arid of countries bordering the Sahara. The superpowers, whose global financial aid helps to maintain peace, simultaneously support or jeopardize that stability by the colossal supply of arms to their satellite allies. China, a super-power in the making, was busy paving the way towards international influence by benevolently supplying sporting stadia to likely allies. Looking at the Atlantic shore across desolate desert and derelict, broken-down trucks on the skyline of poor but dignified Nouakchott, the view was dominated not by a mosque or a modern hotel but by an imposing football and athletics stadium of which Britain, say, would have been proud. It was designed and built by the fraternal Chinese. The temples of the twentieth century come with floodlights. There are a dozen such stadia spread south, north, and east across this vast, emerging, troubled continent. They cost, at that time, some $30-35m each, and were donated by different Provinces of the world's most populous nation: even when they themselves have no such stadia. The stadium in Dakar which we visited had a capacity of 60,000 and a ten-lane athletics track. The area beneath the stand was utilized for halls for Olympic sports such as wrestling, judo, handball and table tennis. It was a monumental hope for a country which in Los Angeles produced a fifth-place finalist in the men's 400 metres hurdles.

When, if ever, Africa has the food and facilities it needs, a continent where at present a home in a tent too often is luxury, I fancy that in some sports we shall see only the dust of their heels. In 1984, Mauritania's Olympic Committee, formed only in 1979, sent a team of five (four wrestlers) to Los Angeles. It was a proud moment indeed when one of them survived the first round. Though their share of the earth's surface is almost twice that of France, from whom they gained their independence, though at the price of surrendering much of their wealth to Senegal from whom they separated, their reward is an unrelenting expanse of desert devoid of anything but some metal ores. Yet here, with sand in your eyes, your carburettor, your toothbrush, in everything, the spirit of de Coubertin lives. It was fostered then by men such as Gabriel Hatti, the president of the NOC and a lawyer who has been the legal adviser to four Mauritanian heads of state. It would be naïve to suppose that there is no link between sport and politics,yet Samaranch was assured by Camera Ali Gueladio, the head of state, that Mauritania would be in Seoul in 1988 irrespective of political considerations.

Freetown, Sierra Leone

In steaming humidity on the airport tarmac, a staff sergeant who spent several months training as a goalkeeper twenty years ago with West Ham United in London, brought his guard of honour – footballers and gymnasts – smartly to attention. On their T-shirts was the slogan 'See you in Seoul'. Samaranch inspected the guard with a broad smile, while a steel band beat out its rhythm with all the vigour of the Los Angeles opening ceremony. At such emotional moments it is difficult to accept Orwell's maxim that international sport is an unfailing cause of ill-will. It cannot be stated too often that countries such as this, ex-colonial territories unobtrusively and vigorously striving for identity, create the Olympic Games every bit as much as any gold medallist.

A little lady of the Sierra Leone committee, in pink dress and pink knitted beret, reminded the IOC of their awareness of women's needs. Dorothy Pyne, the Director of Women's Physical Education, pointed out that in many African countries mothers were reluctant to permit their daughters to be taught by men, and urgent help was required in establishing women's teaching courses.

Mrs Pyne, who studied in Coventry and Liverpool in England from 1951 to 1954, said: 'Development is not advanced because of the shortage of teachers. We have no degree course here, so the overseas courses for women which the IOC has promised are vital.' Freetown's tiny streets, crowded by tilting wooden shops and houses built in the last century, are a nightmare for cars and oblige most people to walk everywhere. 'We walk miles and miles,' Mrs Pyne said. 'What could we achieve if we had coaches to train race walkers!'

Bamako, Mali

Politically unaligned Mali, which appropriately had an education college jointly sponsored by the Soviet Union and the United States, made pleas to Samaranch for assistance through Lamine Keita, the president of their Olympic Committee and also a member of the IOC. By the time of the Games in Seoul, Mali would have had $90,000 in grants from Solidarity over six years for six sports; but in a touching speech, Keita explained that even the unwanted second-hand equipment of a European nation would be invaluable to an underdeveloped country battling on all economic fronts. Mali was one of the most grateful for the television/video sets which Philips had agreed to supply to NOCs and IFs. The favourite local football team, FC Djoliba, were playing in a friendly match at the 20-year-old Russian-built stadium, where thousands of spectators are able to obtain free seats on the adjoining, sharply rising ridge of Red Rock: the 'Snake Stand', as it is known. Mali was then still awaiting its first synthetic track. The red cinders of the Omni-sports Stadium were marginally worse than the old Iffley Road track in Oxford, where Roger Bannister carved his milestone. Yet, watching a performance of the Mali National Ballet, one quickly realized that here was a nation of exceptional natural ability.

Ouagadougou, Burkina Faso

Here was a country with a population 90 per cent illiterate and bereft of all facilities. The NOC had been formed in 1972, but for the past three years the country had been unable to afford to compete in *any* international event, apart from sending a lone runner to the African Championships in Cairo in 1985. It was a crying shame, for a first division friendly football match between Etoile and Civil Service Lazare revealed the kind of skills seen all too rarely in European matches, while a girl runner in the 800 metres showed such promise that she was immediately awarded an IOC overseas scholarship.

Burkina Faso means 'uncorruptible republic', and resident administrators of the World Food Programme and World Health Organization acknowledged the resilience of the people who have almost nothing. The WFP representative said that the rain of 1985 would not solve the crisis of a country which had little to export except Marxism. Everywhere Samaranch went he was accompanied by track-suited athletes chanting: 'Le pays ou la mort. Nous vaincrons. (Country or death. We will conquer.)' By law, everyone was obliged to do an hour's sport at five in the afternoon, even people with only one leg. The cycling ethic had been imported from China: the population of seven million then had five million bicycles and mopeds.

Niamey, Niger

Flying into Niamey from the west, you see a marked difference in the landscape. Green trees and a number of green fields greet the eye. As one of the world's main sources of uranium, Niger is able to afford some of the sophistication of irrigation, electricity and the food and factories which come with both. Niger was still fairly short, however, of international sportsmen. In all the countries we were visiting, Lamine Diack would attempt to convey to the NOC and to the Minister for Sport that the assistance of the government to sport was not a gift but an obligation. 'Sport is not simply a matter of leisure,' Diack said, 'it is part of education, and must be treated as such. It can be one of the incentives in countries where only 50 per cent of the children are going to school.'

Niger had not won an Olympic medal since a boxing bronze in 1972, but that might change, they hoped, in the near future. The Chinese were paying, erecting yet another stadium, one of the eight still left to be finished, in addition to the twelve already in use in Africa. It was to be a multi-sports complex for half a dozen sports, including a hotel with one hundred beds.

Accra, Ghana

The old sign beside the road was peeling: Accra Tennis Club. Colonial days established the game; the roots remained. The Ghana Federation was considering whether to apply for an IOC scholarship for a 16-year-old, Eric Dowuona, who might join a tiny minority of African professionals, led at that time by Odizor of Nigeria. Dowuona, built more powerfully than the then young Edberg, played an exhibition match against the national champion, Joe Atiso, watched by Samaranch. The youngster would mature much faster overseas, yet the NOC was considering instead seeking scholarships to strengthen their re-emerging athletics team, following the encouragement of having their women's sprint relay squad chosen to represent Africa in the World Cup that year in Canberra.

The Minister for Sport asked for more aid from Solidarity to prevent many countries becoming no more than spectators at the duel between the USA and the USSR.

Cotenu, Benin
The conflict between Ministry and NOC, which runs through much of African sport, increasing the instability, was even more apparent here, where the thirst for autonomy in sport had been increased by the upsurge in material status following the new income from offshore oil. Modern offices, factories, houses and international chain hotels were appearing rapidly. There was a pause when an NOC speaker at a conference with the IOC delegation stressed that there must be some independence in the balance between sport and government. An hour later, over luncheon, the Minister was asserting, in defiance of Olympic Charter regulations, that 'there should be a joint hosting in Korea'. He spoke strongly on the sovereignty of African sport.

Malabo, Fernando Po Island, Equatorial Guinea
'Can you turn on the runway lights, please?' The pilot was approaching this densely forested tropical island and offshore capital with about five minutes of fading daylight remaining, and with low cloud among the wooded mountains reducing visibility to no more than 1,000 feet vertically. The pencil-thin strip of tarmac was barely visible in the gloom; a mountain lay to the left, and there was no radar aid. 'Sorry,' Malabo Control replied, 'we don't have lights.' Malabo had little of anything. The touch-down was a minor triumph, not to say a major relief.

The very walls of Malabo were rotting from years of neglect. The port crumbled. The rain and overbearing humidity produces external mould on most of the buildings. There is an aura of decay, a poverty right up to governmental level that I had seen nowhere other than in Central America. Broken windows in one of the main hotels remained unrepaired, curtains flapping in the rain. The corrugated iron roof of the one gymnasium leaked. After three centuries of former Portuguese and Spanish rule, despair now reigned.

This was the occasion on which I became, briefly, deputy for the President of the International Olympic Committee. There was to be a national half-marathon early the next day, Sunday, due to end in the main square at 7.30. With no early sign of either delegation or transport, I set off on foot for the nearby centre of the town, hugging the walls to stay out of the rain. The main square was empty, apart from a small group of European women in drab raincoats: wives of the members of a visiting Russian delegation who were taking part in the run. We huddled under a dripping tree. A short while later a thin young man in a shiny blue suit, also without umbrella, arrived to join us: the Spanish consul. At about 7.29, a dilapidated Morris Mini bumped its way round the corner over the cobbles, pulled up in front of us, and out jumped two men: the timekeepers.

Half a minute later, Diosdado Lozano, who had run the 1,500 metres in Los Angeles two months after Equatorial Guinea's Olympic Committee was registered, strode into the square to give a two-handed winner's wave to a crowd that, including officials, numbered all of eleven. After a while, an open lorry lumbered into sight, bearing a noisy load of passengers: those of the runners who had given up *en route* through heat or lack of preparation.

The Spanish consul was now deep in consultation with the timekeepers, then began to approach me. In the absence of the President of the International Olympic Committee, and indeed of any other senior member of the delegation, would I possibly agree to present the prizes? Or prize. This consisted of a small piece of paper, a docket from the NOC, that entitled Lozano to a new pair of running shoes and a tracksuit. I shook hands as the water cascaded off the end of my nose, wished him luck in Seoul, and squelched my way back to the hotel with no window panes for a belated breakfast. Sad, stoic Fernando Po was in need of more than new shoes.

N'Djamena, Chad

The capital bore the gunfire scars of the civil war which had lasted more than fifteen years, and continued in the north, prolonged by Libyan involvement and occupation; an inheritance going back to French appeasement of Mussolini in the 1930s. The Catholic cathedral and dozens of other buildings are in ruins. Everywhere there were 15-year-olds in battledress. This is a tall, imposing race of people. In the first athletics World Cup in 1977, Chad provided high jumpers in both men's and women's African team. In conditions of dire difficulty - regular cuts in water and electricity, even in the capital, with petrol sold out of glass jars at the roadside - there was immediate evidence on all sides of energy and enthusiasm, an unquenchable will of the people to survive.

An unheralded tour of the city by the delegation revealed dozens of football matches taking place on open pitches resembling Hackney Marshes in London, the only difference being that there was not a blade of grass, and any car which passed kicked up a dust storm. There was no national stadium, as such, merely a pitch formalized by a low surrounding wall with a single rail restraining any spectators, rather as you might find in a tiny town or village in rural Britain or France. At the martial arts school, the training squad included a number of girls whose faces were bright with a sense of participation. In an adjacent boxing ring, where the planks rattled under the canvas, four pairs of young boxers were sparring simultaneously, some of their gloves so worn you could see the shape of their knuckles through the leather. Two of them wore leather shoes without laces. In Chad, they make the most of their pitiful resources, and they do it with a smile.

Bangui, Central African Republic
At dawn, a mist covers the muddy-red River Oubangi, 500 metres wide, which flows into the Congo. The shrouded distant bank is Zaïre. Dozens of dugout canoes, with two men paddling in the stern, and one fishing in the bow, weave back and forth across the strong-running current with the slow rhythm of skaters, just as they have been doing for centuries. Women kneeling in their colourful *pagne* dresses, complete with flamboyant *fichou* head-dress, paddle smaller solo canoes to collect the catch. What might such enterprising people achieve in an Olympic kayak competition, had they the specialized training? Watching the idyllic scene, unchanged by time, and two fish, bigger than a man's thigh, being landed, I was inclined to think they were more fulfilled in their fishing.

In 1974, Central Africa had been African basketball champions. They had a fine, though deteriorating, indoor hall built by the Yugoslavs. There was plenty of evidence of sporting activity, with various leagues, and some rudimentary gymnastics, where enthusiasts were training in near darkness. The roughness of the grass in the tumbledown main football stadium would trouble even an extra-C rugby team, though at every sporting centre dozens of smiling schoolboys were rubbernecking, desperate to shake hands with anyone, all with dreams of being Zico or Carl Lewis. A basketball exhibition between the two top national teams, wearing smart sponsored kit, produced a fine match which neither of the ageing electric scoreboards could keep pace with. The best bit of sponsorship seen in eleven countries so far was that of the national folk dancing group, whose tribal costume carried around the pelvis the legend 'Coastal Beer'. It was the most bizarre contrast in cultures.

Kampala, Uganda
The night was intermittently disturbed by bursts of machine-gun fire. Undisciplined elements of the army, which in effect controlled the country but often received no pay from the government, were marauding after dark to demand food and money from civilians. In the morning, with church bells softly echoing across the city on a restful Sabbath, soldiers could be seen near the market with some of their errant colleagues whom they had arrested. But to what effect? Shopfronts were bare behind locked grilles. An army jeep, blaring its horn to overtake, nearly rammed our car, but accelerated clear with threatening gestures through the rear window. This potentially rich country was still torn by volatile tribal differences.

Somehow, sport was surviving on a shoestring, as did the rest of this relatively modernized community. A first division football match between Kampala City and the army drew a full house at the Nakivubo

Stadium. Constant use of wingers produced a highly entertaining, old-fashioned match, full of shots and errors. The army, fitter and faster, came from behind to draw 2-2. The crowd was knowledgeable, excitable, yet well-behaved, as were the players. Uganda was maintaining, as best it could, its dignity. Over at the pre-independence sports centre, with its cricket field, handsome pavilion, gymnasium and tennis courts, a football squad was in residence at the hostel for training. Later in the month, a boxing team would be competing in Dar es Salaam. Another was at the world championships in Seoul. But Uganda still lived from hand to mouth.

John Akii-Bua, as amiable now as when he memorably won the Olympic 400 metres hurdles in Munich, had returned from working in West Germany to rejoin the police. Samaranch presented him with an Olympic Order in recognition of his continuing prestige.

While driving back to the airport, we saw two women playing golf just below where the Israelis made their spectacular raid at Entebbe. Lake Victoria lapped the fairway. The trees were in glorious blossom.

Djibouti City, Djibouti

If you had to nip down the goat track for thirty miles to find water, and then carry it home, running a marathon would be hardly intimidating. Formerly French Somaliland, this tiny nation on a corner of the Red Sea in the Gulf of Aden, historically populated by shepherds, was producing long-distance runners as readily as Yorkshire in England once produced footballers. Only recently, however, had they recognized the fact. Gaining independence in 1957, and forming an Olympic Committee in 1984, Djibouti had sent a team of three to Los Angeles. Robleh Djama, Ahmed Saleh and Abdillahi Charmarke, having trained at Fontainebleau, finished eighth, twentieth and thirty-seventh respectively in the marathon. Nine months later they had been third, first, and seventh in the World Cup in Hiroshima, to win it; and in the last few weeks Djama had finished third in Chicago, and Saleh second in New York. They were the best ambassadors a new country could possibly have. Pierre Seguy, the French technical adviser to the Ministry of Education and Sport, said: 'The Djiboutians are such a resilient race, able to go two days without water if necessary, that with training and normal food they develop at an exceptional rate. Every two weeks we have a seven-kilometre road race through the city, with five hundred runners.' They were awaiting their first synthetic track; the IOC had promised some help.

The tour had revealed some of the beauty and the bleakness of the African continent. The most enduring impression had been of a tide of goodwill and ambitious intention among hundreds of ordinary people striving, often it seemed without encouragement or realistic expectation, for ordinary objectives which are taken for granted in Europe, against the almost insurmountable obstacles of heat, drought, economic deprivation, poor communications, widespread moral and financial corruption, political manipulation, racial exploitation between tribes, and war. For millions, the inevitable product of such circumstances must be illiteracy and famine. For us there had been many humbling memories: of willing hands in Mauritania attempting to build a stadium without so much as a concrete mixer; of smiling children everywhere with an unblemished faith in the future; of the woman hotel receptionist who, to the sound of Kampala's gunfire, ran into the street as we were leaving to press into our hands the souvenir box of matches with its ironic message: 'The Lion Hotel, for safety and comfort.'

To think of sport in any such surroundings seems an irrelevance. Yet sport represents normality, the tangible, realizable ambition of ordinary people, and one of the more simple demonstrations that they can emulate the rest of the world. Yet even sport presents Africa with a severe challenge, when to travel by scheduled airline from Dakar to Djibouti you must go via Europe.

Two years later, in 1987, the President invited me to cross the southern Pacific by charter, starting from Sydney, with a brief call at Christchurch in New Zealand on the way. This journey was, for obvious reasons, to be more beautiful, though no less informative. For much of the time during the African tour I had seen almost nothing of the countryside because, usually assigned a place in the fourth or fifth car of the cortège, I had lived for a week and a half in a permanent cloud of dust on the unpaved roads. In the south Pacific, I would have a permanent view of the sea, the sky and the luscious vegetation.

Port Vila, Vanuatu

Julius Patching, the Australian who was secretary of the Oceania Association of NOCs, was on the telephone to the Sports Ministry of what was, before its independence in 1980, the British/French condominium of New Hebrides. The President of the International Olympic Committee wished to attend Mass, he said, during his forthcoming visit. 'Hold on a minute,' said the Ministry. A moment later came the answer. 'Yes, that's OK, the spire has gone but the church is still there.' Vanuatu had been devastated by Cyclone Uma, the worst in thirty years. When the wind reached 150 knots, they lost count, because the anemometer was blown away. More than forty people died, many struck by flying refuse. Millions of pounds of damage had been done, hundreds of houses and factories felled, and the Melanesian island was without electricity for two weeks.

As Samaranch toured Port Vila, they were still sorting through the rubble, sawing up the thousands of fallen palms. Corrugated iron rooftops lay twisted in the upper branches of those trees still standing like wisps of paper. Motor fishing vessels were perched at crazy angles on the harbour wall where they had been thrown by the wind. Government offices were felled, and George Sokomanu, the head of state, his residence in ruins, received the IOC President in his temporary hotel suite. Vanuatu epitomizes the Olympic spirit: taking part. They had at the time the fastest sprinter in the south Pacific, Jerry Jeremiah, a semi-finalist at Edinburgh in Vanuatu's second Commonwealth Games, who the following weekend would be competing at the World Indoor Championships at Indianapolis. He trained on the grass track around the national football stadium, where the concrete walls had keeled over in Uma's path.

In 1978, Vanuatu was to have hosted the sixth South Pacific Games, but the French and British governments would not agree on the size of their joint subsidy. Vanuatu eventually received nothing, and relinquished the Games to Fiji, which played host to 2,700 competitors from 21 nations in 19 sports, an event bigger than the Commonwealth Games the same year in Edinburgh. It was touching to witness the formal recognition of Vanuatu's NOC in the ballroom of the one undamaged hotel. Kelman Kiri, president of a genuinely amateur sports federation, received from Samaranch their white Olympic flag which was placed beside the national flag of green, red, black and yellow: palm trees, the common blood of all races, black for Melanesia, and yellow for peace. 'We will try our best,' said Mr Kiri.

Apia, Western Samoa

The young men in the dancing troupe at Aggie Gray's Hotel, swaying from the hips like their sisters to enchanting south Pacific rhythms as they entertained the visiting IOC delegation, looked as though, in slightly different dress, they could have captured a commando platoon. The vivacious Mrs Gray, who was the inspiration for 'Bloody Mary' in the Rodgers and Hammerstein musical *South Pacific*, was now in her nineties and had been singing and dancing in her troupe until a recent stroke had restricted her. The Samoan people, who with five thousand years of civilization are said to be the cradle of the Polynesian islands' race before the arrival of the South American Incas, produce some remarkable athletes without the support of much technical expertise. They have the perfect physique for boxing, wrestling, weightlifting and the back row of a rugby scrum - as Wales were to learn in the 1991 World Cup.

Paul Wallwork, the president of their Olympic Committee, who had been educated at the University of New South Wales and was good enough to have represented Australia at the Olympic Games in 1972, was unable to go to Munich because at that time Western Samoa had no NOC. They had been admitted four years ago. They bring to sport a strange combination of graciousness and stubbornness. When Fiji received thirty seconds' coverage on American television during the opening ceremony of the 1984 Olympic Games, and the march pasts of Western Samoa, the Solomon Islands and Tonga were then blanked out to accommodate advertising slots, the Minister of Sport threatened to take the Western Samoan team home in disgust.

Being a speck on the ocean does, however, make life difficult, not least in communication. A swimming delegation was sent to Western Samoa not long ago by Australia under the aegis of the Solidarity Fund. It was only when the Australian contingent had arrived that they discovered that Western Samoa does not have a swimming pool of any kind. Just a lagoon inside the reef. This was the only country to have staged a South Pacific Games, in 1983, without a swimming competition.

Western Samoa is a good example of a tiny country which knows what it needs. When China, which has one of only three embassies there, offered the same sporting assistance which they have provided in twenty or so African states, the Samoans asked for a multiple stadium, constructed for $3m, including two rugby football pitches, with a horseracing track round the outside, and only a small grandstand. The Samoans retain a tribal wisdom. Before leaving, Samaranch went to visit His Royal Highness Malietoa Tanumafili II, who has been head of state for life since independence was granted in 1962. Did Western Samoa have diplomatic relations with the Soviet Union? Samaranch asked,. After a long pause, the ageing chief shook his head. 'We would not know how to speak with the Russians,' he said. The superstition in the south Pacific is that hurricanes only strike those islands which have dealings with the nuclear superpowers. The farewell in Apia had seen Cardinal Pio, a man of serene Christianity, take part in a formal Polynesian breakfast dance after conducting Mass, rising from his scrambled eggs to take a spin across the floor.

Pago Pago, American Samoa

This US territory, first ceded in 1902, received an Olympic flag from the IOC President in formal recognition of their National Olympic Committee . . . and their government burst into song. For me, it was one of the most beautiful moments in a lifetime of reporting sport. The Samoans have voices as ringingly melodious as the Welsh. They sing with their souls in close harmony and without instruments, and they would, I suspect, win the gold medal at any Olympic Eisteddfod.

At Pago Pago, one of the world's most scenic natural harbours, the IOC President was treated to one of the most spectacular competitions in worldwide sport, regrettably not yet an Olympic event. The Samoans were training for the longboat championships on flag day, 17 April. The boats, once warring craft and massively but finely built in wood, nowadays cost $11,000. They are 30 metres long, and are driven by 48 oarsmen who are kept in rhythm by a helmsman and a drummer. Now, Pago Pago Eagle was challenged by Nuuli Satan, which arrived dramatically through the growing swell for the start at 7.30 a.m. The delegation was perched in vacant spaces at bow and stern in the two craft, though Philip Coles, an Australian IOC member and three times an Olympic canoeist, took one of Satan's oars: and paid for it with blisters. It was an exhilarating experience as two lines of huge knotted muscle drove the boats through the water like floating torpedoes at more than 12 knots. What an Olympic sight this would be.

Nuku Alofa, Tonga

Prior to the 1984 Olympic Games, the gentle, undemonstrative people of Tonga were trapped in what could be seen with hindsight as a piece of sporting expediency. The IOC delegation arrived to try to resolve the problem. Finé Sani was one of many outstanding boxers in Polynesia, but in 1984 Tonga had no Olympic Committee. Sani had been training in Fiji, but was ineligible for their team. Brian Wightman, former England rugby international who had been living in Fiji since 1970 and was secretary of their Olympic Committee and vice-president of Oceania NOCs, had persistently lobbied Samaranch to admit Tonga for 1984. Wightman's argument was that the Games were supposed to be for the youth of the world, and that where there are competitors in small nations worthy to take part, there should be some means to admit them. When the socialist countries boycotted LA, the IOC had suddenly found themselves glad to welcome all countries, so as to augment the number of nations taking part. Tonga had been recognized barely a month before the Games, even though they did not fulfil the Charter requirements that a country must have a minimum of five sports affiliated to International Federations. Tonga had scrambled to get their uniforms made and duly competed with a team of boxers. Yet a few months later, Tonga had been suspended for not having the necessary number of internationally affiliated sports. The problem had dragged on for two years.

Investigation by the Amateur Sports Association revealed that letters of application had been sent to six International Federations, in addition to the three international affiliations already registered. Samaranch assured Langi Karvamelliku, the NOC president and a former Cambridge University second XV player, that the IOC would inquire about the additional affiliations. Meanwhile, Tonga was reinstated forthwith, and eligible for $5,000 per year administrative assistance from Solidarity. All was smiles. Fifty per cent of Tonga's population is under twenty, and with 100,000 people they clearly have a potential in Pacific sport if they could get their act together.

Rarotonga, Cook Islands

An Olympic flame was ignited at sundown, as four anonymous athletes ran a symbolic ceremonial lap of the island's largest swimming pool. The pool, it should be said, was barely as large as a tennis court, belonging to the island's main resort hotel. The torch bearer was a hotel employee who would be taking part in the Oceania Volleyball Championships which the Cook Islands were due to host later in the year. The flame on the podium consisted of three small hurricane lamps. Hurricane was the appropriate word. The southern Cooks had been whiplashed a month or two earlier, by Hurricane Sally, but remained unbowed as they made good the wreckage: their harbour at Avatiu was smashed, and among much inland damage a new rugby ground and lawn bowls club were swamped by a tidal wave. For the spectators around the pool, it was a poignant moment. The Cook Islands, with a total area of only 234 square miles, and a population of 15,000, were about to receive formal recognition of their Olympic Committee, the tiniest among the IOC's 167 member countries at that time. This was not the only significant statistic. The Cooks' population, the more prosperous 50 per cent being on Rarotonga, makes a larger private per capita contribution to keeping their competitors in the international arena than any country in the world.

The government budget for sport is a mere £2,000 a year, so that Hugh Henry, their NOC president, and his colleagues, were overwhelmed when Samaranch announced that there would be an immediate donation of $10,000 towards repairs of the hurricane damage. The Cook Islands are one of the smallest countries to have benefited from the institution of the four-yearly South Pacific Mini-Games, which they had hosted in 1985. They had won three gold medals on the final afternoon, in bowls, rugby and the women's 800 metres. Atina Sawetoo, who competed in the IAAF World Championships in Helsinki in 1983, was the top women's middle-distance runner in the south Pacific. 'Those gold medals suddenly showed our people, in front of their own eyes, what they had been making a financial contribution to for all those years,' Henry said. 'Everyone needs to experience that occasion when their flag is raised on that pole. These mini-games gave the island an understanding of international sport.'

There are those who accuse Samaranch of needlessly visiting such tiny outposts of the Olympic community; of playing to his vanity. Having accompanied delegations on three such tours in recent years, to Asia, Africa and now the south Pacific, I would say the evidence contradicts this. He does not have to do it. Yet as he said, addressing a banquet in Rarotonga attended by the Prime Minister: 'The most important thing for me is not to be able to say I have been to any country, but to try to strengthen our unity and to assist our members. With our unity comes our strength against those who use the Olympic Games as a political tool. The Olympic Games is the largest social event in the world. Last year, the women's volleyball world championship took place in the Soviet Union, and the People's Republic of China played a match against Taiwan. That was achieved by the Olympic Movement. Not bad!'

8 Diplomacy

In 1974, Dr Un Yong Kim, a shortish, thick-set man with glasses whom it would be easy not to notice in a crowd, was attending the General Assembly of the International Shooting Federation in Berne, Switzerland, in an attempt to earn for Seoul, the capital city of South Korea and his home, the right to stage the world championships in 1978. Mexico City, through Mario Vazquez Raña, were offering the Federation a board-and-lodging fee for competitors of $10 a head per day. Kim, with a quick calculation and taking a substantial gamble, offered the assembly $5 a head. Seoul was awarded the championships with 62 of the 102 votes. It may not be an exaggeration to say that by one snap decision in some anonymous Swiss conference room, the future history of the Olympic Games was shaped, and indeed the political/economic balance of power in eastern Asia.

In the story of Samaranch's twelve years as leader of the Olympic Movement, it can be said that Dr Kim, born in Seoul in 1931, educated at Yonsei University in Seoul and at Texas Western College, speaking French, English, Spanish and Japanese, has been the second most influential figure. Yet few outside the Olympic Movement could tell you his name, whereas many would remember that of the high-profile Ueberroth, or of Vazquez Raña and Primo Nebiolo. Like many influential men, Dr Kim did not so much possess power as move close to it. He had been secretary to the Prime Minister, councillor to the Korean Mission to the United Nations and the Embassies in Washington and London, delegate to the UN General Assembly, deputy director-general to the President's office, chairman of the Institute of Korean Studies. In sport, he was experienced in taekwondo, judo and athletics, and in 1974 was president of the Korean NOC and a member of the Asian Games council. As the fastest emerging industrial power in the world took shape during the 1960s and 70s, Dr Kim was close to the heart of things.

'I never calculated in terms of immediate cost at Berne,' Kim recalls, 'but in the long term. At that moment, Seoul had yet to be the stage for any major international championships, though we were already due to host the second Asian Athletics Championships the following year. There followed the shooting in 1978, the first air rifle championships in '79, the eighth women's world basketball championships the same year, and the twelfth Asian weightlifting championships in 1980. That was the sum of our achievements at the time we went to Baden Baden in 1981 to bid for the Olympic Games! During the Games in Moscow, there had been a mood that everyone was the friend of Nagoya of Japan, who were also bidding for '88, but I knew that this was not so. *And* I knew we were capable of staging the Games. Our only handicap was not being known. We weren't that much worried about the cost of staging the Games, but in April of '81, prior to Baden Baden, I was the *only* Korean representative at a meeting in Lausanne between the IOC executive board and the International Federations, taekwondo having become a "recognized" sport only the previous year. We had not even the credibility, during the voting in Baden Baden, of being hosts for the Asian Games of 1986, because that was to be decided in the spring of the following year.'

Only the respect in which Kim was held by South Korea's senior political leaders had put him in a position to be able to go to Baden Baden and stake his country's international reputation on what was at that time a seemingly astonishing risk. To surprise around the world, Seoul, a city well outside most people's consciousness of the Orient, defeated Nagoya, less on account of the influence of Horst Dassler – as previously discussed – than the environmental protestors from Nagoya, who paraded their opposition up and down the streets of the quiet Rhineland spa and undoubtedly helped push the IOC members the other way. Having been influenced, the members themselves then regretted that they had been! 'The boycott threat arose immediately, right there in Baden Baden,' Kim recalls. 'North Korea had been negotiating behind the scene before the election, and demanded a change of site. Samaranch made it very clear there would be no change. For seven years we worked, through him, to make sure everyone knew they would be welcome in Seoul. The absence of diplomatic relations with many countries was going to be an obstacle, yet the Games served as a link to those countries with which we had no relations. Up to the time of the Games in Los Angeles, we still had no contact with *any* of the eastern Europeans, yet after LA it became better. The socialists realized that athletes had been put at a serious disadvantage, and that nothing had been gained politically; and once they realized we guaranteed security, they began to warm. It was Samaranch who persuaded our political leaders to open the continual discussions with North Korea [regarding North Korea's demands to co-host the Games]. We knew we had to accept IOC advice in all matters, so our politicians were always prepared to talk. *We* knew co-hosting could not work, but if the IOC wanted to offer North Korea a share in five sports, say, then were happy to give it a try. It was the same with advice on other issues – equestrianism, for example. We accepted forty volunteer advisers from the Equestrian Federation, who spent several weeks showing us what was necessary, and we did everything they suggested. I don't think we were *too* bad!' His manner is dry.

If Kim's was the initiative that led to Seoul's appointment, it would be a combination of Samaranch's inner ambition – to be seen as the most powerful figure in the world of sport – and sheer will-power that helped enable Seoul to fulfil its responsibilities. 'Samaranch is his own man,' Vitaly Smirnov reflects. 'He has a good smell of a situation, and I never saw him unnerved, or lost for an answer. He is very flexible, and avoids confrontation. I voted for Nagoya, I didn't believe South Korea was possible. The vote created a very bad situation in my country. I called a specialist in Foreign Affairs at our Chinese Ministry and asked: "What now?" He said: "We'll go, that's the IOC's decision." We all have problems in international sport and we ought all to be flexible. Samaranch likes to be adaptable and to help people, it's his nature, but I think I may have been the first to say that he should be flexible with North Korea, not resist their demands head-on. His reaction at first was negative, though I had the same orders from above at first regarding South Korea.'

The success of the Games in Los Angeles, in spite of the socialist boycott, did much to help change the political temperature regarding Seoul; even if it did little to lessen Samaranch's anxiety about a possible *fourth* consecutive boycott. 'He was now terrified about Seoul,' Dick Pound recalls, 'and it was this concern that led to his decision, at the Extraordinary Session, that the invitations to attend the Games should be sent out by the IOC and not by the host city. I think his first trip after Los Angeles was to go to Moscow to test the water, and from then on he went to every annual meeting of socialist sports ministries.'

Alain Coupat observes: 'I think Samaranch felt that the LA Games were not *his* Games, but something that he had taken over from Killanin. The real change in him followed the removal of Berlioux the next year. He became much more active and assured, more willing to *impose*. He turned from Berlioux to Seoul, with total dedication, knowing that he had eight years – being confident of re-election as President – to ensure the success of both Seoul *and* Barcelona, should his home city be elected the following year.'

Kevan Gosper points to the extent to which Samaranch had conditioned the boycott in 1984. 'He moved quickly and corralled eastern Europe,' Gosper says. 'In '80 it had been worldwide, I think Killanin could have done more to minimize it. Yet Samaranch's diplomacy over Seoul was masterful. South Korea in 1981 had diplomatic relations with only sixty countries, yet by the time of the Games there were more than one hundred and sixty there, and North Korea had failed to blow the Games out of the water. The quality of Samaranch which stood out during those years was his anticipation. He has a facility for forecasting the way other people will turn. He realized that unless he worked around the clock in diplomatic circles, and unless he raised the strength of the NOCs numerically, the IOC might be faced with another LA. He knew that a second *serious* boycott really could have the IOC fighting for survival, yet at the same time was determined to uphold the rights of South Korea. By travelling the world, he not only won the loyalty of the NOCs but helped to create new ones.'

Samaranch was anxious about Seoul on several fronts. Not only was there the initial hostility of socialist countries that were major performers in the Olympic arena, but North Korea presented a two-edged threat: incitement of their ideological allies to stay away, and physical obstruction of the Games by unofficial terrorist activity. South Korea was a country itself moving towards democracy from what had been a wholly military state, complicated by the continuing presence of US forces along the border with North Korea. Left-wing organizations within South Korea were becoming increasingly active in political demonstrations. Security would be as much the watchword for 1988 as diplomacy.

'I'd experienced the terrorism of 1972 in Munich,' Samaranch says. 'The organization of those Games was excellent, but the Germans used the Games to show to the world their new democracy, with no evidence of the army or police at events, and "friendly" security at the Olympic Village. We had seen what happened. On a visit to Israel, I'd talked with the head of their secret service, and had discovered the lack of co-ordination there had been during that crisis in Munich between the police of the city, the region, and the state. Israel had asked to be allowed to assume responsibility for dealing with the terrorists, but this had been rejected. I will never forget Willi Daume coming to the executive board meeting, near to midnight on the day of the crisis, and announcing, well-meaningly, "*Wir haben gewonnen* (we have won)", when in fact the hostages had perished.'

A hair-brained plan by the Germans, absurdly motivated by the desire to get on with the Games, had been to airlift terrorists and hostages out of the Village that evening by helicopter – the hostages being already wired with explosives – under the false promise of providing a freedom-flight for terrorists (plus hostages) from the military airfield at Fürstenfeldbruck to a sympathetic Arab destination. The Israelis had refused any deal involving release of their terrorist prisoners. The Germans intended to shoot the terrorists, with marksmen armed with infra-red sights, as they emerged from the helicopters; and in the ineffective operation of this inexcusably hasty solution, both hostages and terrorists perished.

'I knew the potential for danger in Seoul,' says Samaranch, 'and I would remain worried until the closing ceremony was over. I had never thought to express reservations about Seoul before the vote in Baden Baden. My opinion had been that Nagoya was much the best, although the day before the vote I had asked close friends among the members what they thought, and they suggested Seoul was going to win. I was astonished.

'At the Session, there were several attacks on Seoul. Kiyakawa, the senior member of Japan, drew attention to South Korea's then $6 billion debt to Japan, and Titov [the Soviet president of the gymnastics federation] attacked on political grounds. I think Titov pushed some people the other way – they felt that Titov was planted. This was an example of how the IOC can be perverse, cannot be pushed! I am not nowadays happy with the voting system. In '81, I was contented enough about Calgary, but very worried about South Korea, which was effectively still at war with its neighbours. It was hard to understand the members' decision, but the hundreds of protesters were probably decisive. I knew it would mean massive extra work to get everyone there. That was why, immediately after the Games in LA, I went in September with Vazquez Raña to Moscow, to see Gramov [the Minister for Sport] and Gromyko. What I achieved was not to talk of the past but to look at the future. Their position was still not clear, however. I think they were hedging at the time. We attended a seminar on "Future Leaders of NOCs". I could sense an uncertainty about their opinion of the IOC.'

Whatever the Soviet mood, I learned early in 1985, during a tour of East Germany to investigate for *The Times* the continuing dominance of the world of sport by the GDR 'miracle machine', that the intention was to participate in Seoul. This was confirmed during an interview in Berlin with Klaus Eichler, the vice-chairman of the national sports federation TDSB. Eichler implied that there were no objections to Seoul as the venue, but expressed concern about the security of athletes. 'Our NOC has called upon our athletes to prepare well, and we expect from both the Seoul organizing committee and the IOC that they will create equal conditions for all athletes, both in competition and in security. If the 1988 Games cannot guarantee the security of its athletes, then the whole Olympic Movement is in danger. If we do not have the motivation of the Olympics, then we have to have the motivation from somewhere else. We expressed how seriously we view our participation in 1988 when we took responsibility for organizing the forthcoming Session of the IOC here in Berlin in June.' The motivation applied not only to competitors but to the army of coaches, doctors, judges and officials who comprised an organization receiving $170m a year from the national budget.

The defection of Romania from the boycott in 1984 had, critically, set an example. When, before the Session in Los Angeles, the communist countries of Europe, Africa, Arabia and elsewhere had held their customary get-together, the Romanians had been cold-shouldered, uninvited.

'Romania had broken the front-line,' Alexandru Siperco reflects. 'Ceaucescu and his leaders were very touchy on independence from the

Moscow line, more so than the West realized. I belonged to the old guard of Romanian socialists. I knew Ceaucescu from before the Second World War. Perhaps I had some influence to get our Politburo to agree we should go to LA, though Ceaucescu made the final decision. It was a big risk for Romania. At a meeting in Moscow before the Games, Ceaucescu had said, "We can discuss economics, politics, but not sport, that is a different issue and we shall go!" In another meeting in Prague, very near to the Games, after the Russians had declared that they would not attend, one by one the other socialist countries stated they too would not go on account of security, but Alexei Augustin, our Sports Minister and president of the NOC, thumped the table and said we would be there. Ceaucescu balanced independence and evil. He *was* a dictator, but one thing the West should understand: he was not a killer, there were no concentration camps. It *was* a very oppressive regime; his secret service knew *everything*, any meeting of even three people. All intellectuals were against him, and it was impossible to organize anything against him; he was a megalomaniac. That is why the revolution was so spontaneous.'

Samaranch would waste no opportunity for propaganda in the holding together of *his* Movement: even on occasion when such action invited criticism. For two weeks in the summer of '84, Romanians had never gone to bed as the television pictures – which were jammed for Russians, Bulgarians and Hungarians along the joint borders – filled the hours of darkness with the achievements of this small country in gaining the second largest number of gold medals. We would never know what this action of extreme political and financial courage in the name of sport had drawn in the way of economic reprisals; certainly Romania had endured one of the worst winters on record – so short of fuel that street lights were extinguished, restaurants and bars closed at 7 p.m., central heating was inoperative, and in some hospitals people were two to a bed to keep warm. In quiet privacy at the presidential summer villa at Constanta in 1985, in front of a handful of government ministers, Nikolai Ceaucescu was presented by Samaranch with the Olympic Order. It was an action that Samaranch could have come to regret during the overthrow of Ceaucescu's evil regime four years later.

At the opening of the Session in Berlin, Samaranch spoke of the symbolic significance of the hosting of the occasion by the German Democratic Republic, a clear reference to their intended loyalty at Seoul. An Order would be bestowed upon Erich Honecker, another leader of a police state whose days, unknown to him, were numbered. 'There was a major change within the GDR in the winter of '84-'85,' Samaranch says. 'This was the start of the period of decline of Soviet power, the decline of Chernenko. Honecker had made a state visit to West Germany, and received honours there. The GDR was feeling its feet. Honecker told me officially in Berlin that East Germany would compete in Seoul. He said they were very disappointed at being obliged to join the boycott in '84, and that he had never been consulted by Moscow beforehand.'

The Session in Berlin was notable for many developments other than the dismissal of Berlioux. It was now, for instance, that details began to emerge of timing adjustments in the event schedules for Seoul that would accommodate the interests of NBC Television and prime-time coverage in America. Alex Gilady denies to this day that NBC exerted force in this area, though there is ample evidence that the bank balance of the IAAF, if of no other Federation, benefited on account of such 'accommodation'. Also to emerge was news of the first of a series of joint meetings between the two Koreas, that would extend over two years, set up by Ashwini Kumar of India, a vice-president of the IOC. While there was now a great optimism about the participation of communist nations in Seoul, the antagonism of North Korea was coming more into the open.

'The question of North Korea was really a side issue,' Alain Coupat considers, 'but it was handy for Samaranch to have it as a second front on which to focus. The excesses of North Korea made it easier for the other communists. I don't think that Siperco ever understood that Samaranch didn't want to solve the Korean situation! The security would have been impossible. So the worse the controversy, the better the situation. Persuading other people to enter into a nation-to-nation discussion was one of the best things he ever did.'

Dr Kim recalls that during the Session in Berlin he and Tai Woo Roh – then still head of the Seoul organizing committee but subsequently to become state President – met many socialist delegates, including Honecker. 'Manfred Ewald, the GDR Sports Minister, was optimistic,' Kim says. 'He had already had plenty of discussion with Samaranch. Later he really pushed the Korean North-South talks. "That's your problem," he would say to me. "We will only work within the Olympic Charter." East Germany was much more of a leader towards participation in Seoul than the Soviet Union. Hungary and the others were just waiting to be given a guide. Four factors were of influence; the detente between America and Russian, the damage of the boycott to sport, the unifying efforts of Samaranch, and our own efforts to be hospitable, whatever the cost, to show our country was different to what people had heard. South Korea was still partially in darkness.'

The first Korean joint meeting in October 1985, under the umbrella of the IOC at Lausanne – as were all the meetings – was rightly surrounded in scepticism. No competitors from either North or South had as yet taken part in competitions staged in the other country, appearing side by side only when an international event had been hosted by a third country. 'I initially persuaded Roh that some sort of offer would have to be made to the North during negotiations for the signing of the television contract for US rights,' Samaranch says. 'I told him to trust me. I was quite sure in my own mind that North Korea would never organize one single sport, even though they had a brand new stadium that they wished to use. I told Roh that he could offer the North whatever he liked, and of course once we had entered this area of debate, everyone entered the ring, Castro saying that we had to give something more than we had, while I kept on saying publicly that we would never close negotiations with North Korea right up to the last minute.

'It was important for us that the meetings were always on our ground, not at Panmunjom. At *every* meeting there were secret service men in the delegation of both countries. The North Korean delegation was unable to change one comma of their instructions from Pyongyang. Their position was something I couldn't change, but with South Korea, I was always talking with Roh, saying these were not the South Koreans' Games but the IOC's Games, and he had to work with us freely, to offer two, four, six sports or whatever. I repeatedly assured Roh the proposals would never work because North Korea would never agree to accept the free movement of media between North and South that would have to be a part of any such agreement. Fortunately Roh and his colleagues co-operated with us. They realized we were playing for time. I was aware that the Soviet Union wanted us to show we were "doing our best" for North Korea, although they still intended to take part. When I sent a delegation to Pyongyang of Siperco and Coupat, asking them to request permission to return to Seoul through the Panmunjom checkpoint, and this was refused, it was confirmation that the North would never agree to anything. They could not conceivably open the border to television, sponsors and the rest of the Olympic family.

'Un Yong Kim was *officially* not in an important position, but he was the perfect channel to the senior South Korean leaders. I used him to judge how far I could go with offers to North Korea, from the South's point of view. Un Yong Kim was the bridge between the IOC and the Seoul organizing committee, and I spoke with him almost every day on the telephone. The South Koreans eventually became so confident, I had to be careful. If I said one day that maybe something was a good idea, by the next day it had been done! It was so different from Los Angeles. At the same time, I tried to get to know Yu Sun Kim, the president of the North Korean NOC. But at private meetings, translation tended to be a mess: Korean into Russian into English, with neither of us really understanding the other. I went with Yu Sun Kim to the airport in Berlin together with Gramov [Soviet Minister], who confirmed Russia's intention was to participate but that we must resolve the North Korean problem.'

For that first of four joint meetings in Lausanne, in pursuit of a compromise that was wholly outside the terms of the IOC's Charter and without the slightest justification on the part of North Korea, the IOC delegation consisted of Samaranch, Siperco (first vice-president), Berthold Beitz (third vice-president), Sheikh Fahad of Kuwait (president of the Olympic Council of Asia), and Raymond Gafner (Swiss IOC member and interim administrator following the dismissal of Berlioux).

The North arrived with a list of eight demands: joint hosting by North and South, with a single national team; the amalgamated title 'Korea Olympic Games'; sports disciplines equally divided between Pyongyang and Seoul; simultaneous opening and closing ceremonies in both capitals; host cities to make joint guarantees to IFs under the Charter; free exchange in travel for all athletes, officials, journalists, and tourists by air, sea, or land; redistribution of television profits; the formation of a joint organizing committee.

The Wizard of Oz could not have improved on this. At this stage, however, the IOC proposed no more than the two Korean teams marching behind an Olympic flag at the opening ceremony, the course for the marathon and cycling road races to pass through both territories, and the preliminary rounds of team sports such as football to be staged in the North. It would never be the IOC's wish to stage the Games jointly in Seoul and Pyongyang. And the final communiqué stated that further discussion was necessary and would take place in January 1986. The charade continued, making little further progress, beyond debating the holding of preliminaries for men's handball, volleyball and football in North Korea, their involvement in the cultural programme, and the joint entrance of both Koreas to the opening ceremony in Seoul. The debate was further adjourned until June the same year.

The interminable conference-speak continued. By the third meeting, the South was now offering: a joint opening ceremony march by the North-South teams; allocation of some preliminaries to the North; a cycling road race through both territories; more involvement of the North in the cultural programme. By the end of discussions the IOC had proposed the further offer of two full sports to the North and additional sports to be partly relocated in the North. The two Koreas would communicate their willingness by the end of the month and a fourth meeting would then be convened.

Meanwhile, the Asian Games were about to be staged in Seoul. Attending these, I took the opportunity to pay a tourist's visit to the border at Panmunjom, to observe their weird division of a single people by an ideological fence, as was then still the case in Germany. The little former farming village on the 38th parallel, which was obliterated 35 years before, lies no more than an hour's drive or so north of Seoul. A zephyr ruffled the muddy waters of the Imjin River, catching the sunlight. Duck and pheasant cried overhead. A gentle peace, an autumnal tranquillity, caressed the rice fields and the rolling hills. Yet the peace in the air was as fragile as a pheasant's egg. Along the northern side of the four-kilometre-wide demilitarized zone was then assembled the largest permanent peacetime armoured force in the history of mankind. Standing there, at this volatile symbol of armistice, it was difficult to believe in any kind of Olympic fraternization between communist North and republican South two years hence,

It had been intended that Samaranch should visit the scene of the little 'Bridge of No Return', the one forlorn remaining road link on Highway 1, where prisoners of war were exchanged in 1953 and across which the Olympic family would pass, were North Korea to accept the current offer of the IOC and the South Korean organizing committee. Tactfully, Samaranch decided against such an appointment, which would have brought him within a stride of North Korean territory while still standing provocatively on South Korean soil. Had he visited the invasion tunnel of the North – driven through granite 70 metres under the demilitarized zone, discovered by the South in 1978, and the third such secret tunnel to make a mockery of the armistice, capable of carrying 30,000 armed troops and armour and emerging a mere 44 kilometres from Seoul – Samaranch's altruism might have waned. His eyes would have widened at the insensitivity in this diplomatic no-man's-land, a security Disney World where men and machines of surveillance eyed each other minute by minute, hour by hour, across a harmless-looking line of white posts which signify the military demarcation line. It was high noon at Panmunjom that day, the way it had been for every second of every day for 33 years since 1953. Could sport seriously penetrate this aura of impending war?

The two projected sports now planned for Pyongyang were table tennis and archery; the partial sports were cycling and football. It was inconceivable that, supposing the draw for football should throw together Italy and West Germany for a match in Pyongyang, North Korean security could contemplate not only a horde of photographers and television camera crews but 15,000 western European supporters pouring through the Berlin-type wall and continuing the 80-kilometre journey to Pyongyang through countryside bristling with armed soldiers. For the moment, however, Samaranch's skill in the negotiations on shared events had yet again left the ball squarely in the North's court. Meetings of sports ministers of non-aligned nations in Pyongyang and then of non-aligned prime ministers in Harare had both rejected the North's suggestion of joint hosting. Now, the larks were singing in Panmunjom, in the heart of a demilitarized zone which had ironically become a wildlife sanctuary, saviour of the threatened Manchurian snow crane. Yet human hearts fluttered. 'When the sun goes down,' a United States corporal said to me, gazing out at dusk at the invisible armaments around Mount Jin Bong to the north, 'this is the eeriest place on earth.'

As the 27 nations and a record 4,797 competitors marched into Seoul's magnificent brand-new Olympic Stadium for the opening ceremony of the 1986 Asian Games, a 16-day event of 25 sports, the most politically relevant fact was that the Chinese People's Republic, with their squad of 391 competitors, outnumbered only by Japan and South Korea, had given a massive socialist vote of confidence and approval to one of the world's most successful and confident, though controversial, capitalist states. South Korean, laid bare by civil war thirty years ago, was about to stage a Games that represented part of the ambition of three billion Asians. It was similarly relevant that the first visit by a prime minister of Japan to the country which it colonized from 1910 to 1945 should have coincided with this ceremony. As Park Seh Jik, the president of the organizing committee, prophetically said in his address to a 100,000 crowd: 'A new era for Asia is dawning. With Asia's advance into the world arena, and the world's people gathering on our soil, this new era is for all of us to share.' We could optimistically expect Korea to surpass this triumph in two years' time, so long as they could stay on top of their security crisis.

'The talks between the two Koreas,' Zhenliang Hé of China reflects, 'gave both countries, and all NOCs, the chance to think more deeply about Olympic ideals. I think it became apparent that the Olympic Movement *can* bring people together, can be a universal bridge. Although we in China had no relationship with South Korea, we felt obliged to contribute to the success of the Olympic Games, and therefore before that the Asian Games. Our participation in Seoul was an occasion to let our people know better the people of South Korea, and vice versa.'

Samaranch had for some time been advised by international experts in security and terrorist analysis that the most dangerous time would probably come during the period two years before the Games. 'This was particularly the view in Europe,' Samaranch says. 'Opinion was that once the Games began, once the teams of the USSR and China had arrived in Seoul, then Seoul would be one of the safest places on earth. There was, of course, considerable alarm arising from the several air crashes, of which the terrorist one in Burma was the worst, immediately following the Asian Games. We were obtaining intelligence information all the time, from the CIA and FBI and the intelligence units of many countries. The best information on the Korean peninsula came from Japan, America, and West Germany.' Dr Kim estimates that in the period of seven years between the election of Seoul and the staging of the Games, Samaranch made fifteen visits to South Korea.

The level of anxiety was indeed beginning to rise during the winter of 1986-87, and the summer following, as bloody political demonstrations in South Korea, fiercely put down by the police, made headline news around the globe, vividly supported by dramatic photographs. I was approached by several British journalists with wives, mortgages and children, inquiring whether I thought they would be safe the following year, now about to fill in their pre-accreditation forms. Hysteria and over-reaction at political unrest in South Korea was reaching a peak in America, a country that possesses some of the world's most destructive weapons and many of the world's most neurotically nervous civilians, as demonstrated by the emptiness of American aeroplanes during the Gulf War in 1990 on scheduled flights at least 10,000 miles from the scene of action. (For some, that period was one of the most comfortable there has ever been for travelling by air.) The hysteria in June 1987 was typified by the journalistic columns of Howard Cosell in the *New York Daily News* and Jerry Eisenberg in the *New York Post*. Cosell: 'You read it here first. You read it this time last year. William Simon, former head of the United States Committee, told you. So did Peter Ueberroth, former head of the Los Angeles Olympics ... this reporter told you, too. We all told you that the 1988 Summer Olympics would never be held in Seoul, South Korea. Not for the citizens of the United States, at least . . . What does it take for the IOC to respond to threats to the safety of its athletes? A limited nuclear engagement?' Eisenberg: 'There is blood on the streets of Korea these days but, apparently, even in 1987 the word is sent by sea. Nobody at the IOC in landlocked Switzerland has blinked an amateur eyelid. When the time comes when they must comment, they will give you the same self-serving answer as always: "Politics (or murder, or genocide, or war) has nothing to do with us." Instead, they will dust off the words of Baron Pierre de Coubertin, founder of the modern Olympics: "The Olympic Movement attempts to bring together in union all the qualities which guide mankind to perfection." There is one hell of a gap between that wish and the deed.'

The demonstrations in Seoul and elsewhere were certainly disturbing, although reliable sources did suggest to me that some of the demonstrations were carefully staged performances, the demonstrators informing the police where they would assemble, some rocks being thrown and deflected by riot shields, and after half an hour or so both sides going off for a coffee together. This is no doubt a cynical exaggeration, although, having observed two such demonstrations at moderately close quarters, I thought I detected certain elements of stage management on both sides which may well be a part of Asian psychology. It is only too possible, moreover, as is well known from experience in Britain, for the dimensions of civil unrest to be hugely exaggerated by the distorted media use of one or two photographs of isolated scuffles.

Throughout the spring and early summer of 1987, the respective Korean NOCs had stuttered towards their fourth direct meeting at the beginning of July. A reliable eastern bloc source had disclosed to me, at the time of the Session in May that year at Istanbul, that there were some twenty points on which the North would have to satisfy the IOC, that the government in Pyongyang and its puppet NOC were well aware that all of these points would not be met, and that they would continue to stall. The mood at Istanbul was, moreover, that communist allies of North Korea were running out of patience. Samaranch's plan appeared to be moving according to schedule. When the parties gathered in Lausanne, Samaranch kept up the pressure on the North by playing a testing lob towards the Pyongyang baseline: the additional offer of women's volleyball as a full sport in the North, to join table tennis and archery and a share in football and cycling. Women's volleyball was a major sport in socialist countries, and apart from anything else this move should have strengthened the allegiance of the Soviet Union and others to attend the Games. Furthermore, it was the most attractive sport, in television terms, yet offered to the North, and would substantially increase the television sales by NBC to the socialist countries. Samaranch was killing the North Koreans with generosity.

In this bizarre game of political chess that had been going on for two and a half years, North Korea, in spite of having nothing much left on the board besides pawns and maybe a straight-up-and-down rook, would nevertheless still play as though going for checkmate in three moves. Not content with the latest additional offer, in a situation in which they had no legitimate or moral rights from the start, the North Koreans now continued to push their luck; perhaps in the knowledge that they couldn't win, and therefore simply attempting to embarrass the IOC and the South as much as they could. An official press statement by Chin Chung Guk, vice-president of their NOC, was more aggressive and more overtly political than at any stage in the negotiations previously. 'The situation in Seoul is telling the world that the IOC took the wrong decision,' Chin said, with reference to South Korea's political volatility. 'Seoul is insecure.' The IOC's official communiqué stated that both sides had been given until 17 September to accept the proposal just related, that being the date for official invitations to be dispatched around the world. Samaranch declined to agree that it was a deadline, though he did say: 'After that date, any negotiation will be much more difficult.' He continued to insist that the IOC would not close the door, but that administrative necessity would eventually oblige them.

Chin had quickly made it apparent, at the conclusion of the fourth joint meeting, that North Korea was anything but appeased.

The proposals, he said, were an improvement but still less than the

North's demand for eight sports. He declined to be specific about the additional three. The aim of Kim Il Sung, the North's President, continued to be an opening and closing ceremony in Pyongyang with Samaranch in attendance, and accreditations issued by the Northern government and not by Seoul. Such an attempted distortion of the contract with Seoul was out of the question. Equally naïve was the demand for the whole football tournament. It was only recently that North Korea had been disqualified by FIFA for refusing to take part in an Olympic qualifying match, a decision that FIFA insisted was final. It seemed that the North Koreans believed that by being given the whole football tournament by the IOC, their own entry would be reinstated, this time as hosts.

Samaranch, meanwhile, confirmed his intention to visit Seoul again that November, irrespective of any decision from North Korea by 17 September. It was his plan to meet the political opposition leaders and Tae Woo Roh as a contribution towards stability. Dr Kim points out that, for the South, negotiations for better relations with the North had never been a direct part of the overall objective, merely coincidental. 'The aim was to raise South Korea's profile in economics, culture, industry, science and sport. It happened coincidentally in the development of Korean democracy, that we would have a Presidential election at the end of 1987, and that political demonstrations were taking place concurrently with the run-up to the Games. There was an element among the political opposition to Roh [who was standing as democratic successor to the military presidency of Chun Doo Hwan] that supposed the IOC *ought* to have been supporting co-hosting, that the IOC had not been doing enough. Samaranch offered to meet the opposition leaders, Dae Jung Kim, Young Sam Kim, and Jong Pil Kim. After that meeting they began to understand more about the IOC, about the Charter, and there was no more opposition.

'Throughout the negotiations, Samaranch had never been dogmatic. He's very much a man of consensus, co-ordination, persuasion. It is true to say that he helped set a pattern for future negotiations between North and South after the Seoul Games were over: a joint film festival in New York, the programme of football matches in Seoul and Pyongyang following the Asian Games in 1990; even the prime ministers' exchange that year; and the sharing of supporters at the Asian Games in Beijing. All these were joint policy decisions that were easier following our many talks prior to 1988. Yet Samaranch's anxiety had been there right to the end. On the day of the Presidential election, he was calling me every half-hour in the early hours of the morning, and I was saying to him, "It's Roh, go back to sleep again", and he would insist, "If there's no stability, there will be no Games." The next day he apologized for his nervousness and for bothering me.'

edding Day with Maria-
heresa, December 1st, 1955, at
Barcelona Cathedral.

2
Present and future IOC Presidents, 1967: l/r Pablo Negré, Spanish Hockey Federation president; Marius MacMahon, honorary IOC member; M-T; Avery Brundage, IOC President 1952-72; JAS.

3
Lord Killanin, retiring Presider
1972-80, hands the keys to Samaranch, on his election in Moscow, 1980.

4
Horst Dasler, master-mind of Adidas, a massive sports benefactor and shrewd analyst, with JAS in Seoul.

5
The late Tomas Keller (left), president of international rowing and opponent of the IOC, with Denis Oswald, current rowing president and IOC member since 1991.

6
Power-struggle: JAS at Los Angeles Games with Monique Berlioux, the IOC Director, whose authority he challenged. She 'resigned' the next year.

7
Acknowledging the crowd at the Opening Ceremony, 1984, together with Peter Ueberroth, organising president, who transformed Olympic revenue.

8
Together with Nancy and President Ronald Reagan behind bullet-proof glass of main tribune, Opening Ceremony, 1984.

9
Carl Lewis, successor to the legendary Owens, with four gold medals at LA; here, after the 100 metres victory.

10
Sebastian Coe, appointed by JAS to the new Athletes' Commission in 1981, uniquely retains his Moscow 1,500 metres title.

11
Evelyn Ashford of America, fifth in 1976, absent in 1980 boycott, wins 1984 100 metres from Alice Brown (US), right, and Merlene Ottey (Jamaica), left.

12
Joan Benoit, winner of the inaugural women's Olympic marathon, in 2hrs. 24mins. 52secs., just over two minutes outside her World Best time.

13
Joachim Cruz wins Brazil's first ever track medal, the 800 metres, consigning Coe to another silver. Jones (909) is third, Konchellah (585) fourth.

14
Global politiking: attending the 35th anniversary of Chinese Republic, whose Olympic return JAS had finalised: l., Xu Xianqin, Military Vice-Chairman, r., Ulanhu, CPR Vice-President.

15
Sychronisation: Dr Un Yong Kim, guiding light of Seoul's nomination and successful staging of the 1988 games, with JAS at GAISF Congress, Lausanne 1988.

16
Building for the future: JAS lends a hand with the National Stadium construction at Ougadougou, Burkina-Faso, during trans-African tour, 1985.

17
See-saw negotiations: keeping North Korea in the ring prior to Seoul Games, Lausanne Conference 1986: l/r, Raymond Gafner, (IOC), Alexandru Siperco (IOC), Chong Ha Kim (S.Korea), JAS, U Sun Kim (IOC/N.Korea), Ashwini Kumar (IOC), Berthold Beitz (IOC).

18
Most famous cheat in history: Johnson 'wins' 100 metres, 1988, from Lewis (r) and Christie (centre).

19
Below left Absurd margins: Daniela Silivas of Rumania, arbitrarily judged to have lost the gold medal at Seoul to Yelena Shushunova of USSR by 0.025 pts.!

20
Below right Gregory Louganis, the first male to win the springboard and platform diving events twice in a row, prepares for take-off at Seoul.

21
Tennis returns: Men's singles medal winners, 1988: (l/r) Stefan Edberg and Brad Gilbert, bronze; Miloslav Mecir, gold; Tim Mayotte, silver.

22
Kristin Otto, unknowingly a representative of the last swimming team of the German Democratic Republic, heads for one of her six gold medals in Seoul.

23
Olympic reality defeats totalitarian ideology: Lutz Long, Hitler's supposed protégé in 1936, shares cameraderie with Jesse Owens, who has just beaten him in the long jump.

24
King and counsel: JAS presents an inscription to King Juan Carlos, 1990.

25
Niclolai Ceaucescu may have been a cruel dictator, but he led Rumania against the Soviet boycott of LA: and here receives an Olympic Gold Order from JAS.

26
When JAS had this audience with Saddam Hussein early in 1990, Iraq's invasion of Kuwait was still eight months away. Sheik Fahad, IOC member of Kuwait who died in the attack, introduced JAS and Hussein on this occasion.

27
Latin leaders: Primo Nebiolo, president of athletics (left) and Mario Vazquez Rana, president of Association of NOCs, for whose IOC involvement JAS campaigned.

28
South Africa re-admitted: IOC delegation meets President De Klerk at Cape Town, 1991. l/r Gosper, Boetha, M'Baye, De Klerk, Ganga, Moses (partly hidden), Adefope, Lamine Ba.

29
Above left Visiting US Olympic Centre, Colorado Springs, in 1990, together with Anita DeFrantz, the IOC's first black woman member.

30
Above right Richard Pound, Montreal lawyer, architect of commercial development of IOC and a leading candidate as presidential successor.

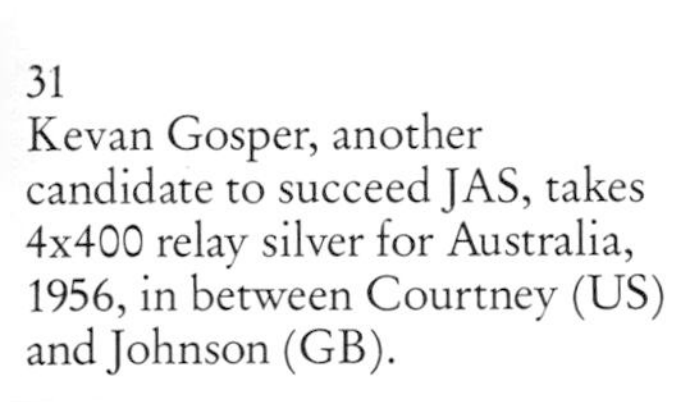

31
Kevan Gosper, another candidate to succeed JAS, takes 4x400 relay silver for Australia, 1956, in between Courtney (US) and Johnson (GB).

32
Never a dull moment: JAS surrounded, as always, by the media horde, this time at Pan-Am Games, Havana, 1991.

33
Three generations of Juan Antonio: father, son and grandson at holiday villa near Gerona.

If the South Koreans had reason to be grateful to Samaranch, he in turn was fortunate to have had a man as emotionally stable as Dr Kim with whom he could communicate almost daily on the other side of the globe. At the time of Roh's election, the leading financial newspaper in Japan had listed Kim in twentieth place among the fifty men who 'run' South Korea. His rise through sport had been inexorable, if to a degree unobserved. After Samaranch had destroyed Thomas Keller as leader of GAISF, it was Kim who began to re-establish that organization as the forum for all sports, and his was the guiding hand at all times for Seh Jik Park, the president of the Seoul organizing committee, a politician put into the job by the then military government and short on sporting experience. I do not pretend to understand the Oriental mind, but for a Westerner such as myself the avuncular Kim has an almost definitive, all-seeing Asian wisdom. Commenting, at the time of Samaranch's visit in November 1987, on the $80m development of the new Kwachun equestrian centre, with its equine hospital and swimming pool, 2,000-seat, six-storey grandstand, and projected regular racecourse, Kim had observed self-deprecatingly: 'Six years ago, we had nothing more than a few donkeys.' The modest, almost shy manner of many of the Koreans was in sharp contrast to the assertive Albertans of Calgary, whose Mayor Klein had been so crassly insulting about Seoul a few weeks previously.

The North Koreans chundered on: first announcing that they would not accept the invitation for '88, then radically shifting their ground and saying that they would seek a joint North-South team. This, however, had been while they were hoping that Roh might be defeated by the opposition, a hope in which they were disappointed. Another of the IOC's regular nightmares, however, was beginning to rear its head towards the end of 1987: threats from within Africa to take action against the inclusion of tennis players in the Olympic tournament who had participated in the South African championships in Johannesburg that November. (The African problem and its relation to the Games in 1988 is dealt with in a subsequent chapter.)

The North Korean problem had, by Christmas-time in 1987, for all practical purposes, ceased to be an issue. Administratively, it was becoming increasingly impossible to consider their involvement, however much they might try to keep their hat in the ring. Discussing the issue with me in Calgary before the start of the Winter Games, Seh Jik Park said: 'There's been plenty of time to negotiate a final solution, but North Korea has not responded positively, which was most disappointing. We had sincere hopes of some mutual agreement. We saw the possibility of a visiting North Korean team, but never envisaged joint hosting, which is not in the Charter. We agreed to the various IOC proposals, in the interest of the stability of the Games. It is hard to say what

North Korea will do now. This is very unpredicable. I do not think they could find a logical reason for staying away – for not competing as an individual National Olympic Committee, even if not as joint hosts. I would hope that North Korea might see there are substantial gains to be had from combining internationalism and idealism. The present selfish, short-range attitude is negative thinking. Why not contribute? By doing so, North Korea would learn a lot. We believe the Olympic Games in Seoul are removing barriers, giving the Games back to the athletes, putting the Olympic Movement back on the track after a series of boycotts which left a sense of damage. I think everyone, not just South Koreans, wants Seoul to be the best-ever Games.'

The following day in Calgary I talked with Marat Gramov, the Soviet Minister of Sport, who, though continuing to carry that air of gravitas of an old hard-liner, was becoming both less dogmatic and less powerful within the changing Soviet face under Gorbachev's regime of *perestroika*. How important was participation in Seoul? 'We think there should be as many nations there as there are IOC members,' Gramov said, 'and conditions should be created so that every country does participate. The Olympic philosophy is to promote co-operation. That is why we always support, and always will, the Olympic Movement and consider it is our duty to promote its development. Now is the time when all countries, irrespective of social systems, believe it is better to live in co-operation and find ways of better understanding. The Olympic philosophy is an integral part of those ideals which the world seeks. In Calgary, we're involved in sport. Nobody tries to make political propaganda regarding social differences. I do not mean to say that social differences do not influence the development of sport. Some athletes from the Third World cannot come here because of material disadvantages, yet we should not concentrate attention on *social* differences. The essence of the Games is for people to make friends and establish stability.

'Each country makes its own decision [about Seoul]. I can tell you firmly that we shall participate. As Minister, I can say we have been in full co-operation with the IOC for the last four years, that we've tried to help provide an atmosphere so that all can participate. President Samaranch has said the door is still open [for North Korea]. We consider the position of the IOC and Samaranch has been quite realistic. I think we should do everything possible to the last minute to enable all countries to attend. The Olympic Games are a real help, a forceful benefit. Any communication helps.'

Zola Budd, the controversial South African runner, who had acquired a British passport at the last moment by a discreditable route in order to gain inclusion for the British team in Los Angeles, was doing her bit to help in 1988. She withdrew her request again to be included in the

British team. Having fluctuated in her residence between her natural and adopted homes, she had re-aroused African hostility, the Supreme Council stating she was unacceptable, the IAAF threatening to ban the British team if no action was taken against Budd. Her withdrawal cleared the air.

As for Howard Cosell, he might have broadened his understanding had he been present on a sweltering afternoon not long before the Games at the Full Gospel Church in Yoido, alongside the Han River that flows majestically through Seoul. 'The Olympic Games are just ahead of us, and the world is coming to Korea,' Choi Yong Kim the leader of one of the world's largest religions, said in addressing his congregation. 'Let us pray there is no terrorism to disrupt them.' The congregation that day was 18,000 strong, and Choi's Full Gospel Church was one of the phenomena of the new South Korea. In 1958 he had five followers. Now the Church had 530,000 members, and the vast glass and brick church is one of the sights of Yoido, in a growing business centre of Seoul. 'Our country is poor in natural resources, but God poured his blessings on to this land because our people began to accept Jesus,' Choi told the congregation. 'There was remarkable growth and as a result our country has been able to host the Olympics.'

Out of town, at Kimpo International Airport, a Korean Air charter flight, having made the first stop ever in a communist country, arrived from Budapest carrying the Hungarian Olympic team: part of South Korea's determination to use the Olympic Games as a vehicle for diplomacy. Prior to the airline's arrival, it had already been announced that permanent Missions had been established in Seoul and Budapest as a prelude to full diplomatic powers. Hungary was the first communist country to create formal links with Seoul, capital of a country where communism is banned. The barriers, in every sense, were crumbling; and perhaps the word was also travelling by sea to Jerry Eisenberg.

As late as 10 June, Samaranch had telexed Yu Sun Kim, president of the North Korean NOC, that he was still ready at any time to fly to Pyongyang if that might help facilitate participation in the Games. It was a genuine wish. The IOC, aware of the degree to which their leader had campaigned for four years literally to bring the world together in Seoul, rewarded him at the time of the Session prior to the Games with a unanimous request that he should extend his eight-year term. Wajid Ali of Pakistan had gathered more than sixty signatures inviting Samaranch to carry on; in fact, his period of office was officially due to continue until the next year, following the approval of Killanin's proposal to avoid elections in the year of a Games.

If the IOC was grateful, the South Koreans believed him to be the most valuable person ever to have set foot on their Asian peninsula. They would reward him two years later with a solemn Peace Prize.

Samaranch had brought to South Korea the most valuable gift that anyone can bring to a nation: status. With status comes respect and recognition. And with the staging of the Olympic Games began an accelerating trend of trade and diplomatic relations with the communist world which had pretended since 1953 that South Korea did not exist. Their gross national product was now increasing at the rate of 12 per cent a year, three or four times that of any nation in Europe. In 1981, when awarded the Games, South Korea did not have colour television. Seven years later it had become one of the ten largest television-trading countries in the world. Their profit on the Games, for all their immense generosity towards many competing countries, would be an astonishing $500m. Among other donations, they would give $20m to the Disabled Olympic Games taking place later that autumn. They contributed 450 cars to the Asian Games in Beijing.

'Since the Games, we have established diplomatic relations with all socialist countries except Cuba, Albania, North Korea, and China, and with China we have a trade office,' Dr Kim says. 'Who could have believed there would be a Gorbachev-Roh summit meeting in San Francisco? All this has stemmed from the Olympics, yet the success of the Olympics is primarily due to Samaranch. What happened in 1988 was the biggest turning-point in the history of South Korea, in the mentality of our people. They now think they can achieve anything, though the problem with that freedom is that we've now generated too much consumption. We used to have seven newspapers in Seoul: now there are thirty dailies and weeklies. If we had a weakness in the organizing of the Games it was that we were too warm-hearted. Mario Vazquez Raña asked for twenty personal invitations and ten cars, all of which were on us. Nebiolo wanted to keep everyone together within ASOIF, whatever the price. If it hadn't been for me, there would have been serious complaints within the organizing committee, but in the end we had more participants than ever, and therefore more prestige.'

As I walked away from the closing ceremony of the 1988 Olympic Games, just before the end, a haunting Oriental chorale still drifting upwards into the clear night sky, I was more than ever in love with Korea. Confronted with the largest Games ever, they had been the perfect hosts. The debt which the Olympic Movement owed them was immense. The Koreans had the organization of the Germans, the courtesy of the Orient and the financial sense of the Americans. They could hardly fail. It is undoubtedly true that the Games always tend to bring out the best in a host nation, but few, if any, have given so much, and on such a scale, as had these remarkable people. The worst had been expected. The IOC and Samaranch had been condemned for allowing the Games to proceed. Yet what had been achieved by a nation that thirty years ago had been a bomb site was phenomenal. The North Koreans did not terrorize us, the socialists did not boycott, the students threw only a handful of token petrol bombs.

The largest Games in history – in size, technology and publicity – had been an exceptional success, never mind a drugs scandal of sensational proportions. The Games provided competition facilities without parallel, and the Koreans had advanced the public perception of the Games more than anybody since the West Germans in 1972. The friendship had overflowed. At the closing ceremony, Arabs and Israelis walked around the track with total informality, side by side. The Koreans have a cultural tradition in music and singing, in theatre and dance, which had made their ceremonial accomplishments, at the opening and closing, no surprise. They had welcomed us and bidden us goodbye with such warmth that it was sad to be leaving.

'I was never relaxed,' Samaranch reflects. 'My happiest moment was when I closed the Games. They were, I think, the best Games there have been, but it was a desperate anxiety throughout those two weeks.'

9 Cheats

—

To avoid being caught by random drug testing, which is now beginning to pervade most Olympic sports and NOCs, a cheating competitor no longer needs a week's warning, as has been claimed to be sufficient, but a mere ten minutes. Those competitors who know they are liable to be found guilty allegedly carry with them in their kitbag wherever they go a 'clean' urine sample, conveniently provided by a friend. By the macabre, and I would suppose not unpainful, use of a catheter, it is possible at short notice to insert the urine devoid of drug elements, then to produce it upon request by the 'natural' process. Alternatively, sachets of clean urine can be concealed within other orifices. If this sounds grotesque to the ordinary reader and non-athlete, it must be said that it is no more than an extension of the manipulative world of mechanical medicine, as illustrated by surrogate parenthood.

The problem was emphasised by the irregularity, revealed in February 1992, in a test in South Africa on Katrin Krabbe, the world-sprint champion from former East Germany, in which she and two other athletes appeared to have identical urine from an alternative source. Her four-year suspension was subject to appeal at the time of writing. Prince de Mérode, chairman of the IOC Medical Commission, revealed during the Winter Games at Albertville that reliable blood testing was now available. Some NOCs, such as USOC, are resisting on ethical grounds; but exploitation is so profoundly unethical that blood testing, in my opinion, should be introduced immediately. The stance of Anita DeFrantz, one of the IOC's most principled members, on this issue seems out of place. 'Blood testing is an invasion of the body,' she argues. But what is taking drugs? Urgency following the Krabbe affair is paramount: especially as there is the prospect of the IOC or the IAAF being sued by Krabbe's equipment suppliers if she is prevented from competing.

Given the extent of such deceit, together with the long odds against randomly obtaining scientific proof that a competitor is guilty – admitted by the medical technicians, who acknowledge that their cheating, professionally qualified colleagues tend always to be one step ahead – it may well be that, however vigilant the medical commissions of the IOC and other organizations, whatever the money spent on officially accredited laboratories, whatever the uniformity among administrators in pursuing and punishing the cheats, the situation will remain in favour of those who seek to win by devious means. The world athletics championships of 1991 in Tokyo showed a marked decline in performance in the 'heavy' throwing events, and in some women's running – times between one and two seconds slower in the 400 metres than eastern European women were achieving in the early Eighties – but, reality suggests there is still an undetected army of competitors anonymously furthering their prospects with the help of illegal anatomical chemistry. When 900 Canadian athletes were interviewed, in the wake of the Ben Johnson scandal, the majority said that, in spite of potential health hazards, if given the opportunity to take enhancing pharmaceutical aids, they would do so.

It was therefore essential that, at the IAAF Congress immediately preceding the championships in Tokyo, agreement was reached on extending the suspension in athletics for positive tests from two years to four, on the proposal of Great Britain, Canada, New Zealand and others. It should be said, in passing, that it was regrettable the British should be obliged to have done a deal in the lobbying beforehand: gaining support for their motion in return for abandoning their opposition to the proposed second world championships in the four-year cycle. Such is the world of power-broking. At least there was now discouragement, however, for those on a daily diet of anabolic steroids, testosterone and other performance-enhancing substances. A positive test would now mean, in effect, a ban for life. The Athletes Commission, formed by Samaranch in 1981, had long demanded a life ban, but had been resisted by a cautious IOC Medical Commission under the direction of Prince Alexandre de Mérode, a Belgian. The IAAF decision would specifically include the next championship in any four-year cycle, even where this happened to be a month or two beyond the four-year period. There are few competitors who, even when competing regularly, are able to maintain a nine-year span at the top of their sport that enables them to qualify for three consecutive Olympic Games. Deprived of competition, it is unlikely that any competitor can return to the sport at all after a four-year exclusion, let alone at the same level. In terms of dissuasion, the IAAF had established an important psychological as well as technical advance. Dr Manfred Donike of Germany, foremost of the scientists working against drug abuse in sport and the man who technically supervised Krabbe's most recent random test, is against uniform four-year suspension, being unfair to minor non-steroid offenders; whereas he advocates life suspension for such as Johnson. He also expressed the hope, at the time of writing, that Krabbe and her two colleagues would challenge the suspension in court, where they would be obliged to testify under oath. Dr Donike referred to the athletes' signed confirmation, given twice, that they were satisfied with the testing procedure and the authenticity of the samples.

The IAAF, not unreasonably, in 1991 wished to persuade the IOC to try to enforce uniformity of penalties for positive testing among all IFs.

It clearly made no sense to have a range of suspensions; from three months in cycling to life in weightlifting, four years in athletics, and discretionary periods in yachting. The IAAF's own record in the past was an unhappy one, with a period in the late Seventies and early Eighties during which an 18-month and then two-year suspension was sometimes lifted for the reinstatement of the guilty athlete; a notable example was the reappearance of Finland's 10,000 metres runner Vainio at the European Championships in 1986, after being found positive at the Olympic Games in 1984. A British middle-distance runner, Christine Benning, withdrew on principle from the Olympic Games in Moscow, stating she had no wish to run against competitors previously guilty and now reinstated. Athletics had long been dragging its feet. By September 1991, Willi Daume, the chairman of the Eligibility Commission, was proposing there should be a minimum level of random testing by every NOC in order to be eligible to receive an invitation to compete in the Games. The strength of this idea, in my opinion, was to take part of the control of drug testing away from the Medical Commission, which has tended to be a shade too academic in its approach, and to put responsibility within the eligibility camp; and at the same time to make action preventive rather than reactive. Daume at this point did not have a clear enough proposal to put to the executive board. A complication would be the huge difference in the financial scope between large and small NOCs.

Dr Roger Jackson, chairman of the Canadian NOC, a former Olympic oarsman and a practising physiologist, had been working along the same tack as Daume for several years. Addressing the 29th Session of the International Olympic Academy in 1989, with an audience of over two hundred former Olympic champions, students, journalists, and a dozen members of the IOC, Jackson said that the national federation of a sport in any country with more than one competitor found positive should itself be suspended from the next Games. He branded national federations as the fourth guilty party in drug abuse, together with the athlete, the coach and the doctor. Manuel Guerra, the IOC member for Cuba, went further still. He believes that NOCs, having the ultimate responsibility for competitors entered in a Games, should also be suspended: in other words, the exclusion of a country's whole team where several competitors are found guilty of drug use. Jackson is also pressing for more governments, as in Canada and Scandinavia, to introduce anti-trafficking laws to control the import of steroids in the way they control marijuana or heroin. 'We, as NOCs, have the ability to prevent athletes from competing in the Games,' Jackson said. 'The Olympic Games epitomize excellence. Because of the philosophy of the Olympic Movement, the banning of individuals from the Olympic Games is different from other international sport.'

Jackson is not in favour of permanent exclusion from sport for drug offenders, other than from the Olympic Games, on the principle that penalties in other walks of life allow for rehabilitation and a second chance. At that session of the Academy, I met Lee Evans, the 1968 Olympic champion at 400 metres and 4 x 400 metres relay in Mexico City. His world record there was lowered later by another American runner, Butch Reynolds, who would be found positive, though not on the occasion of his record run. Evans recalled he had been aware, when eliminated in the US trials for a place in the Munich Games in 1972, that some of the athletes who defeated him were using drugs. 'I had the chance, too,' he admits. 'I was offered handfuls of the stuff. But I thought, if I could run 43.8 without pills, why should I bother?' Evans said that he suspected at the time that David Jenkins of Britain, who, when I talked with Evans, had recently been released from a prison sentence for massive importing of steroids into California from Mexico, was using drugs when he won the American Athletic Union 400 metres in 1971.

It has been my own opinion since the late 1970s, when the prevalence of drug abuse began to become widely apparent, that this factor presented a much more ominous threat to the Olympic Games, and to sport in general, than did, for instance, professionalism or commercialization. Cheating by drug-taking strikes at the root of sport's credibility, destroys public confidence more fundamentally than any of the other abuses which have plagued sport throughout this century. I have repeatedly made this point to Samaranch during our various travels. He, following his practice of delegation, has I think tended too optimistically to expect that the breadth of attention being applied through technology to the drugs controversy would resolve the situation. The emotions that are aroused by the controversy, both among innocent competitors and among spectators who are more than cursory voyeurs of a passing event, are passionate. Repeatedly Samaranch has said, in reference to the suspension of Johnson in Seoul, where the Canadian sprinter tested positive after winning the 100 metres in world record time: 'The IOC uses action, not words, in the fight against doping.' The IOC's action up to the present time, except in the notable instance of Johnson, has been undemonstrative, to say the least.

Consider the most consistently abused of all sports: weightlifting. There is a widely acknowledged, and all-too-obvious, link between body-building clubs and weightlifting, a short step away. People close to both sports tell you that body-building, especially in America, is the most rampant source of muscle and strength-building aids that there is; and weightlifting consistently has had the worst record of any Olympic sport in its proportion of positive tests. Yet the IOC has been persistently reluctant to take positive, let alone draconian, steps to bring weightlifting under control. Everyone has been easily charmed by the smiling assurances of an eminently agreeable Hungarian, Tamas Ajan, secretary-general of the International Weightlifting Federation, that next week everything will be in order. At a meeting of the IOC executive board coinciding with the Congress of ANOC in Vienna in 1988, Dick Pound, then IOC vice-president, proposed that the weightlifting federation should be suspended from Olympic membership, following excessive malpractice in Seoul three-and-a-half months before. Yet Samaranch and the board resisted Pound's proposal, leaving the Canadian to say, disappointedly: 'We had a perfect opportunity to take positive action. I am disappointed and surprised that my colleagues on the board did not accept my recommendation. We could have helped weightlifting in the long term by a temporary suspension now.' Pound was all too aware that the Games were in danger of being perceived as rotten, and that there would be no continuing sympathy without radical discipline. The Canadian Weightlifting Federation – in line with Roger Jackson – had proposed that if a team member had a positive test, then the whole team should be banned from the next equivalent competition, whether continental, world or Olympic.

There was a growing fear in the United States, indeed, that it was only a matter of time, given the perverse legal system of that country, before an individual, medically damaged by voluntary drug-taking for sporting performance, brought a legal action against a sports federation or Olympic body for offering the incentive of medals and financial reward without providing adequate protection against drug inducement. Following the Johnson revelation, there was an *upsurge* in demand for performance drugs in America among *schoolchildren*. At an Australian inquiry in Canberra, weightlifters had testified that they were obliged to take steroids, by the risk of losing their 'scholarships' and by the standards set by the national coach, which were otherwise unattainable. It did seem, at the Commonwealth Games in Auckland at the beginning of 1990, that Samaranch's patience with weightlifting might be finally exhausted, with yet more scandals of positive testing. Still nothing of consequence was to happen. Samaranch was presiding at a boardroom table of which one of the legs was progressively being eaten away by woodworm; but none of those sitting around the table would get down on their hands and knees underneath to discover how serious the situation was. At Auckland, the competitors were subjected only to random testing, for economy measures. Sam Coffa, president of the Commonwealth Weightlifting Federation, said he was disappointed that *all* medallists had not been tested. Subratakumar Paul, an Indian tested positive in the lightweight division, had not been tested previously because India had no adequate testing facilities. At Auckland, the samples for testing were being sent to Sydney at a cost of $180 a time.

Pound's proposal in 1988, though rejected, may have had indirect influence, by frightening the weightlifting federation into action under the realisation that their Olympic future was seriously threatened. The sport's next two world championships showed a marked improvement, free of positive tests and with a significant fall in the level of performance; and the federation introduced life suspension for offenders. Ajan's re-assurance at last reflected genuine action behind the scenes. While weightlifting has been one of the most conspicuously guilty sports long term, its removal from the Olympic programme would by inference incriminate many in sport; weightlifting, athletics and gymnastics represent the three basic disciplines of all competitors strength, speed and agility.

Auckland had revealed the impediment to the installation of Daume's proposal of minimum NOC levels of testing is cost. Accredited laboratories are exceedingly expensive in technology and personnel. To Samaranch's credit, it had been his initiative that launched the idea of a mobile IOC laboratory for random testing; in practice, the difficulties confronting a successful operation of that scheme were such that the proposal had to be abandoned.

The IOC Medical Commission had been first formed, during Brundage's presidency, in 1961 under the chairmanship of Sir Arthur (later Lord) Porritt. The initial need had been for the determination of femininity, at the time a factor causing controversy in relation to specific female competitors. The need had intensified following the death through drug-taking of Knud Jensen of Denmark in the cycling time-trials at the Games in Rome the previous year. By 1968, when the Commission began systematic examination at Grenoble and Mexico City, de Mérode had succeeded Porritt as chairman. It was in 1976 in Montreal that the first positive tests were revealed, with seven competitors disqualified for the use of steroids . . . including three weightlifters. Five more weightlifters suffered disqualification in tests not completed until after the Games. The following year three Finns and an East German woman shotputter, Slupianick, were found guilty at the finals of the European Cup in athletics. At a meeting of the IFs at Lausanne in 1979, Ajan was assuring colleagues that weightlifting had overcome its difficulties.

Samaranch, to this day, continues to be defensive on the topic: concerned at the genuine need to catch and punish not just offending competitors but the many collaborators and even initiators of the abuse among the ranks of coaches, doctors and other professional advisers. 'We need a clearer definition of what exactly is cheating, not just having taken "a substance on the banned list",' Samaranch says. 'Drawing a line is not easy, but we urgently need it. Doping is against the health of the athlete, sometimes dangerously, as well as improving performance.

There are many substances you can take to enhance performance that are not on the list [for example, forms of ginseng]. Why? We have to have clearer definitions of what is and is not harmful. Most athletes are taking something, from relatively innocuous vitamins to painkillers. Are painkillers not harmful, if they leave you with what may be afterwards a worse injury? These people are not villains. We now have a more critical situation than ever, with revelations of systematic drug-taking by competitors in Germany over the years, not only what was East Germany, but in the West. This could be seriously damaging financially, with the loss of sponsorship. We in the IOC can control events to some extent within the Olympic Games, but not at championships in between. That has to be the responsibility of IFs and NOCs.'

Unintentionally, Samaranch points to one of the shortcomings of de Mérode, the chairman of the IOC's Medical Commission. Following a lengthy period on the executive board, including several years as vice-president, de Mérode retired from the board, a statutory requirement, before seeking re-election at the Session in Birmingham in 1991, where he was defeated by Pal Schmitt of Hungary. 'Alexandre is not a fighter,' Samaranch observed. 'He did not lobby for his re-election, that is not his style, and the members failed to realize the value of what he did over many years. Indeed there were those who considered that the suspension of Johnson in Seoul would be harmful. Fortunately, many governments are also now fighting against drugs in sport, and we can say that in many competitions there are fewer positive tests than there were.'

de Mérode is a genial Belgian aristocrat, his lineage going back to the twelfth century. He is not the kind of person who *needs* to lobby for position; and he brings to his conscientious work within the IOC an independence and intelligence that characterize the better traditions of that body. It is beside the point, as three presidents have recognized, that he is not medically qualified; this does not prevent him bringing to the chairmanship the ethical consideration that is paramount to the job. I would say, however, that de Mérode's attitude has leaned on the benevolent side, taking the legitimate view that, in many instances of positive tests, it is not possible to know the extent to which the competitor might have been manipulated by others. de Mérode could not have been more positive on the case of Johnson, threatening to resign if the automatic suspension was not effected. There are those who had considered, during de Mérode's time on the executive board, that his independence from political stereotypes, his lack of ambition for personal prestige, his acceptability to all branches of the Olympic Movement, might make him a potential successor to Samaranch. Yet that lack of ambition, a nicely balanced belief that the organization he joined in the 1960s was still the seat for gentlemen and for respectability, somehow disqualified him.

His tendency to break into an irreverent laugh disguises the degree to which this hereditary prince takes life seriously, though it is probably true that he does not live *for* the IOC. If not to do so once was a virtue, it may nowadays be considered a handicap. de Mérode does not *have* to catch the bus. His views on Samaranch are worth giving.

'He has a good feeling for public opinion,' de Mérode says. 'He knows where he wants to go, but takes his time. He is a winner, but doesn't take risks, and doesn't do anything in such a way that it could later be undone. Moves one small step at a time, so that people tend not to realize what is happening. When he was elected, some thought he had no influence, but I told them, "Wait and see, he *may* be a President." He seemed to be a grey man without personality, but people were surprised, for after six months they realized we had a President with a large P. During twelve years the IOC has been transformed. With the evolution in sport, social and financial, what was previously acceptable is no longer so. When I arrived in '64, there was just enough money to pay Brundage's secretary and to rent a room for meetings. Now, the IOC is a big company. The chairman *had* to be in residence. Berlioux was filtering the information getting through to the President. I think she believed it was her job! She was unable to compromise, she was omnipotent. With any development you had to go through her. A company grows, and if you don't change, the company will be destroyed. Maybe Berlioux believed she was indestructible. It took five years [to depose her], but that was Samaranch's style. Samaranch knew he needed money to develop the IOC, that without it we were beaten, but the problem with money is that you are under the influence of it. Yet money was the only way Samaranch could protect the influence of the IOC. He trusts his own capacity to convince people, and is very open: a curious mixture of autocrat and democrat. He used people for the benefit of the Movement, and nothing can disturb his preoccupation. You rarely find people who are as involved as he is. Whatever he does is for the benefit of the IOC and the Olympic Movement. If he is without power, the Olympic Movement will not have power. The two are integral, though if the Movement has power, inevitably he will have more. Up to now the line has been wholly positive. That's why he was re-elected unanimously.'

The partial failure in control of drug-taking by de Mérode and Samaranch, if failure there has been, has come through liberalism: de Mérode's attitude that the Commission must work towards positive as well as negative attitudes, that athletes must be shown how they can escape from the temptations of drug aid. 'Cheating will go on until the end of the world,' he admits, 'but our job must be as much to expose the health dangers, of depression, of glandular and cardiovascular damage, as to *ban* people. We know that there is blood-doping, the injection of an athlete's own oxygen-fortified blood, which cannot be detected. But do the athletes know that it is only three-tenths effective, and has the risk of accident?' It is with his views on restricting the workload of athletes' training that de Mérode is most radical. There is too much competition for the human body to endure, he suggests, and training should be limited by regulation, just as it is in other forms of working employment. 'In sport there is no time limit, but administrators should become interested in this field. Certainly, it would be a type of social regulation. But so is "saving" money, as with trust funds. There cannot be *absolute* freedom, even in the rights of a professional sportsman, any more than there are in medicine, or piloting an aeroplane.' In the area of academic, ethical argument, there is no one better informed than the chairman of the Medical Commission; yet the historic principle of discipline, that setting an example with an individual will have a significant influence among the crowd, was perhaps not fully brought home until the incident involving a global star such as Johnson.

While the Medical Commission, in order to be able to take punitive action, needs to have scientific evidence, visual and circumstantial evidence has been available for many years. Harold Connolly, the 1956 Olympic hammer throw champion, testifying to a United States Senate Committee in 1973, said that in the American team of 1968 there were athletes that had so many puncture holes from injecting drugs that it was difficult to find a fresh spot to give themselves a new shot. 'The overwhelming majority of the international athletes I know would do anything, and take anything, short of killing themselves, to improve their performance.' Connolly admitted to having been hooked on steroids for eight years.

Suspicions have frequently been aroused by the sheer physique of some athletes. Dr Leroy Perry, a Los Angeles chiropractor, who had treated Olympic athletes around the world, was sceptical, for instance, about Jarmila Kratochvilova, the Czechoslovakian who won both the 400 and 800 metres in the 1983 world championships. He told the *Los Angeles Times*: 'I believe her condition now is a physiological impossibility from what she was five years ago. That is not a normal physiological female body. . . . I've treated Olympic female athletes in thirty-four countries, but I've never seen a body like that. I think there is something chemically different about her physical make-up, and it hasn't come from weightlifting.' In 1979, aged 27, Kratochvilova, who failed to qualify for the European championship final the previous year, had a best time for the 400 metres of 51.47. Five years later, she became the first woman to beat 48 seconds. In experimental tests made in Cologne in 1981 on unidentified samples taken from competitors at the Moscow Olympics – where Kratochvilova took the 400 silver – more than 20 per cent were found positive for excess of testosterone, a substance which was not on the list of proscribed drugs in Moscow, and predominantly detected among women.

In 1987 Sandra Gasser, a Swiss runner, was banned for two years by the IAAF after she failed a test during the world championships in Rome. The high court in London upheld the ban. At the IAAF Congress in Rome before the championships, a ten-point plan had been adopted: increased penalties for doping offenders, ranging from two years for a first offence with a 'heavy' drug, and life for a second offence; more accredited laboratories; more controls at major events; all national federations to accept IAAF anti-doping testing at national championships; obligatory random testing for all national federations; senior athletes to endorse the campaign; termination of kit contracts for positive athletes; a youth education programme; continuing financial support of medical research; supply of anti-doping equipment to national federations. So dismayed by this time was Andreas Brugger, a former Swiss shotput champion, by the prominence of drug-taking, that, as promoter of the Grand Prix in Zurich, the sport's most prominent non-championship event, he now refused to accept throwing events. Because Grand Prix events carried testing, it was impossible to find throwers willing to compete.

Professor Benzi, an Italian expert on pharmaceutical manipulation by the sport, has claimed there are performance-enhancement substances not included on the list of banned drugs, so fast is the technology of human chemistry developing. Evidence of this became available during the Winter Games in Calgary in 1988, with an as yet undetectable drug, said to be able to increase endurance performance, for instance in cross country skiing, by as much as 9 per cent. The drug is used to resist kidney failure, and is called erythropoietin. de Mérode said that EPO, as it is known, would be on the open market under prescription within a few months. It is manufactured in America, West Germany and Japan, and was then believed already to be in use as a performance-additive. It is said that all traces of EPO used in competition disappear within 48 hours of injection. This demands the degrading process of inspecting an athlete's body for injection puncture marks.

There was inspection by the Medical Commission in Calgary, without positive results, on the day that Marty Hall, Canada's cross country skiing coach, accused the medal-winning Soviet women's team of blood-doping. Hall's accusation caused recriminations, with Otto Jelinek, Canada's Minister for Sport, apologizing to his opposite number Marat Gramov. Hall remained adamant. 'I just want to see something done,' he said. 'Sport right now is in trouble.' The two Soviet medal winners, Tamara Tikhonova and Vida Ventsene, both denied using blood-doping.

Hall's comments were given support by Anders Lenes, a former

Norwegian cross country champion. Lenes, who coached the Canadian team in 1984 at Sarajevo, alleged he had accidentally witnessed the blood-doping of Aki Karvonen, a Finnish silver medal winner. He said that he and a West German walked through the wrong door into the Finnish team's suite: 'We walked in and there it was,' Lenes said. 'What do you do? You can't run and get the police.' Karvonen has since admitted blood-doping in an interview with *Sports Illustrated*, the American magazine. Blood-doping was made illegal only in 1985.

de Mérode already had evidence at this time that the US cyclists, who had been taken ill and were unable to compete in Los Angeles, had been blood-doped. His Commission is confronted by scientific advances moving faster than detection methods can keep pace. 'We need, as much as anything, the collaboration of governments,' he said. The pace of advance was apparent at the European athletics championships at Split, Yugoslavia, in 1990. Professor Arnold Beckett, a prominent researcher at Chelsea College in London, revealed: 'The immediate problem is the replacement of blood-doping by EPO. The increasing use of endogenous substances, those already secreted naturally in the body, make our job exceedingly difficult. How do we determine the "extra" amount present in any athlete? We can measure EPO, but where should we set the limit that is allowed?' Beckett recommended a government mandate that would require manufacturers of EPO to insert an inert 'marker' agent, free of effect on competitors but instantly identifiable. Even more alarming was the relevation, at the world athletic championships in Tokyo in 1991, by Dr Arne Ljungqvist, head of the IAAF medical committee, that there will soon be on the market a testosterone contraceptive pill for men. This will raise exactly the same indefinable problem of establishing *normal* levels in a normal male.

There had been no doubt about the levels evident in the testing of Ben Johnson, which showed a pattern of continuous use of Stanozolol. The fall from grace, within 72 hours, of a victor who had been hailed around the world for a seemingly magnificent triumph, was demonstrably the greatest single deterrent in the history of the campaign against cheats. In the early hours of Monday morning, some thirty hours after Johnson's victory, a note was pushed under the door of Carol Anne Letheren, *chef de mission* of the Canadian team, informing them that the first test was positive and inviting Johnson to attend the second test with NOC officials. Dick Pound was called mid-morning by Samaranch, who informed him that 'the worst' had happened. Pound, as a lawyer, had an initial instinct to defend Johnson, but was warned by Samaranch to be careful, and Pound departed for discussions with the Canadian delegation.

There arose an allegation of a 'mystery man' being seen with Lewis, with dark suggestions that a harmless beverage in Johnson's kitbag might somehow have been 'spiked'. However, at a meeting with the Medical Commission it was demonstrated to the Canadians that the 'profile' of the test on Johnson left no possible doubt, the analysis showing absorption of the drug over a long time. Some members of the IOC executive board considered it unethical for Pound to appear with the Canadian delegation, as though siding with the case for Johnson's defence, which did not really exist. de Mérode had already stated to the Medical Commission that if the executive board did not immediately pronounce Johnson suspended on the evidence before them, then he, de Mérode, would resign. Killanin, attending the Games as honorary President, had been irritated in 1980 by the lenient attitude of the IAAF towards positive tests in those Games, and now said that Johnson ought to be banned for life.

Samaranch was shocked by the revelation: the leader of every sporting event likes to bathe in reflected glory, a natural emotion. He now tried to cut the losses. Johnson had been smuggled out of Seoul on a flight back to Canada on Monday evening, and the news began to break in the early hours of Tuesday morning. 'The bad news we can transfer into good news,' Samaranch stated to the world's press. 'This is not a disaster, for it shows the IOC is very serious, and that we are winning the battle for a clean Games. The gap between our aims and those who are cheating is narrowing. I am very sorry for Johnson, who is a great athlete, and he is not the only person we have to blame.'

Evident here was Samaranch's wish not to be vindictive. Those eventually to be convicted of complicity were Charlie Francis, Johnson's coach, and Dr Jamie Astaphan, who had helped administer the drugs; the path of justice would take some time. Few were bothered at this moment when Dr Robert Dugal, a Canadian who was a member of the doping sub-commission, said that the side effects of Stanozolol included cancer of the liver. Cancer of the Olympics was currently top of the charts; Samaranch's warning in his address to the IOC Session a week beforehand, that 'doping is Death', now seen to have carried a prophetic ring. 'We are all involved,' Marat Gramov said, heavily.

The impact of Johnson's suspension would send ripples to every corner of sport. The repercussions were inestimable, yet they all stemmed from a single motive force: money. In creating greater wealth for the IOC and the Olympic Games, Samaranch had helped create greater wealth for the competitors, at least in those sports where it was professionally available. For Johnson, and to a lesser extent for Francis, the fruits were substantial. Johnson's victory could have been worth an estimated $8m over the next four years. He was currently driving a $150,000 Ferrari and was having built in Toronto a house valued in the region of $750,000. In the years ahead, 'Johnson v. Lewis' would have been a draw-card spoken of in almost the same terms as 'Ali v. Frazier'.

Overnight all that had gone; replaced by a lengthy inquiry in Toronto under Judge Dubin at which Johnson, after months in which he had protested his innocence, finally admitted under cross-examination his wholesale involvement with Francis and Astaphan in defrauding his sport, the Olympic Games, and the millions in Canada who had emotionally celebrated victory over the American foe on that supposedly glorious Saturday evening in Seoul.

The benefits, if they can be called such, that began to flow from the example set by Johnson's suspension were many. An initiative, first proposed before the end of the Games in Seoul between the Soviet Union and the United States, led to the signing, at the second World Conference of Sports Ministers the following year organized by UNESCO, of an agreement for mutual cross-testing for drug abuse, twice a year, for the period until December 1992. Regrettably, the fulfilment of this would be largely frustrated by the extraordinary political developments that were about to take place within the Soviet Union.

Yet a radical move towards testing by the Soviets was encouraged by their elimination from the World Cup, in 1989, by a positive test in the European Cup finals of their shot-putter Alexander Bagach. That positive test forfeited team points, and resulted in East Germany replacing the Soviet Union in second qualifying place for the World Cup in Barcelona. Bagach had taken testosterone *after* being passed clean by the IOC-accredited laboratory in Moscow prior to the European finals. 'The punishment has to go to both the athlete and his coach, Palamarchuk,' Marat Gramov said during the IOC Session in San Juan, Puerto Rico, that autumn. 'Everyone in the Soviet Union, including press and television, has been highly critical. Reinstatement will depend on whether the athlete is still in training in two years' time.' Gramov confirmed that, at the time of the Session, cross-testing under the previously mentioned agreement was under way, a group of American analysts being in Moscow to test a hundred Soviet competitors, selected by the Americans. Gramov stressed that research had to continue urgently. Manfred Donike had been able to expose, at the IOC-accredited laboratory in Cologne, the use of steroids by fifty unnamed competitors who had gone undetected during the Games in Seoul. The spectacular performance improvement of Bagach was characteristic of drug involvement. Ranked only eleventh in the Soviet Union in 1988, he had moved to fifth in the world within a year. A whole team had been excluded from the World Cup, with all the loss of financial benefit that this would entail, on account of one competitor's positive test.

The work of de Mérode and his many colleagues on different medical committees was indeed beginning to take effect, yet all suspensions stood at risk of legal challenge. Particularly worrying for the IOC, in the autumn of 1991, was the successful appeal by Butch Reynolds to TAC, the American federation, upheld on the grounds of alleged imperfections in the testing administrative procedure and analysis detail by the accredited Paris laboratory of his samples from a Grand Prix meeting in Monte Carlo the previous year. The International Amateur Athletics Federation (IAAF) would therefore be obliged itself to challenge this appeal; in the event of failure by the IAAF, on a test conducted by Dr Donike, foremost of those in his field, both IAAF and IOC would be damagingly undermined in their long-running campaign. Details of the grounds accepted by the TAC appeal tribunal, however, suggested that the IAAF's counter-appeal could withstand the legal test.

At an international symposium on legal issues in Monte Carlo in 1990, under the aegis of the International Athletic Foundation – charitable arm of the IAAF – Robert Armstrong, QC, counsel to the Dubin Inquiry, criticized both the IOC and IAAF. Armstrong alleged a failure of leadership, and a lack of reaction to available evidence prior to the Johnson incident. For example, Dr Robert Kerr, of San Gabriel, California, had testified that he had prescribed steroids to twenty US medal winners in the 1984 Games. A US Senator's judicial committee hearing on steroid abuse had been told by Pat Connolly, a coach to the US women's track team, that almost *a quarter* of the team were on steroids in 1984, and even more in 1988. The defence against such allegations, by de Mérode, Ljungqvist and others, is that they can do nothing without names and evidence. The most disturbing suggestion of the symposium came, however, from Gary Roberts, of Toulane University, USA, a specialist in the anti-trust laws of America. He suggested that regulations of the IAAF, and by implication of the IOC, too, could be torn apart in legal analysis, unless those two bodies became more professional in outlook. The IAAF was in difficulty, he said, once it crossed the line from being an amateur body to being professional; it would then no longer be exempt from anti-trust ruling on commercial issues by the Amateur Sports Act of 1978. In other words, individual competitors would be much more free to pursue individual commercial activities even where they were not in the interest of the governing body. Existing IAAF regulations, Roberts suggested, were too often acting as a cartel for the protection of its own commercial interest, and would not be defensible in American courts.

Thankfully – in my opinion – the year of 1991 began with the conspicuous failure of Ben Johnson to recapture the form that had made him appear unchallengeable in Seoul. Two years without Stanozolol for breakfast brought him to the starting line a much changed athlete. The muscular explosion was gone, and much of the muscular definition. Admittedly, Johnson was now 29; the oldest Olympic 100 metres champion there has been was Allan Wells, at the age of 28 in Moscow. Two years without racing would also have had its effect on Johnson. When, at Hamilton, Ontario, the first of a series of indoor races that was expected to earn him $300,000, win or lose, Johnson was defeated by Darron Council, I was convinced Johnson was unlikely to rewrite his epitaph. The fractions by which he had gained his false fame would now prohibit his finding recycled glory. Francis, meanwhile, had just been banned for life by Athletics Canada, the national federation, and was busy proclaiming that his ban had only occurred because, unlike the majority of coaches in a worldwide cover-up, he had gone into the witness box at the Dubin Inquiry and given evidence on the widespread use of drugs, and of trafficking: evidence which was still being ignored.

What the race in Hamilton told us was more about Canadians, or maybe about human nature, than about Johnson, never mind the irony of Johnson being defeated by a narcotics-prevention deputy sheriff from Gainsville, Florida. Canadians, so often in the shadow of neighbouring sporting supremacy, had been humiliated 28 months before by the exposed cheating of their champion. So much did the sporting soul of Canada *need* Johnson, a simple, adopted Jamaican, that at the Copps Coliseum all moral reservation and former sense of shared guilt were banished by forgiveness and by wounded, resurgent national pride. 'He was framed,' protested one of the many welcoming banners naïvely. It would have been a misjudgement to suppose that the largest indoor crowd in Canadian athletic history, over 17,000, represented a uniform national opinion. It represented both a sympathetic, subjective element, and the expedient element; the latter including the Canadian federation, amnesiacs to a man if we recall how Jean Charest, the then Sports Minister, had said in Seoul that Johnson would never again represent his country. In Tokyo later that summer at the world championships, he ran in the relay.

The forces against cheats were closing in, even if they may never be wholly successful. Steve Heynes, the chief executive of the Australian Sports Drugs Agency, told the 25th Congress of the General Assembly of the International Sports Federations (GAISF) in 1991 that positive tests had dipped in the past two years. In 1988, of 47,000 tests at IOC laboratories, 2.45 per cent had been positive. In 1990, of 71,000 tests, 1.31 per cent were positive. If this was encouraging, the revelation in December 1991 by a report of the united German Sports Federation (GSF), that nearly all coaches, doctors and other officials in former East Germany were strongly suspected of having taken part in systematic long-term doping in at least fourteen sports, revealed the relative past failure of the drug testing programme against wilful cheating.

A clause in an agreement between the IOC and the World Federation of Sports Goods Industries, initiated by Horst Dassler and Walter Tröger, secretary-general of the then West German NOC, and encouraged by Samaranch, has stipulated that any sponsor may withdraw from a contract, with an individual or organization, in the event of positive drug testing. Thus the financial factor which has so encouraged cheating may now – as evident within alarmed German federations – have the effect of helping to stifle it.

Vigilance on all fronts will have to intensify. Following the Krabbe case, Jacques Rogge, a member of the Medical Commission, revealed that there will soon be a recommendation for competitors being random-tested to have to take a harmless pill a few hours beforehand; this will temporarily 'colour' the urine for identification of its authenticity, preventing the substitution of donor-urine. Sophisticated cheating requires extreme prevention measures. The best answer lies outside sport: legislation by government to make unauthorized possession, importing, handling or conveyance of the major drugs a punishable offence, and further legislation to enforce pharmaceutical manufacturers to include harmless marker agents in drugs that will make their presence easily identifiable. Such steps are in the interest of society, never mind sport.

10 Solidarity

'Why,' asks Wolf Lyberg, for many years the secretary-general of the Swedish NOC, now retired and devoting himself to a history of the Olympics, 'do the International Federations come before the National Olympic Committees in the IOC directory? Within the family, the NOCs are closer, it is the NOCs who bear the costs of taking the competitors to the Games. Should not the NOCs have the right to decide how their share of the money is divided? That was something Monique Berlioux always refused to discuss, the division of NOC money, with either Brundage or Killanin . . . and she decided most things.' Jacques Rogge, president of the Belgian NOC, estimates that NOCs contribute $150m to the staging of a Games, divided equally between sending their teams and preparing them at qualifying events.

The feeling of being the 'working class' of the Olympic Movement is not uncommon among the nations who take part. 'The NOCs were ignored in Seoul, to an extent,' Dick Palmer, Britain's secretary-general, reflects. 'Queuing for food, little furniture in the apartments, no one standing up for us. But you don't complain too much, because you're not wanting retribution on your NOC.'

It has always been much the same. The NOCs were the cannon fodder; they only had glory from the Games on those days when somebody won a medal and the national flag was raised, and then it was mostly the same old countries and the same old anthems, with a hundred other secretary-generals scuffling around trying to protect the interests of their team, getting the transport, the passes, the 'phones, the food, the hundred items that make the difference between a national team having a pleasant or disagreeable Games. Brundage, extraordinarily, wanted little at all to do with NOCs, and resisted their collective organization. Killanin, recognizing the elements of a genuine family, initiated the Tripartite Commission. Samaranch consolidated that trend by bringing the new 'Commission for the Olympic Movement' within the realms of the IOC; yet he still maintained a slightly ambivalent attitude. 'The strength of the NOCs lies in the strength of the IOC,' he has said repeatedly. He considers that the power of the NOCs resides primarily with their competitors, and that many international competitions can be organized without any involvement whatever of NOCs. Today, with the growth of the Olympic Games to a point where the number of competitors has to be controlled if not reduced, the body-physical of the Olympic Movement is threatened. Dick Palmer acknowledges this:

'The BOA took a policy decision in 1990, following Seoul, that future

Olympic squads would be more competitively selected, carrying no driftwood. The political reality of having a Western Samoan Olympic Committee, say, or a Cook Islands or Guam NOC is one thing, but technically it's a nonsense. To what extent are they able to compete? They go out in the first round. Now there are twenty more NOCs applying for admission, which means many more competitors: an imbalance of the ecology that is unhealthy to the Movement. If you get Samoa v. Cuba in the boxing ring, the Samoan is likely to have his brains scrambled. Arguably, the Cook Islands have no place, yet the expenses are paid for six competitors and two officials. The Solidarity Fund is fine in principle, yet it tends to be used too much on a political basis in its allocation, and not enough strictly on development. South Pacific islands need US boxing coaches for five years, not for two weeks. With the size it now has, the IOC *could* be a rudderless ship, and therefore I have the greatest admiration for the way Samaranch has been able to control the machinations of the Olympic Movement Commission.'

There are few with more administrative experience at ground level of the Movement than Palmer, who came from humble surroundings in a Welsh village, he and his brother both achieving university degrees; he then was apprenticed in university sport, and learned just what it means to be a minor competitor or official, before moving to the more high-powered environment – if that is not an exaggerated phrase – of the BOA.

Palmer's view on the imbalance created by the increasing catholicity of the Movement is predictably challenged by Mario Vazquez Raña, president of the Association of National Olympic Committees (ANOC), a man who would never wish to see reduced the breadth of his empire. 'If the day comes when we had to agree to this,' Vazquez Raña says, 'that would be the end of the Olympic Games. The IOC would then have just another world championships of International Federations. We would have to find some new name for "high level competitions". I think such a day is far away. We have to help maintain the participation of those small countries. If the Olympic Games were to become dedicated to high society, to an élite sport society, I wouldn't want to be part of the Olympic Movement. That is why we have International Federations, and why they have their international championships. There are many objectives within the Olympic Games that we have to consider, not necessarily following de Coubertin one hundred per cent. We have to change, and I believe in the Samaranch revolution. What I am doing is making an effort to organize Games for smaller groups of countries – regional, sub-regional, as well as continental Games.'

If Samaranch takes a pragmatic view of the relative strengths and weaknesses of the NOCs, his appreciation of their emotional significance within the Movement has been endlessly demonstrated by an unflagging willingness, over twelve years, to travel to meet them in pursuit of unity. In the twentieth of the regular information letters that he has sent to IOC members since he took office, he wrote:

> Several days ago, I returned from a long trip of almost 60,000 kilometres which enabled me to visit five new NOCs in an especially vast area: Oceania. It is certain that neither Vanuatu, Western or American Samoa, Tonga nor the Cook Islands represent important powers, whether from a political, economic or sport point of view. They are nonetheless NOCs like any other. And I can assure you, by my own experience, that they do not merit less than others, and even frequently merit more, given their enthusiastic and admirable efforts to spread our Olympic ideals to the youth of their country. I believe that it is through personal contact with such realities that one can truly realize the force, the impact and the power of our Movement, the respect and admiration of which it is an object, even by those who are not familiar with it, or who, by their culture, their position or their isolation, are far removed from it. On many occasions, I have encouraged you to take an active part in the sports life of your country and to follow it carefully, and keep me informed of the developments, needs, or problems encountered. Once again I should like to draw your attention to this matter, as it seems to me primordial . . . I can assure you that my visits to the 151 NOCs out of the 167 upon whom we can now count, my contacts with all the IFs, many international organizations, heads of governments, and leaders at all levels, have only served to strengthen my conviction from the beginning: the Olympic Movement is one of the most, if not *the* most important of the social forces of our time.

'The IOC must try to balance,' Samaranch says, 'between NOCs and IFs. Sometimes this is not easy, because there are many more members from NOCs than there are from IFs. I understand the NOCs, because I was president of the Spanish Olympic Committee, and I well remember when Giulio Onesti tried to pull together the NOCs within one voice. Brundage fought against this idea, but I and others knew this was futile if the NOCs wanted to be united. The problem continued, to a degree, under Killanin, Onesti having the backing of a powerful NOC, CONI, which was very rich with all its money from the national pools. Mollet [Raoul Mollet, then President of the Belgian NOC] did a good job with Onesti and others in the creation of ANOC, but I always felt Mollet's view was much more for NOCs than for the Movement. I wanted to elect him to the IOC late in his career, but I found there was not strong support [Belgium were entitled to two members, but already had a French-speaking member, de Mérode, and a second member would have had to be Flemish-speaking]. Mollet has been an important figure. He has a clear idea of what the Movement could be in future, and in his time he was a great help.'

Aware of the need for the NOCs to be brought more closely within the Movement, but acting on the principle of divide and rule in order to contain their power, in 1981 Samaranch embarked on two policies: the creation of continental associations of NOCs, and the formation of the Solidarity Fund, with its own administration, for the purpose of distributing the NOCs' share of Olympic Games income, an ongoing sore point. Anselmo Lopez, a long-standing and dependable friend from Spain with the personal and financial independence that would allow him to devote the time, was given charge of the Solidarity office, with a staff of four secretary/clerks, and would supervise the distribution of more than $12m annually.

The Association of National Olympic Committees (ANOC) had taken shape at the end of the 1970s, with Vazquez Raña elected President in 1979. In 1981 Samaranch flew to Lomé, Togo, to create, under the leadership of Anani Matthia, the African association of NOCs (ANOCA). There was already an association of European NOCs, and those of Asia, Oceania, and Pan-America would follow. Samaranch had thus dissolved the central financial power base of ANOC, from which Vazquez Raña might have posed uncomfortable dilemmas for the IOC.

'ANOC *could* have challenged the IOC on the distribution of money,' Samaranch reflects. 'But now we were following the true meaning of *solidarity*. Those who needed the money most were Africans. At that time, Africa alone was receiving more than $500,000 a year, but how was it being spent? It was going direct from ANOC to the NOCs. For this reason, the channelling of the money through continental IOC federations made them very strong, and this was a main aim for us [in the IOC] because it avoided many problems. When we had a meeting in Lausanne in '91 of thirty of the leading NOCs from around the world to discuss the future of commercialization, I reminded them that their strength depended on *our* strength, and that it would be unwise to challenge us. How else would they receive many of their benefits; for example Andorra, now with its own office of two hundred square metres, a competitive swimming pool and international tennis and shooting facilities? The NOCs have to remember their weakness. The Goodwill Games [a particularly controversial topic, the more so after the relevation in September 1991 of the consultancy fees received by Robert Helmick as intermediary negotiator with Turner Broadcasting in his position as USOC president] were able to be organized by Turner without reference to the NOCs. In 1984, at a time when we did not know how widespread the socialist boycott would be, we *needed* additional NOCs where we could create them: Tonga, Western Samoa and others. Now, for Barcelona in 1992, it is the other way: we don't have the room, and the Barcelona organizing committee has requested that we elect no more NOCs, though constitutionally we felt obliged to *readmit* the three Baltic states. In all, with places like Gibraltar and Macao, we have nearly thirty in the queue, although those with their papers in order are maybe no more than four or five. Perhaps I do now regret the degree of expansion. One is regretting many things in one's life. What I have to say is that we are the only international sports organization in which the member countries do not pay fees, but receive every year subsidies from us, and in which we pay part of their expenses for the Olympic Games.'

'Power groups attempting to influence the decisions of the IOC in Luxembourg were yesterday severely criticized by Avery Brundage,' James Coote reported for the *Daily Telegraph* of London in 1971. Brundage, by now 83, specifically attacked the newly formed Permanent General Assembly of NOCs, which had met the previous week in Munich. It was an indication of the extent to which Brundage was losing his grasp of reality when he described the PGA as 'unnecessary agents'. Brundage saw the PGA as a threat to the authority of the IOC. That might indeed have been true, but required shrewder analysis than Brundage was now capable of bringing to the problem. The IOC was a paternal oligarchy, whereas the PGA, under the presidency of Onesti, himself also a member of the IOC, was a democratically based organization, though without executive power.

Raoul Mollet, today approaching 80, was a prominent equestrian, golfer and tennis player, who was president of the Belgian NOC from 1965 to 1989. The Belgians are unusual for a western NOC, in that their administration embraces 86 national sports; similar to Italy, France and Luxembourg and, from 1992, Denmark, Holland, Poland and Czechoslovakia. Mollet, a colonel in the Belgian armed forces, was for many years the secretary-general of the International Military Sports Commission (CISM). He had finished fifteenth in the modern pentathlon in Berlin, but suffered a serious accident in London in 1948, when the quality of horses provided just after the war was poor, and Mollet's horse threw him badly at the last fence. Earlier that year he had been champion in the world military épée event. 'Before the war, Belgium had no sporting traditions like those in Britain,' Mollet recollects. 'We wore straw hats for the march past in Berlin! Our situation was ridiculous; our three officers in the modern pentathlon only had two pistols between them, the German officials having rejected one for being worn out, and the British loaned us one. That day I swore I would create money for sport. I spent five years as a POW on the Polish border, and then was evacuated from Lübeck in northern Germany during the

Russian advance and sent to Aldershot to supervise air crew selection.

'In 1965, Onesti convened a meeting of NOCs in Rome. That was a turning-point, with 86 NOCs represented. At an IOC executive board meeting that year, to discuss preparations for the Mexico Games, Brundage lost his temper with Alain Danet, of the French NOC, and I had to protest. Sport in France and Spain was still relatively disorganized. General Jiminez of Spain was working with me in the CISM, through which I was able to arrange some coaching in Spain, where sport was restricted under the Franco regime. That was probably why Samaranch, when he was elected President, invited me to Spain to discuss unification of the Movement. When I was proposed as an IOC member in '72, there were objections from Brundage, of whom I was a big opponent, and also from the USSR and GDR, who thought that because I was with NATO I must be in the pay of the CIA! On reflection, I regret not being elected. CISM then had the biggest budget in world sport, with bases in Brazil, Congo, Nigeria and elsewhere. The Chinese were members of CISM long before they returned to the Olympics, and I think I could have been a useful contact with *real* sport. I think Samaranch valued my experience. At the time of the IOC Session in Tehran in 1967, Onesti, Danet, Crespi, Gafner of Switzerland, de Sales of Hong Kong and I had dinner together. We knew we would succeed in the creation of ANOC, because without our competitors, there were no Games.'

Tsuyoshi (Bob) Myakawa of the Japanese NOC was another figure central to the formation of ANOC. In the early 1970s he was responsible for Japanese international sports relations. 'Following a meeting in '73,' Myakawa recalls, 'I was appointed under Killanin to the IOC Press Commission, representing NOCs, and it was then I met Samaranch for the first time. He was chairman of the Commission, and I realized he was enthusiastic about the media. I'd not expected this, after all my dealings with Brundage. At Sapporo [Japan] in '72, I'd been in charge of the foreign press centre, and we'd had a senior press officer who didn't speak English! That was the Japanese conventional bureaucratic way of doing things. The press in the Seventies were still poor relations. When Tokyo bid for the Games of '64, during the IOC Session prior to the Asian Games in Tokyo in '58, there were few Olympic reporters in Japan. It was good to find someone like Samaranch who cared about us. In the Seventies, Berlioux was doing the real work, was the power in the background. I soon discovered, before he was elected President, that Samaranch was more of a diplomat than either Brundage or Killanin. He wanted to bring in more sports that had a wider interest. Although initially I didn't think he was a man of principle, I began to understand the way in which he could manoeuvre situations for the benefit of the Movement. I think Samaranch is a very lonely man at times. That's how it is when you are using people. He's used Igaya [the younger Japan member, a slalom silver medallist in 1956], one of the new generation, a self-made man who has been useful commercially, because the Japanese tend to be conservative and traditional. Igaya was willing to ignore the past, to jump in even if he got into trouble with the NOC, doing things that would have been more difficult with Kiyakawa, then our senior member. When Kiyakawa was chairman of the Press Commission, he did little. I was doing the work. Kiyakawa was asking, "What do I do next?" '

Anton Geesink of the Netherlands was a judo world champion who won the demonstration event Olympic gold medal in Japan in 1964. He is one of a number of younger former athletes whom Samaranch has brought into the IOC, being elected in 1987. A measure of the esteem in which he is held in Holland is that he lives in a street bearing his name. Geesink is one of those who come under the category defined by Dr Fredtjof Nansan of Norway, an athlete, scientist, author, and statesman, who said that to be a true internationalist, you must be a true nationalist: that it is necessary to understand your own nation's genius and take a pride in its contribution to international civilization. 'Samaranch has shown that every NOC has the same value,' Geesink says, 'that USSR and USA were in principle no more important at an Olympic Games than Malta. If he has shown that money matters, he has shown too that *people* are more important. Without him, the IOC would not be the institution it is today.'

Geesink, I would say, represents the definitive style of IOC member of the past, moulded in a contemporary framework. He is too much without personal ambition ever to be a prominent leader, yet personifies the quality of neutrality essential to the long-term survival of the IOC. He mirrors the attitude about which Lord Philip Noel Baker, a British IOC member elected the same year as Lord Exeter in 1933, wrote in a contribution to *Olympic Review*, at the time of his ninetieth birthday in 1980:

> I say without hesitation that some of the greatest moments in my life have been when I have seen the Union Jack at the top of the Olympic flag pole, and have heard the stadium band play 'God Save The Queen'. I remember Douglas Lowe's victories in the 800 metres in 1924 and 1928; Godfrey Brown's magnificent win in the 4 x 400 metres relay at Berlin in 1936; David Burghley's 400 metres hurdles victory at Amsterdam in 1928, and David Hemery in the same event in Mexico City in 1968. I am not ashamed of the exultation I felt on those occasions. . . . Yet there were three victory ceremonies on one day at Munich in 1972 which I found deeply moving, none of them for Britain but deeply moving all the same. The first was for Valeri

> Borzov, the Soviet sprinter, whom I class with Douglas Lowe as the perfect artist of the track. Borzov had just added the gold medal for 200 metres to that he had won in the 100 the previous week. He had won decisively, and had proved himself not only one of the fastest men, but also one of the most beautiful movers of all time. The second ceremony was for Kip Keino of Kenya. Keino had won the 3,000 metres steeplechase, one of the most exacting of all Olympic contests, with a Kenyan compatriot close behind for the silver medal. Keino won the 1,500 metres at Mexico in 1968, and his universal reputation for fair play and good sportsmanship endeared him to the sporting public of every land. His victory was as popular as Borzov's. The third ceremony was for a local schoolgirl, Ulrike Mayfarth, 17 years old, who had won the women's high jump for West Germany. She had jumped superbly, creating a new Olympic and world record at 1.93 metres. In Munich, it was natural that the joy and the excitement were great indeed. On that Monday afternoon there were 80,000 people in the stadium: perhaps 50,000 West Germans, 10,000 East Germans, and 20,000 Americans, Russians, British, French and others from around the world. The three victory ceremonies were moments of great triumph for Russians, Kenyans and West Germans in the crowd. But much more important, the raising of the Soviet, Kenyan and West German flags, and the playing of the national anthems, evoked a full-throated, passionate, standing ovation from the vast international assembly, an ovation that was the same for the communist runner from Russia and the black man from east Africa as it was for the German schoolgirl. Those ovations were a tribute to the national honour of the victors' countries, a cosmic tribute to the glory that had come to their flags and anthems. Even more, they were a witness to the worldwide solidarity of all nations and the universal glory of Olympic sport. They are a witness, more precious perhaps than any other in any realm of Olympic activity, to the unity of the human race, to the common interests, the shared ideals, and friendships, of all nations everywhere.

In Noel Baker's words lies the essence of the meaning of the Olympic Games, so utterly different in concept from ordinary world championships, and it is this that binds NOCs and IFs with the IOC in unique fashion. It is because the Olympic Games have been, and we must all hope will continue to be, the soul of sportsmanship, in spite of all the corruptions that have assailed them, that Jacques Rogge, the president of the European Association of National Olympic Countries (EANOC), may be a valuable figure in the years ahead. He has proposed to Samaranch that all NOCs should be encouraged, within the boundaries of their own national laws and customs, to become representative of all sports, as is the Belgian NOC. Rogge's principle touches on a long-standing controversy in Britain, for instance, where the debate on 'who runs sport' has rumbled for twenty years, in the confusion between Sports Council (government orientated), Central Council for Physical Recreation (independent forum of governing bodies for all sports), and the BOA.

Rogge, who succeeded Mollet in 1989, is the first Flemish-speaking president in Belgium. Three-quarters of the top competitors are Flemish-speaking in a country that was under Dutch rule in the early nineteenth century, before experiencing a French-speaking revolution in 1830. 'Election to the IOC was an honour Mollet deserved,' Rogge says. 'It was he who first developed marketing in the late Sixties, helped by van den Eede, whom he had promoted. Then, there was an NOC budget of $15,000 a year, whereas now we have fifty people with an annual budget of $10m. In the Sixties and Seventies, I was a yachting enthusiast, competing in three world championships and three Olympics, training as an orthopaedic surgeon, and playing a bit of rugby in my spare time. I wasn't thinking about administration, and as a competitor was always complaining. I was suspended for three months in '68 for telling the president of the national yachting federation that he was an idiot. Mollet brought me on to the NOC, telling me to sit in silence and learn, that I could contribute seriously later. It was in '88 that Dick Palmer informally suggested to me that I should stand as president of the European NOCs. What could I and EANOC contribute? I'm not a boaster, but the fact is, whether others like it or not, Europe is the leading Olympic continent: in the number of competitors, medals, the range of experts. Western Europe saved the Games of 1980. We don't have continental Games, and we don't want them, because the calendar is full. What we want to do is expand the levels of youth and school sport – and also to change the attitude of the Solidarity programme. There is enough expertise at the top already, and we felt that Solidarity money was helping IFs rather than NOCs. EANOC is not there to help train pole-vault coaches. We want to reinforce the role of each NOC to become the leading sports body of its country, to be able to speak on behalf of *all* national federations. In Belgium, we funded the national team for the World Student Games in Sheffield in 1991, and for the Disabled Games. We are a truly inter-federal body. I regret to say the influence of British sport internationally is ten per cent of what it should be because of the conflict between Sports Council, CCPR and BOA.

'The reduction in size of the Olympic Games, the raising of qualifying standards, would inevitably strengthen Europe and weaken others. Of course the strong *should* take what they can from television and commerce, but the *universality* of the Games must allow the weaker continents and nations to send their athletes. EANOC has proposed an elaborate formula for this, endorsed by ANOC: for example, in wrestling, the top eight from the world championships *plus* the best two from each continental championship. The circumstances of each sport are different. We could isolate ourselves in Europe by maintaining or raising standards, because we take 85 per cent of the medals in the Winter Games and 75 per cent in the Summer Games. The fact is that 50 per cent of all medals, Winter and Summer, are won by eight NOCs. My fear for Europe is that although the eastern Europeans will still be strong in 1992, having the money to send teams of three hundred competitors, they will no longer be investing in youth to the same extent, and will have slipped back by '96 or 2000. If eastern Europe slides, who replaces them? At the moment, western Europe, but eventually probably Asia.'

Mollet claims that the name Solidarity, for the Olympic charitable fund, stems from him; that he, Onesti and Gafner began the fund, initial contributors including Agnelli, the Fiat millionaire. Whatever the origin, Killanin established the Solidarity Commission in 1973, with Herman van Karnebeek of the Netherlands as chairman. Killanin had a large Commission, on which Ordia and Ganga were prominent in pressing the demands of Africa. The distribution of funds, direct to NOCs, remained a matter of controversy and dispute until the time of Samaranch's creation of continental NOC federations. The biennial general assemblies of ANOC produced in the 1970s a variety of proposals for the distribution of mounting funds, without ever achieving central agreement.

'One Olympic medal provides the motivation to keep a National Olympic Committee going for the next twenty years,' Ashwini Kumar reflects. Few are more aware of the problems of maintaining motivation where there is a lack of success or money, or both, than Kumar. At the Seoul Games, India, with the second largest population in the world, failed to win a single medal. 'Money made available to International Federations does not reach national federations,' Kumar says, 'and there needs to be more going to NOCs.' As Louis Guirandou-N'Daiye observes: 'If you want to see amateurs, come to Africa! Even the Ministries don't have money. Killanin created the Solidarity Commission, but it was not solidarity at all, just a few gifts to those they knew. There were lots of good words and promises, tours of inspection, but people were travelling to see what *might* be done. The money only really arrived with Samaranch. Brundage and Killanin, being part-time, didn't really have the opportunity to think about Olympism around the world.'

The story in the Third World, as in health and education, is not a matter of the need for benevolent donations, but of creating a social structure that will generate a degree of self-sufficiency. That is why, of course, black Africa has begun to modify its attitude to South Africa, aware that

South African wealth carries a key to the future development of the rest of the continent. Kumar's comment on motivation is also true. Akii-Bua's gold medal in Munich might have done so much for Uganda, had it not been for the suppressions of Amin's hideous regime. What will the victory of Samuel Matete, in the 1991 IAAF world championships, now do for Zambia?

I did not attend the African Games of 1991 in Cairo, but I had seen, four years before, at the African Games in Nairobi, the brimming potential of black Africa, if and when the threads of administration and finance can be pulled together. You hear it said that Africa is a lost cause. In Nairobi in 1987 such cynicism was energetically dismissed. The opening ceremony of the fourth All-Africa Games, and the ten days of events that followed, were a heartening festival of pride and optimism. They proved that black Africa is able to stage major public events with some style. The Kenyan organizing committee might have lived close to chaos up to the last moment; on the day, the most dignified of faces was presented to the outside world when teams from 39 out of the 45 African states marched colourfully into the stadium. Like every continent, Africa has its deceits, greed, exploitation and inhumanity, but Kenya gave their opening ceremony an unaffected charm. The Games had been postponed three times, awaiting the completion of another gift from China, a $28m stadium with Kenya's first synthetic track. This fact escaped mention in the programme at the opening ceremony – but then who admits borrowing the money to get married when there is a marvellous wedding reception?

The worst African problem, any European resident there will tell you, is corruption. Consignments, from toilet paper to tanks, simply go missing. A dozen Mercedes Benz limousines, the manufacturer's gift to the Games, were still untraced in Nairobi a year later. In the long term, Africa has a bright future, if and when it can fully get its act together, and if it is not betrayed by those current leaders who claim to be rescuing it. To achieve this, Africans need progress, self-discipline and diplomacy, none of which regularly comes easily to many of them. In 1989, the last year for which complete figures are available at the time of writing, Africa had received $2,253,044, more than half what it had received in total during the previous four years, thanks to the success of the Games in Calgary and Seoul. Yet I fear this would not even scratch the surface of Africa's sporting famine, because ultimately the generation of facilities must come from a modern internal structure which is as yet missing in the majority of their 45 countries.

The first charitable work of all in the Movement came in 1961, with the formation, on the initiative of de Beaumont, of the Commission for International Olympic Aid. It was this that Killanin effectively transformed into the Solidarity Commission, and the following are the sums that have been made available to the fund since 1972:

Sapporo and Munich (1972), $2,833,540; Innsbruck and Montreal (1976), $3,475,727; Lake Placid and Moscow (1980), $7,407,837; Sarajevo and Los Angeles (1984), $20,929,525; Calgary and Seoul (1988), $42,094,000; Albertville and Barcelona (1992, projected), $54,500,000.

These are some of the general developments in funding for NOCs in the past eight years:

1984: for the first time, 48 NOCs received aid in equipment, travel and accommodation for the Winter Games, total $445,368. For the Summer Games, 140 NOCs received aid of $3,155,316. Also for the first time, the responsibility for allocating Olympic Solidarity courses was given to NOC continental associations.
1985: an annual grant of $5,000 introduced for each NOC for administration. Aid for organization of regional Games, such as the Asian Games, introduced.
1986: creation of the Itinerant Administration School, providing mobile courses.
1987: the first Olympic Day Run, contributing $1,500 per NOC.
1990: a new scholarship programme introduced both for athletes and officials.

The following have been amendments to the Charter which have affected NOCs:

1984: flexibility for professionals to take part in such sports as basketball, football, ice hockey and tennis; NOCs who withdraw from the Olympic Games to be suspended and executive board to be responsible for application of this measure; the period of the Winter Games to be extended from 12 to 16 days.
1985: (indirect: athletes tested positive to be suspended by IAAF for two years); the IOC to send invitations to the Games, rather than organizing committees; the eligibility code included on entry forms signed by competitors; Arabic accepted as a working IOC language.
1986: a separate cycle of Winter and Summer Games with effect from the 1994 Winter Games.
1987: host cities to be nominated seven years in advance instead of six; introduction of quotas for certain sports.
1988: demonstration sports to be eliminated after 1992.
1990: joint IOC/IF/NOC Evaluation Commission for bidding cities, replacing three separate Commissions; NOC applicants to be composed of at least five affiliated federations (previously three); Athletes Commissions recommended within every NOC.

It would be wrong to prejudge the qualities of individual officials according to the coincidence of whether they happen to belong to the IOC, to an International Federation or to an NOC. Nevertheless, it is my experience that the more philosophic, in the deeper sense, among people in sport tend to be those working with NOCs: probably because they are more concerned with the interests and affairs of people rather than with the creation and promotion of events and projects. Such a man was the late Professor Nicolaos Nissiotis, vice-president of the Hellenic Olympic Committee as well as an IOC member, and president of the International Olympic Academy. The thoughts of Professor Nissiotis on Olympic ethics could fill this book. Perhaps we should forgive him for having opposed the torch relay of Los Angeles in 1984, and recall some of the fundamentals that he raised when addressing a special session of the IOA for National Olympic Committees in 1979:

> The unquestionable success of the Olympic Games is mainly due to the following reasons:
>
> A) The realization of the need of all the people in the world to meet at periodic intervals together, away from things that divide them racially, nationally, religiously, politically;
> B) The progressive participation of more and more nations, in particular the presence at the Games of new nations, mainly of Africa, as independent and free people;
> C) The spectacular development of sports performance in the last fifty years and the achievement of almost superhuman records, something which gives them an indisputable grandeur, with the competitive spirit that prevails in all Olympic sports;
> D) The equally spectacular technical progress, especially in the field of mass information media, as a result of which, in addition to the few thousand spectators who can watch the spectacle, the Games have reached those millions who can now enjoy them through television as if they were present themselves. . . .
>
> Education as provided through Olympic principles should *not* be:
>
> A) Autonomous and self-made, since it is the distillate of wisdom, religious faith, humanitarian culture, the pre-existing rich, spiritual tradition of mankind in its evolution towards the higher values of life: beauty, greatness, truth;
> B) Fanatical and partisan, since it refers to the most unifying principles of the transcendent that constitute the basis of human dignity and family, and whatever is transcendental and eternal can become panhuman;

C) Self-sufficient, as it is only through co-operation with the other values from which it originates that it can fulfil its higher purpose. . . .

NOCs should in particular:

A) Maintain close contacts with education officials in their countries;
B) Extend efforts to attract the interest of educationists in general about the Olympic Movement, and not only physical education teachers;
C) Use every opportunity to promote the value of Olympic principles as an educational tool among school pupils and students;
D) Organize seminars during the holiday period so as to introduce these principles to as many students as possible from universities and technical and professional schools, who will meet jointly, independent of their individual field of specialization.

As it rides the ever steeper big dipper of financial enticement, the Olympic Movement is tending to forget much of what it once knew, of the wisdom of generations, of centuries, that preceded the modern Olympic era. I was invited to dinner in Taipei by Ching-Kuo Wu with nine of the NOC who in the late 1970s had fought for their existence, when Taiwan was threatened with removal from the IOC in the attempt to re-admit mainland China. In a rare way, the Taiwanese come closer to de Coubertin's conception of sport than any contemporary nation taking part in the Olympic Games. Their government spends 15 per cent of its annual budget on education, and 6 per cent of that on sport. Yet this is not aimed at producing international medals; the money goes primarily on facilities and grassroots development, rather than élite coaching. 'The Confucius conception of fitness of the body is to fulfil the completion of the person,' Professor Hsu Din, a former diplomat and veteran adviser to the Taipei Olympic Committee, said to me. 'We are not looking in sport for the creation of stars. Sport has lost its way and its meaning. It is now merely manipulated by governments. What is important in sport is education.'

The 'China problem' was one of the longest-running in the IOC, following the withdrawal of mainland China from IOC affairs after the Games in 1952, proclaiming there would be no further association until recognition was taken away from Taiwan. With the evacuation of General Chiang Kai-Chek and his forces to the island of Formosa, as it used to be called by the Americans, in the late 1940s, the original China NOC also transferred itself to Taipei. Intransigence on both sides, together with the enduring incapability of the IOC to find an answer, resulted in a 29-year period before both the mainland and the island would be reunited as sporting brothers. A new Olympic Committee had been formed by the People's Republic in Peking, and the IOC had initially attempted to deal with both, until mainland China voluntarily and formally withdrew its own affiliation in 1958. In 1954, the IOC had voted 23-21 to recognize the Committee in Peking, and it seemed that the situation was resolved, to the exclusion of Taiwan. Brundage, echoing American sympathy towards Taiwan, unilaterally attempted to maintain recognition of both bodies. Thereupon Peking withdrew from the Games of 1956, claiming unlawful recognition of Taiwan as a separate entity, Taiwan having been a province of China prior to the Sino-Japanese War. Brundage, who had been disposed to arrange for the two Germanies to compete jointly in 1960, 1964 and 1968, when few countries recognized East Germany, made comparatively little effort to resolve the Chinese puzzle.

In 1970 the situation was further inflamed by Brundage's nomination of Henry Hsu as an IOC member representing Taiwan, forcing the election against unanimous opposition from the executive board. This was another of the inflammable controversies that Brundage would pass to Killanin. The sympathies of the new president lay with mainland China; not least because, as he remarked in his autobiography, *My Olympic Years*, the IOC had neglected its own regulations. In 1952, a team of 38 men and two women went from Peking to take part in the Helsinki Games, though being represented by no official Olympic Committee; whereas the Olympic Committee that *was* recognized – the one in Taipei – was not resident in the country it claimed to represent and therefore was equally illegal.

Killanin, who had worked as a young journalist on the Sino-Japanese War in 1937, took a personal interest, and considered firstly that the name of the Committee in Taipei should be changed. Those Chinese in Taiwan were as politically orientated as their Maoist rivals on the mainland. By 1974, the Asian Games Federation – an organization superseded in 1981 by the Olympic Council of Asia – was recognizing Peking and not Taipei. The Taipei Committee still existed, however, and planned to send a team to the Games in Montreal in 1976.

This move, disputed by the communist Chinese and accepted only disapprovingly by Killanin, was frustrated by the (equally political) refusal of Prime Minister Trudeau to admit the Taiwanese team. de Beaumont and others claim that Killanin should have upheld IOC principle by threatening to cancel the Games if Canada did not honour the signed agreement to admit all competitors, irrespective of other diplomatic relations, or lack of them. Trudeau, sensitive to the threat posed to valuable grain export deals with the People's Republic, dug in; Taiwan were obliged to fly home.

Michael Lee, one of those deeply involved with negotiations over the years for the Taipei NOC, recalls: 'Before the Games in Montreal, there was an awareness, I think, that the majority of the IOC wanted two Chinese Olympic Committees. There was discrimination against our participation, considering that we were members, Trudeau deciding that our anthem and flag could not be used, as a pre-condition. Our team waited in vain in Boston for Canadian visas, but they were not issued. At the Session of 1978 in Montevideo, a resolution for two Olympic Committees was adopted, but the question of flags, anthems and names remained subject to further debate, and this was delegated to the executive board, which had meetings scheduled in Puerto Rico and Nagoya, Japan. Killanin paid us a special visit in Taipei, and we told him the IOC had violated their own Charter. Nevertheless, the People's Republic sent a delegation to Nagoya, and the executive board there decided on a change: there would be a postal ballot of the IOC. It was a technical manoeuvre, though it seemed legal. It was decided that our name, flag and anthem would have to be different, whatever happened. We knew that Berlioux was pro-Peking, as well as Killanin. When IOC lawyers decided that the Taipei NOC had no legal rights, Henry Hsu, our IOC member, sought an injunction that the IOC's decision to reject us was illegal. The Swiss court found in our favour late in 1979.

'The Lake Placid organizing committee [Winter Games, 1980] said they would accept us, with a different name and flag. We refused the conditions, and began another litigation before the US Supreme Court, under the US constitution which says that "all aliens must be treated equally", claiming that the organizing committee should not carry out an illegal IOC resolution. We won the first round, but President Carter then intervened, also under the constitution, on the basis that the US President can overrule on a political issue "in the interest of the state". So Taiwan withdrew and, pending a solution, would not send a team to Moscow. The position now was that the People's Republic was eligible for Moscow, but withdrew because of the boycott; and it was following the Moscow Games that Samaranch began fresh negotiations in Lausanne. By now, because of the controversy, we had been ousted from various International Federations, including volleyball, swimming, athletics and boxing, and were down to eleven affiliations from eighteen. We challenged Samaranch on how the IOC could lose face and principle, but he stressed that even if a Swiss court found in favour of Taiwan, then the IOC would move the registration of their office to Paris. We kept talking on the issue of the name and the flag. Samaranch was right on wanting to keep sport together, but we know that we were *legally* right.'

My view, as a non-Asian, is that, whatever the emotional ties binding the Taiwanese Chinese to the mainland, and to their millions of relations living under the communist regime, it was wholly unrealistic to believe that the title 'Republic of China NOC' and the pre-Maoist Chinese national flag could be acceptable to such a multinational organization as the IOC, which was attempting to defuse political dogmas. While the stance of Taiwan may have been legally correct under the IOC Charter, it was totally naïve in the context of world opinion. I may not understand the Oriental complexities of 'losing face', but it is my belief that the rational compromise eventually accepted, under Samaranch's persuasion, for the name of Chinese Taipei NOC, might have been achieved long before, given common sense by the Taiwanese. In so many other ways they exhibit such humanity that their immovability on this technical issue seems the more strange.

In so many respects they are more rational than their ideological mainland brothers. After the severe flooding in southern China in the summer of 1991, Taiwan and Hong Kong donated substantial relief funds, Taiwan a massive $15m. Yet at the 1989 congress of the Olympic Council of Asia, representatives of the China National Olympic Committee had solemnly condemned the bid by the Chinese Taipei NOC to stage the Asian Games of 1998, on the grounds that the People's Republic team could not compete in the land of Chiang Kai-Chek. Even now, though the two countries compete jointly in the Olympic Games, the Beijing government tries to pretend that the island does not exist. When Taiwan has the world's second largest trading reserve of $76 billion in 1991, and is the thirteenth largest trading country in the world, the Beijing government's attitude is absurd. No People's Republic team has yet competed in Taiwan, though more than twenty Taiwanese teams have been to mainland China since their gymnasts broke the ice in 1989. One wonders why the Taiwanese could not have accepted a compromise ten years or more before they did.

The Baltic states, though denied by occupation the physical independence that the Taiwanese have enjoyed, maintained throughout forty years a moral independence. With the dissolving of the Soviet empire, the re-admission of the Baltic states, at the executive board meeting in Berlin in 1991, was a happy inevitability. The disintegration of the former centre of the other twelve republics, and attempted reformation by Boris Yeltsin within a new commonwealth in the winter of 1991-92 presented not only the IOC but all International Federations with unprecedented problems of recognition and competition reorganization. The Soviet Union team, which had won the most medals in Seoul, 132, left the World Athletics Championships in Tokyo – where it took 28 medals, two more than the United States – correctly expecting that this was the last championships they would attend as the Soviet Union. The most powerful sports machine the world had known headed for home and the prospect of disintegration.

Igor Ter-Ovaneysian, a former long-jumper at five Olympic Games and president of the Soviet Athletic Federation, was in a daze. Born in Armenia, educated at Lvov University in the Ukraine, and having spent all his adult life in Moscow, capital of the Russian republic as well as of the Soviet *republics*, he was reduced to wondering who *he* was. 'I had so many ambitions as a sports leader,' Ter-Ovaneysian told me, 'to do all I could for track and field for my country, the Soviet Union. As a competitor, I always felt we were as one, and I cannot imagine competing separately. I don't wish to say independence is bad, and as a democratic person I understand the independence that some people want. Yet there are many difficulties.' Indeed there are: the Russian Republic itself extends from the Baltic some 9,000 kilometres to the Sea of Japan at the Sakhalin Peninsula, and had provided the majority of Soviet competitors. Since the Soviet Union entered the Olympic Games in 1952, they had won 1,204 medals (473 gold, 376 silver, and 555 bronze). Before 1952, and before the Revolution in 1917, it had been the 'Olympic Committee of All-Russias', and their first five IOC members were either princes, counts or generals.

Shortly before the Winter Games in Albertville, Samaranch flew to Moscow to meet Boris Yeltsin, President of the Russian Republic. Together they historically restructured the world's foremost Olympic nation, achieving stability for the Games of 1992. This was my report to *The Times*:

Outside women with ice-picks, some of them grandmothers and some in their teens, chip away at the pavement, tidying the approach to the Kremlin that sits in familiar picture-postcard frozen splendour. Aspects of Russian life and economics remain unchanged. Or are worse .

Across a small bowl of freshly-picked daffodils on the cabinet table within the Kremlin Palace, Boris Yeltsin, president of the Russian Republic, smiles from deeply bloodshot eyes at Juan Antonio Samaranch, the president of the International Olympic Committee. Only four hours of sleep a night, moving from one crisis to the next, is taking its toll on the man who replaced Mikhail Gorbachev.

A week ago, Yeltsin postponed at eight hours notice his scheduled meeting with Samaranch. Now, he apologises. It was a misunderstanding of communication, he says, and those responsible have been fired. As the two shake hands for official photographs, beneath the red-white-and-blue Russian flag, Yeltsin, a former prominent volleyball player, stands a head taller than the small Spaniard. Yet this is familiar ground for Samaranch: he has met more heads of state than Yeltsin as yet has had foreign flights.

As the discussion proceeds on the formation, identity, flags and anthems for the 1992 Olympic Games, Yeltsin shows himself to understand the delicate position of both IOC and his volatile republic. He is proud of his own sports heritage and physique. 'If I wasn't fit from sport, I wouldn't have been able to leap up on to those tanks," he says, with reference to the demonstrations at the time of the failed coup against Gorbachev.

It is evident, as Samaranch makes his proposals for a unified team as a prelude to acceptance of independent republic National Olympic Committees (NOC), that Yeltsin would like the national prestige associated with Russia flying its own flag at medal cermonies this year. Such exposure would enhance him personally, but he readily agrees to the compromise that is necessary to harmonious continuity of the Games, and shows himself pleased with the day's outcome.

Although external sporting equilibrium has been maintained for Russia, internal stresses remain acute, primarily economical. The rouble, and savings, have become valueless. Muscovites hedge against inflation by storing vodka to pay the plumber, or buying semi-valuable goods – on Saturday it was a new delivery of expensive vanity boxes at Gum, the government department store – which may be twice the price next week.

On Saturday, Samaranch arranged for $1.5 million owed by Russian television for Games coverage to be deferred. An endorsement contract with Adidas has covered the $800,000 cost of sending the team of 147 competitors to Albertville next week. Vitaly Smirnov, president-elect of the Russian Republic NOC, calculates that $3.5 million will be needed for Barcelona.

As yet, they have one-seventh of that. It is unique that the budget of an Olympic team is being met wholly by a foreign source. All existing contracts with the former USSR have become void. Almost 90 per cent of the Equipe Unifiée (EUN) for Albertville will be from Russia, and much the same for the 510-strong team for Barcelona, which is only 20 less than for Seoul.

Smirnov calculates that EUN will win the same number of gold medals in Albertville as in Calgary, 11, and two more, 53, in Barcelona than in Seoul. Yet financial hardship plus the fragmentation from 1993 onwards will reduce the power once held by the USSR.

Fragmentation poses many problems: who will fund the 'national' training centres, some of which are in Armenia, Georgia, Latvia and the Ukraine? Yeltsin promises that the Russian sports budget will be expanded, not contracted, but the exchange rate and food shortages could cripple Russian sports in the long run.

Many of the republics are unaware of the extent of the responsibilities they are gaining. The creation of NOCs will be the manifestation of independent identity, but not achievement. 'This is not the work of the sportsmen but of politicians,' Smirnov says, 'The small republics will suffer the most.'

Moldavia, for instance which supplies three players to the EUN volleyball team for Barcelona, can never expect to qualify independently for the Olympic tournament. 'Where are our medical supplies/petrol/tractors?' some republics are already crying. Scottish Nationalists might pause to study the uncertain fate of the Asian end of the Soviet giant . . . Thus was marked in Moscow the end of one remarkable sporting era and the uncertain beginning of another. Never again shall we hear that heavily melodious Soviet anthem. The two leaders collaborated to ensure a combined team of the 12 independent republics would be sent to the winter Games, starting next week, and the summer Games in Barcelona, and for provisional recognition of 12 new NOCs, conditional upon acceptance of a combined team, Equipe Unifiée (EUN). 'I am a man of sport, and during my presidency I will do my best to help sport in Russia,' Yeltsin, a former volleyball player, said at the end of talks that have helped preserve the quality of this year's Olympic events amid post-USSR political turmoil.

A single problem remains. At a subsequent separate meeting with the leaders of the unofficial NOCs of Russia, Ukraine, Belorussia, Kazakstan and Uzbekistan, Valeryi Borzov, the former Olympic sprint gold medal winner, strongly requested an independent Ukraine team for Barcelona. Borzov privately agrees to the unified team but is under political pressure from Leonid Kravchuk, the president of the Ukraine.

'Why can you not treat us equally with Croatia and Slovenia?' Borzov asked, the former Yugoslav states having been given emergency recognition ten days ago to enable participation in the winter Games. 'Because the problems are not equal.' Samaranch answered. With Yugoslavia torn by war, the normal formal procedure had not been possible, he said.

'The agreement by Russia to a unified team for this year was fundamental,' Samaranch said afterwards. 'Without Yeltsin's support, for this, all the other republics would have wanted separate teams, and the organising team in Barcelona could not have handled the logistics of this sudden increase of nations.'

'The politicians are wanting to hear their anthem.' Alexander Ratner, the editor of Moscow's *Olympic Panorama* and the official Russian/Spanish translator for the discussion, observed wryly afterwards. A key figure on Saturday was Shamil Tarpischev, the president of the Russian Tennis Federation and recently appointed as Yeltsin's personal counsellor on sport. Francois Carrard, the IOC director general, accompanied Samaranch.

'The openness and speed of the agreement was quite untypical of Russian tradition,' Alexander Kozlovsky, a vice-president of the former USSR NOC, said. 'It was clear that Yeltsin recognised the prestige of having an IOC vice-president, Vitaly Smirnov, as president of the Russian NOC.'

Vladimir Vasin, the acting president of the Russian NOC, had made a press statement last week presumptuously saying that 'we will have to consider the election of the IOC members', misunderstanding the prerogative of the IOC in this matter.

In fact, Smirnov and his committee that transfers en bloc from the USSR to Russia decided on Friday that the EUN flag at the Albertville opening ceremony will be carried by Igor Zhelezovsky, the Belorussian world champion speed skater.

If Samaranch had cleverly negotiated a formula for the 1992 Games, the agreement with Yeltsin to transfer the USSR NOC with its staff of 30 to new Russian offices was even more significant. Samaranch thereby not only protected the position of Smirnov, one of his most experienced IOC members, but effectively raised the status of the NOC above the former level of the sports minister.

These were the agreed points:

Winter Games, Albertville: A united team, EUN. Olympic flag and anthem for team and individual gold medal winners, the republic name of individual winners to be announced. The name and flag of the respective republic to be carried on the arm of the competitors' uniform.

Summer Games, Barcelona: EUN team. Olympic flag and anthem for team gold medal winners. Republic flag and anthem for individual gold medal winners.

Recognition of 12 new NOCs from 1993; dependent on acceptance of the above conditions, and for other important sports events this year.

Transformation of USSR NOC to become Russian Republic NOC (similar to the United Nations transfer).

Vitaly Smirnov, the senior IOC member from USSR, to transfer to Russian Republic and to be NOC president.

The Soviet upheaval, together with the radical change in socio-economic policies in other eastern European countries, is going to mean a major long-term alteration in the balance of Olympic power on the field. The rivalry, as a feature of every Games, between eastern socialists and the USA and western Europe, has gone. 'Those days are over,' Ivan Slavkov of Bulgaria says. 'The duel, day by day, counting the medals, between two opposed ideologies will be replaced by something more like the Tour de France. All kinds of competitive rivalry are helpful to the prestige and importance of a major international event. In *some* ways, I think what has happened will be a loss. But the acceptance of full professionalism, that *was* a necessity – you can't separate sport from other forms of human activity. What was there before was a fake. Our countries in eastern Europe have troubled economies now, it's no longer convenient that we should spend a similar amount on sport. We are not yet market-orientated. Barcelona will be the last Games, I think, at least for the time being, with eastern European teams of the strength we have known. I think there will now be a problem for Samaranch and the IOC to help maintain sport within the former communist economies. We are facing a period of major change. The inherent danger of the increased professionalism of many sports is that it will take strength *away* from the International Federations.'

Samaranch questions whether the loss of eastern European power on the field will be detrimental. 'Maybe it will be the other way,' he says. 'The Soviet Union was absent in 1984, and the Games were still a major success. The most important countries, in the creation of the financial success of the Games, are the western Europeans and America. The fact that other countries will be winning medals that previously might have gone to the Soviet Union and other eastern Europeans will be a benefit to *those* countries.' Smirnov says that what is needed for Russian sport to continue at anything like the same level is a transfer of power from government to national federations. 'The Olympic Charter is still something not really familiar within Russia,' Smirnov says. 'Our Olympic Committee was created by special decree from Stalin, and up to now it never had real status; no staff, no independence. We are looking for this government recognition *now*. . . . The old bureaucratic administration, with dozens of ministerial officials, was bad. We don't want state *projects* any more, like "fifty gold medals in 1972", for the fiftieth anniversary of the state. Of course there will be more professionals as competitors seek to gain personal reward for success. And *that* personal ambition will continue to generate Olympic winners, rather than the glory of political status. The old system tended to devalue everything else. We are trying to establish a new order, in which everyone benefits. In this, Samaranch can still be helpful. His contribution to international society has far exceeded anything connected with sport.'

The situation for sport in the former socialist countries is indeed serious. At a 1991 annual meeting of sports leaders at Varna in Bulgaria, Dr Georgi Hristov, the president of the Union of Fiscal Education and Culture in the host country, revealed that the Bulgarian government had *no* budget for sport that year, and that the Ministry for Sport was almost totally dependent on a substantial sum that was to have been paid by the former East German sports ministry for high altitude sports training facilities in Bulgaria. It was not now known whether this contract would be honoured. Nikolai Rusak, then still the USSR Minister for Sport, expressed concern at the movement of athletes from country to country with changes of citizenship, though he raised the possibility of athletes from the eastern Soviet Union taking part for the first time in Asian championships. Bogdan Duviez, the Romanian sports minister, said that western countries were literally buying athletes from the poorer east. Hungary and Czechoslovakia, where the economy is comparatively stable, are two countries presenting a more optimistic forecast. Rezho Galov, head of the Hungarian Department of PE, said that sports budgets were being maintained by the government, though the Hungarian delegation echoed Samaranch's doubt about the value of future such meetings, saying the Hungarians felt a closer identification with the Association of NOCs of Europe.

One of the most moving scenes I have ever witnessed of a country attempting to hold together its Olympic ethics was in Poland in the summer of 1990. On the tenth anniversary of the foundation of *Solidarnosc*, the Solidarity movement of working people begun in Gdansk, I attended the half-marathon of the Solidarity Games, run from Gdansk to Gdynia, the adjacent Baltic port: part of a dozen sports events being staged as a symbolic, unaggressive recognition of Solidarity's triumphant revolution 'without a broken window pane'. There was no shouting, no feeling of vengeance, just an overwhelming, silent sense of freedom as the 1,100 runners gathered for the race. Mothers with prams, heralds of the new generation of hope, watched the jostling runners as they warmed up, in mute appreciation of the significance of the moment. A cheer was heard. Lech Walesa had arrived at the scene of a decade of proletarian heroism to start the race. He would fire the gun for the start at Gate 2, alongside which stands the 20-metre-high memorial statue of three crosses, bound by an anchor at the top, forged by the shipyard workers. The three crosses represent the three uprisings of Polish workers: at Poznan in 1956, and in Gdansk and Gdynia in 1970 and 1980. Even this foreigner was near to tears as, unaccompanied, the national anthem was sung under a weeping sky: yet one more soulful moment for a people historically trapped in middle Europe's political rivalries.

The finishing line in Gdynia, twenty kilometres away, was also poignantly sited: alongside the town hall where, during the 1980 uprising, many strikers were imprisoned and Janek Wisniewski, a leading solidarity activist, was killed. When the building was liberated, the walls were found to be covered in blood. Outside, on the city square where the ancient trams rumbled past, stood a wooden cross, a temporary memorial to Wisniewski and others that was to be replaced by a monument similar to that in Gdansk. The impact of the scene in Gdynia was its representation of the average: ordinary people with ordinary lives harbouring similar ambitions, unostentatiously proud, resilient and, when necessary, defiant. Their response to historic change was to treat it with maturity.

Grzegorz Perski is a large, amiable man. He does not talk much about the fact that his liver was permanently damaged by the beatings he received when arrested in 1981 for being a member of Solidarity. 'Not that bad. I'm still alive,' he said to me, dismissively. Now, he was preoccupied with trying to revolutionize Polish sport. Aged 51, and a qualified coach in tennis, boxing, volleyball and basketball, Perski was chairman of the Solidarity Committee of Olympism and Health Education, a body attempting by democratic process to become Poland's NOC, recognized by the IOC. The then official NOC, whose members had been elected in 1989, before the fall of the communist government, was almost wholly unrepresentative of the people or of Polish sport. Worse still, many Polish delegates to the IFs, elected to international office by unwitting foreign colleagues, were Marxists who had been responsible for imprisonment, loss of jobs, censorship, or merely ethical or moral intimidation. 'In our economic situation,' Perski told me, 'the future of the nation, never mind the future of sport, could be dark. We cannot think too much about competitive sport. The first goal must be to regain general healthiness. Yet competitive sport must not be excluded, because people need rôle models. One of our problems, however, is the emigration of coaches: domestically, into better-paid jobs, and abroad to more professional sport.' Observing Perski and his Polish colleagues involved in their altruistic work, driving around Gdansk with him in his little 500cc Fiat and experiencing his unbounded optimism, was a lesson in magnanimity. In their transition from forty years of obligatory communist thought and practice to free social democracy, the Poles were providing a blueprint not merely for their eastern Europen neighbours in sport, but for life itself.

11 Gigantism

'The programme for the Olympic Games is obsolete,' Raoul Mollet, the veteran Belgian, asserts. 'How can it be possible, for example, and realistic, that in athletics a competitor can win perhaps two golds whereas in swimming it is possible to win five, or even seven? [as Mark Spitz of America and Christine Otto of East Germany did].' The degree to which the Games have run out of control – in the number of competitors, sports, and events within each sport – must be one of the criticisms of Samaranch's term of presidency. The problem had been there, and growing, throughout the previous twenty years. Although Samaranch promises that there will be action by the time of the Centenary Games in Atlanta, and major reform by the Games of 2000, up to the time of the Games in Barcelona in 1992 little has been done to restrain a growth that has become administratively unmanageable.

'We are at the limit,' Samaranch said, at his final press conference of the Games in Seoul. He did indicate then that demonstration sports would be excluded after 1992, and that additional events within existing sports would be halted. Such steps are insufficient. Several sports have multiplied their events, for no more than self-aggrandisement, out of proportion. It was significant in Seoul that, out of the sixteen competitors with three or more medals, thirteen came from two sports, swimming and gymnastics. The total of ten thousand competitors had become an almost intolerable burden upon the host city: in security, technology, transport and accommodation, for both competitors and media. Any weakness in any one part of a host city's organization is likely to lead, at the least, to chaos, and at worst to disaster. Seoul, brilliantly conducted as the Games were, was the largest yet, but at what price? There were alleged to be 67,000 uniformed police, soldiers and plainclothes detectives on duty around the marathon course on the final Sunday, which was about one every two feet. Security in Barcelona was expected to be as much of a nightmare, on account of Basque separatists and other potential terrorists, in conjunction with the expected presence of more than 40 heads of state. The Games in Seoul demonstrated that any host city needs total backing by the national government to stage the event satisfactorily and safely.

The dilemma for Samaranch and the executive board is where to begin the reduction. IFs will fight tooth and nail to maintain their number of events, in some instances their very existence; while ANOC, as stated here earlier by Vazquez Raña, will resist the setting of qualifying standards that eliminate lesser nations. The Games contain a fundamental figure skating, gymnastics. We need a clearer definition of what a team sport is. Sculling is an Olympic sport, but what about an eight? In sailing, is a pair a team?' The Princess's views tend to be idiosyncratic and not always in touch with global reality.

The sub-commission under Chatrier for Summer Games includes Franco Carraro of Italy, Bashir Attarabulsi of Libya, Sinan Erdem of Turkey, Anita DeFrantz of America, Shun-Ichiro Okano of Japan, Jacques Rogge, Boris Stankovi c and Walter Tröger of Germany, all IOC members; together with Milan Ercagin, president of wrestling (representing IFs), Luc Niggli, secretary-general of GAISF (representing recognized non-Olympic sports), Mario Pescante of Italy (representing NOCs), Peter Tallberg (representing Athletes Commission), and Charles Palmer of Britain, the former GAISF secretary, as an individual. Tallberg, who has been on the Commission since 1978, says, with exasperation:

'We've not taken *one* decision. Mostly, things are postponed. On short track speed skating, we were unanimously against it, yet the executive board approved it for inclusion in 1992. I feel the Commission has no influence. When the skiing federation were allowed to include freestyle, I think they should have been told they could do so only if they eliminated another event. And I think we need a younger Commission. All sports should be told that they have a fixed number of events, that they can only introduce a new event by losing another. This was the principle we adopted in yachting once we reached ten events.' It remains to be seen what influence Chatrier exerts in a situation seemingly controlled by the executive board.

The British Olympic Association took a policy decision, in 1990, that in future their teams would be selected more strictly, inclusion to be confined to those competitors with a chance of success, as opposed simply to those eligible to take part. The decision was partially pragmatic, on account of rising costs, but also based on a realistic assessment of the contemporary nature of the Games and the problem of over-crowding. The decision would exclude, for example, such fringe competitors as Eddie Edwards, a ski jumper, who in 1988 at Calgary gained temporary acclaim – causing offence to the rest of the British team, though this was not publicly expressed – for being 150 feet behind the leaders. Taken up by the international media at a Games that were short on stories, Eddie the Eagle was a somewhat wingless phenomenon who stretched the philosophy of 'taking part' beyond acceptability. Edwards was 'a story' only in that his presence was a farce.

Voluntary reduction of the size of their teams by the larger NOCs is too imponderable a factor to be relied upon for solving gigantism. This must come through directives from the IOC, prompted by both the Programme and Olympic Movement commissions. Stankovic, working on the Congress schedule, is well aware of the urgency; though his own sport, basketball, is clearly defined, with its single men's and women's competitions. 'Samaranch must decide between attracting those sports which appeal to spectators and to television, and those which are healthy participant sports,' Stankovic says. 'Clearly some sports have too many medals, and there has even been a proposal for *beach* volleyball. If you have team gymnastics events, why not team skating? Some sports, that are old, such as bobsleigh and modern pentathalon, are there because they are traditional. The problem with multiple sports, as I see it, is that they tend to combine sports which are already there individually on the programme.' Beach volleyball has more competitors than fencing, for example, as Ruben Acosta, the president of volleyball, would argue.

As long ago as 1981, addressing the GAISF Congress, Samaranch stressed that because IFs now predominantly all had their own world championships, independent of the Olympic Games, the IOC considered that the programme for each sport in the Games should no longer be a replica of world championships. Yet in the interim, Samaranch acknowledges, this principle has not been properly addressed.

'The only way to cut participation in the Games is through the IFs,' Samaranch says. 'I remember how synchronized swimming was added, in Moscow. Killanin was discussing with members at the Session the acceptance of rhythmic gymnastics, when someone from the floor suggested synchronized swimming as well, and it went through almost without debate. We have to investigate the affiliation of member countries to IFs, checking whether IFs genuinely qualify under the number of countries required by the Charter for Olympic qualification, and whether the national federations themselves are legitimate. Luge and bobsleigh, for instance, have country members that have never taken part in any competition! We have countries who are applying for IOC membership with the required affiliation to five IFs, yet are not competing. Gibraltar were not at the world indoor championships for athletics in Seville in 1991, even though they were invited, and I don't think they were at the world championships in Tokyo. Yet they were busy campaigning for their IOC membership on "home" ground during the Session in Birmingham. I know that we must take some positive action soon. I will study the programme for the Congress in '94 after the Games in Barcelona. We need a "brainstorm" meeting of fifteen to twenty people really to thrash out the main issues regarding the programme. However, I don't know if I can be strong enough to remove those sports that are without a really broad base among young people, and are there only by tradition. Modern pentathlon is included only because it defined de Coubertin's ideal of the complete competitor in his day, embracing shooting, fencing, riding, swimming and running. Now it is a minority sport, and is so expensive because the organizing committee must buy sixty to eighty horses for the riding pool. I am convinced that triathlon (swimming, cycling, running) will be included by the Games of 2000.

'There are some sports that do nothing to modernize themselves, to provide more public appeal. Fencing, for instance, still has a gauze mask behind which the competitor is invisible. Why could it not be transparent? Why should there not be colour introduced in the uniforms of competitors from different countries, or better technology for registering hits? There are so many questions that need answering. Should the Olympic Games, which are intended to promote peace in the world, include shooting? [That question arises in biathlon in the Winter Games as well as shooting in the Summer.] Do we have too many fighting sports: wrestling, boxing, judo, taekwondo? Some of the wrestling events could be said to be obsolete, yet the sport has *twenty* gold medals. I'm not sure that archery is sufficiently widely practised to retain inclusion. We have to look at the number of medals available in some sports, such as swimming and gymnastics. It is too late for us to make other than minor changes for the Centenary Games, though we have withdrawn demonstration sports. We must have a *new* schedule in time for 2000. The Olympic Movement must reflect the current trends in the world today.'

Personally, I shall regret the elimination of modern pentathlon, if and when that happens, even if the justification for retaining the sport is insufficient. Of all the sports at an Olympic Games, modern pentathlon perhaps more than any personifies the relationship between competitors that is truest to the ideal. Because of its demands on versatility and endurance, it promotes between rivals a mutual respect equalled nowhere except perhaps in the decathlon. As the hard men among the pentathlon wait, exhausted, at the conclusion of the cross-country on the fifth day, for the announcement of the team result, there is a mood of shared fulfilment that I regularly have found to be one of the most moving experiences of any Games. Modern pentathlon will now probably suffer from the fact that for twenty years the IOC has consistently permitted expansion in pursuit of prestige: in 1976 the addition of ice dancing and 1,000 metres speedskating; in 1980 additional events in athletics (three, all for women), canoeing (one), cycling (two), gymnastics (women's rhythmic), judo (one), swimming (four), shooting (four), yachting (one); 1988 tennis and table tennis; and in 1992 additions to the biathlon (women's event), skiing (freestyle), skating (short track, men and women), athletics (women's 10k walk), yachting (women's single-handed dinghy), and badminton.

There have been nominal attempts to restrict the number of competitors. Following the Congress in Varna, the Session agreed to restrict archery to two competitors per country per event; reduced fencing teams from 20 to 18; and removed some minority events from cycling and shooting. It must be said, of course, that expansion in order to widen the involvement of women competitors was overdue, and to this day women have grounds for complaining that prejudice and male chauvinism continue to operate against them. In many countries, especially in the Middle East and Asia, and parts of Africa, the prejudice has religious derivation. Dr K.F. Dyer, in his book *Catching up the Men*, has drawn attention to the deplorable attitude in Ireland of the late Archbishop McQuaid, who pronounced that women undressing beside the track would be an occasion of sin for male athletes. Dr McQuaid's sexually repressed disapproval of women's athletics, which sports administrators accepted rather than confront the Roman Catholic church, seriously impeded the development of women's athletics in the Irish Republic. Even with the advent in liberal societies of women jockeys, racing car drivers and footballers, it must be doubtful whether the full emancipation of women within the Olympic Movement will be achieved until well into the twenty-first century.

As Stankovic has implied, one of the more difficult issues for Samaranch, and his colleagues on two Commissions and the executive board, to decide is the relative ethical merits of competitive sports as representative of the interests of society. As outlined in an earlier chapter by Nikolaos Nissiotis, the Olympic Movement must be sure never to lose sight of the intended relationship with education. In the context of re-aligning the programme for the twenty-first century, it is worth quoting from an article by Horst Dassler, the initiator of many benevolent moves for sport, in *Olympic Review*:

> Élite sport has almost entirely lost the ethical value which it owes to the Olympic ideal, and it is of no use to lament what is already gone, because any change in the situation would no longer be either possible or one which could be controlled. Today, the functions of élite sport have a quite distinct aura: 1) political propaganda; 2) economic propaganda; 3) spectacle and entertainment; 4) business interests (especially promotional sports); 5) to assist promotion of mass sport; 6) sociological influence on the masses. However much these six points seem to oppose one another when viewed individually, they do as a whole offer more advantages than disadvantages. The question posed is how these factors can be channelled in such a way that they do not begin to take control of sport, but be co-ordinated in order to assist the sports [Olympic] movement.

Dassler's accusation against élite sport is true enough. The extent to which the ideological forces of east and west have attempted to exploit the Olympic Games to prove, quite falsely, the moral superiority of one or other system, capitalist or communist, is abundantly evident. That is not something for which the IOC can be held responsible. The IOC's binding duty is to ensure, as far as possible, that the ethics under which the Olympic Games are conducted retain the traditional element of sportsmanship. This ought to mean that the rules of each individual sport, and the regulations of the Charter, are upheld rigidly and unfailingly. The strength of the Olympic Movement rests in its ability to demonstrate to the world that sportsmanship and fair play are paramount to the conduct of sport; and that breaches of this conduct necessarily forfeit participation in the Games. It is by maintaining an aura of exclusivity, in behaviour as much as in performance, that the Olympic Games will continue to hold a greater appeal in the public mind than the ordinary world championship. This is why, in my opinion, the IOC leaves itself so exposed when it fails to respond to persistent breaches of ethic by, say, weightlifting. The IOC, led by the President, should have a sufficiently strong nerve to say to any sport that failure to uphold ethical standards will result in suspension. The authority to say to any sport that the Games do not need that sport, and if necessary can survive without it, is the very basis of the unique strength of the Olympic Games.

Why, therefore, does the IOC not grasp the nettle and tell swimming to cut out some of its contrived medley relays, or tell athletics that throwing events, so randomly abused by cheats, are no longer acceptable; and the same for race walking, which is impossible accurately to judge? Weightlifting should be suspended for one Olympiad and told to re-apply for admission when it has established a sequence of other championships – utilizing IOC testing laboratories – that have been free of positive tests. It is by imposing its will in such arbitrary ways that the IOC is capable of defending the future not just of the Games but of sport itself.

Although the Princess Royal has put forward an arguable case against team sports' exclusion from the Games, it must be said that apart from the two most basic of all individual sports, athletics and boxing, those sports which most lend themselves, in both practical and emotional terms, to the developing countries are team sports: basketball, football, handball, volleyball and baseball. The development of basketball, for example, runs in parallel with its development within the Olympic Games. Brundage was on the technical committee for basketball at the Berlin Games in 1936, yet thereafter never attended a match, even when President from 1952. Throughout the Sixties and Seventies, basketball received only moderate collaboration in its promotion from the IOC. Arenas at Tokyo, Mexico, Munich and Montreal held only four or five thousand; it is only since Moscow, thanks to Killanin's interest, that basketball has moved to indoor stadia holding fifteen to twenty thousand.

With 176 national federations, second only to athletics, basketball has become one of the world's most prominent sports, the Olympic tournament comfortably maintaining its superiority and appeal over continental and world championships. The 'failure' of the United States, which has dominated Olympic basketball since 1936, in Seoul, where it took only the bronze medal behind the USSR and Yugoslavia, persuaded famous American professionals such as Larry Bird of Boston Celtics and Michael Jordan of Chicago Bulls to jump at the chance to be involved in the competition in Barcelona. In the four years from 1986 to 1990, the basketball federation had an annual budget of two million Swiss francs. Between 1990 and 1994, assisted by ISL Marketing, this would rise to SF15m. Although some spectators in, say, Spain and Yugoslavia are drifting away from football to basketball, the indoor sport is as yet no rival globally to football, but its eminence and its grass-roots popularity are substantially due to promotion within the Olympic Movement.

Much the same is true of volleyball. Twenty years ago the international game was dominated by two socialist nations, the Soviet Union and Poland, and Japan. In the early 1980s, a tactical revolution took place, introduced by Doug Beal, previously a player in unsuccessful US Olympic teams. Beal introduced strategic innovations adopted from other American professional sports, which, copied by Cuba, Brazil, Italy and others, have transformed the game. Indeed, the problem with volleyball today is that, as a spectator sport, it is almost too clever, beyond the comprehension of the non-playing spectator in much the same way as the best table tennis. Yet the game now has millions of recreational players, and is outstanding, socially, because it can be played satisfactorily by teams of mixed age and sex. Good women's teams will defeat hesitant men's teams. In terms of social and educational value, volleyball, avidly promoted by Acosta, its president, must rate substantially higher than, say, canoeing, judo or wrestling.

'The challenge to the Olympic Games in the immediate years ahead will come from an upsurge in world championships,' Sonny de Sales of Hong Kong says. 'This is as much on financial as sporting grounds. All multi-sport Games are threatened by the increasing frequency of single-sport championships.' How much this is a perceived rather than a real threat remains to be seen. I do not think it applies to basketball or volleyball, each of which for the moment values its Olympic involvement too highly. The two obvious sports that substantiate the theory of de Sales are football and athletics. While, on the one hand, the Olympics does not need football – and vice versa – an Olympic Games without athletics is inconceivable. This cannot be overlooked by Primo Nebiolo, the president of athletics, in his quest for a higher profile for both his sport and himself. The outcome of the power struggle over the next [illegible] letics and the IOC will much depend [illegible] is successor – to call the bluff of athlet- [illegible] of IAAF member countries would tol- [illegible] pic participation an under-23 event – as [illegible] rnament – though undoubtedly, acting [illegible] ebiolo is capable of exerting considerable [illegible] ter 13). It is worth recalling that Nebiolo's [illegible] Paulen of the Netherlands, once said that if [illegible] the athletics programme, the IAAF would [illegible]

[illegible] s an anomaly which many would like to see [illegible] nt the IOC to go in its attempt to impose uni- [illegible] on? There are IOC members belligerent on this [illegible] newly elected Vazquez Raña of Mexico, who consider that FIFA [illegible] d be given an ultimatum. 'Why should we have a problem with Olympic football?' Vazquez Raña asks. 'I respect IFs, and FIFA has its own outstanding show, the World Cup, every four years. Now, they're effectively trying not to take part in the Olympic Games. They are already filling the world with football: under-17 tournaments, under-21, and so on. I would tell them "goodbye". If the IOC is not careful, we will soon have other IFs doing the same. This is something we have to decide at the Congress in '94. The difficulty is that all IF leaders want to have the best for themselves, yet we *all* have responsibilities to sport. I have supported continental Games, as president of ANOC, because we have to be able to give lesser athletes an alternative to the Olympic Games.'

Both Samaranch and João Havelange, the FIFA president from Brazil, attempt to play down the conflict. In two previous Olympic tournaments, FIFA had a regulation excluding former World Cup players of Europe and South America. Their present condition clearly flies in the face of an *open* Olympics, for which Samaranch has battled. 'Havelange is a heavyweight, though he's very keen to be active as a member within the IOC,' Samaranch says. 'Of course we have a problem with the age limit; this will have to be discussed again after Barcelona. I hope a solution can be found. Football is not vital to the IOC, or the Olympic Games, and we could live without it, although that would be difficult for a Games in a country with such a strong football tradition as Spain. World opinion, however, considers the Olympic football tournament is not a first-class event. The principle of the age limit is not only against our Charter, but is an unsatisfactory solution.'

Football clearly has a stronger hand here than athletics, on two counts: one emotional, one technical. The status of the World Cup in football is so glamorous that the Olympic Games is bound to be secondary in consideration; at the same time, the qualifying tournament for the Olympics takes place simultaneously with the qualifying competition for the continental championships of Europe and Africa; and national senior teams cannot simultaneously play in both. The IOC's answer to *that* should be: play the best team available in the Olympic qualifying tournament and *then* play the top players in the final Olympic tournament.

Havelange remains bland to the point of being casual. 'In my view, there is no serious difference of opinion between FIFA and the IOC,' he says. 'The IOC always respects IFs, because sport belongs to the IFs. The idea of an age limit was first proposed in 1981. We took seven years to come to a conclusion, and it was finally accepted unanimously at the Session in '88. We have a *record* entry for the tournament in 1992, higher even than for the World Cup. In my opinion, the football decision will be seen as a *positive* point in Samaranch's administration, because of the success of the football tournament within the Olympic Games.'

Sepp Blatter, FIFA's secretary-general, elaborates on the justification of the age limit. 'Under this system, a team can progress naturally, from the youth side to the under-21 team, then to the Olympics, and finally to the World Cup,' Blatter says. 'It is good for progress and development of the game, and our members, in particular the Africans, were emphatic about this.' An additional strength of football is that it consistently attracts some of the largest live audiences at the Games; for the last three, the largest. The irony is that it was FIFA which, in the late 1970s, was helping the IOC edge towards professionalism and an end to the sham-amateur era, in which eastern European nations had won every football tournament since the Second World War. Now the IOC has altered its standpoint so radically that it is demanding more professionalism than FIFA is willing to concede.

Blatter admits to Samaranch's efficiency. 'He has put a kick into a conservative and old-fashioned organization, drawing it into modern social and economic conditions,' Blatter says. 'He has given the Olympic Movement more impact, copying the travelling programme of Havelange, when *he* was first elected in 1974, projecting the IOC and developing the Solidarity programme around the world. Samaranch was fortunate to have a good adviser in Horst Dassler, who suggested to Samaranch that he should promote the IOC through himself. "You're in a glass palace," Dassler told him, "a figure like the Pope to whom everyone must come. *Reverse* the process." Doing this helped Samaranch accelerate the expansion of the IOC. I know about those conversations, because Dassler talked with me in the early 1980s. With all the visits Samaranch has made, meeting heads of state, he has given the Olympic Movement so much prestige. He is tenacious and self-disciplined, and once you are in the spiral of success, popularity will grow and grow. I admire how he withstands the stress of his position. His fault is that he has listened too much at times to the socialist countries, when they have pressed for an increase in the number of disciplines to raise the number of medals by which to promote their ideology. Samaranch has been susceptible to this.'

The restraining influence on Nebiolo, besides the wish of IAAF member countries not to break from the Olympic Movement, would come from individual athletes. The prestige of an Olympic gold medal is still worth at least twice as much, in commercial negotiating terms, for sponsorship and advertising as a world championship title: more so now that there are to be two world championships in every four-year Olympic cycle. It was significant that during the world championships in Tokyo in 1991, gold medallists repeatedly said, when asked, that they valued victory the next year in Barcelona even more highly. The strength of the Olympic Games, especially in relation to athletics, is that it has the rarity value of its infrequency. Furthermore, it is not an event which is open to manipulation in the way of Grand Prix meetings; and, in due course no doubt, even world championships, for which the leading performers would be demanding appearance money.

In my opinion, Nebiolo ought to see his main concern in the future being not so much for a better financial deal from the share of revenue generation in the Olympic Games, as for the protection of the reputation of athletics from manipulation by agents. With the increase of fixtures throughout the four-year calendar, and intolerable physical pressure being placed upon the competitors, there is a growing threat to the degree of athletic involvement in subsidiary Games, such as the African or Commonwealth Games; leading competitors will prefer the financial inducements on offer from promoters in Europe. As athletics becomes increasingly professional – which is fine for the development of some national federations – what is urgently needed is a form of contract for tournament participation similar to that operating in tennis and golf; and, crucially, within the jurisdiction of the IAAF and national federations rather than independent agents. It is not inconceivable that IMG, for instance, could come to control the field – or market – for certain events, such as the 100 metres or pole vault or 400 metres hurdles, simply by signing the majority of the appropriate group of performers.

For their own protection, all sports need to look critically at their rules of competition and at the face they present to the public. Conspicuously doing so are, for example, table tennis and yachting. Because table tennis is played at such a speed and with such a small ball that it is difficult for all but the most experienced followers fully to appreciate, Ichiro Ogimura, the president of the International Federation, and his executive committee have worked hard to adjust the presentation. The ball is now coloured yellow, and there are microphones beneath the table to pick up the sound of the ball on bat to make identification of shots an audio as well as visual quality. Players are nationally identified by their kit, and multiple electronic scoreboards give instant verification of the state of the game to a spectator in any position.

The International Yacht Racing Union (IYRU), under the direction of Paul Henderson, former Olympic competitor and chairman of the committee for 'The Future of the Olympic Classes', is seeking to establish boat classes that are universally available, do not have a prohibitive cost, and fall more easily within the terminology of 'sailing' as opposed to the more exclusive-sounding 'yachting'. In the Olympic event at Pusan in 1988, two minor nations – Virgin Islands in Finn Class and Netherland Antilles in Board – won their first ever medals in the Games. The IYRU is also studying submissions regarding preferences between fleet racing and the more attractive practice of match racing, head to head, which is better suited to television coverage and at the same time substantially reduces the number of competitors.

Other sports need to examine themselves in the same way. In view of the need, and the IOC's desire, to reduce the number of Olympic sports, the price of failure to do so could be very high.

12 Freedom

In the spring of 1988, there were rumblings of unease from within Africa that might have threatened participation at the Games in Seoul. Rebel cricket tours of South Africa, busting anti-apartheid agreements, were still a sore point; and there was mounting irritation at the possible selection by Britain of Zola Budd, who not only had spent much of the time since the Olympic Games in 1984 returning to live in her native South Africa, but had allegedly been involved 'illegally' in the promotion of a race or races in South Africa. It was now that Samaranch played one of his more masterful strokes: something so simple, indeed, that it was a surprise, on reflection, that he had not put it into effect some time before. Four months prior to Seoul, the IOC staged in Lausanne a meeting of African sports officials, specifically for the purpose of establishing publicly the IOC's unanimity on anti-apartheid policy in sport. Following this meeting, and the adoption of a declaration regarding apartheid, Samaranch created the 'Apartheid and Olympism Commission', with the mandate of gathering facts for the reinforcement of the anti-apartheid policy. This African sports summit convinced black Africa of the IOC's goodwill, and achieved in the process much more than that: not only was any talk of boycott of Seoul reduced, but the base was laid for steps that within three years would lead to South Africa's readmission, with remarkable swiftness, into the Olympic Movement.

Major-General Henry Adefope of Nigeria, elected to the IOC in 1984, took a degree in general medicine at Glasgow University between 1947 and 1952, then followed a career as a doctor in the Nigerian army before becoming Minister for Foreign Affairs in 1978-9. He is a moderate radical: a man of resolute moral principle with as agreeable a disposition as you could wish to find. 'The conference in Lausanne in '88 was Samaranch's initiative,' Adefope says. 'Everyone who mattered was there: the president of the Supreme Council for Sport in Africa, Laval of Nigeria; there was Diack of Senegal from the IAAF, Vazquez Raña, Nebiolo, nine African IOC members. There was a general acceptance that apartheid in sport was not acceptable to the IOC, followed by the establishment of a new Commission. What this did was enable the Supreme Council, as an arm of the Organization of African Unity, to realize that the Olympic Movement was against apartheid, and indirectly to establish that a boycott per se was not the solution to any problem. That in turn led ANOCA to approach leaders of sport within South Africa, in order to enlighten them on *our* points of view, and to hold a meeting in Harare in November '90. The meeting in Lausanne was a watershed. Over the years, there had been so many pressures, so many attempts to bring South Africa out of the cold by using cricket or rugby or athletics or boxing to by-pass the anti-apartheid movement.

'We in Africa had to make clear what was the only way South Africa could tread in order to get back. What we see now in South African sport is the direct result of the efforts of Samaranch. The effect of sport on ordinary social/political life in South Africa is tremendous. The exclusion of South Africa sport has been painful for them, white *and* black. I know that over the years there have been a good number of whites in South African who would have liked to see South Africans of all races competing together to form teams to represent South Africa. I know also that existing laws had made that impossible. The laws made it illegal to travel together, or to change in the dressing-room together, but the impression I've always had from genuine whites, like Dennis McIldowie, was that some of them wanted it different. I believe that human beings are human beings, whatever their colour, but when a situation is established by law, there is very little that individuals can do against it.

'The time it takes to find normality will depend on the South Africans themselves. When they return to the Olympic fold, if South Africa wins a gold medal, no one's going to ask what colour he or she is, they will simply be South African. Yet they will not achieve normality if there is not access to facilities which are predominantly in white areas. *They* have to solve their problems. The Olympic Movement could have stood aloof, and said that unless South Africa abided by the Charter, they remained excluded. Instead, the IOC had bent over to help them realize their ambitions. Now it's up to not just the leaders but everyone else: to decide when they're ready to come back at every level. I believe de Klerk has been sincere, a better politician than he was thought to be. If he can see this situation [sport] through to the logical conclusion, it will help in the solution of the political problem. In the society where there have always been rigid barriers between the races, it's not easy suddenly to allow mixed use of facilities. There is, too, the probability that clubs with membership subscriptions will be out of reach of the majority.

'So how does South Africa achieve integration of sport if the majority of the population has no access to facilities? There has to be a pragmatic approach on both sides, by white and black. Facilities will *have* to be made available. In Nigeria after independence, clubs became integrated; we have white and black chairmen. In South Africa the government has to give a push, otherwise things may remain intractable for a long time. The Olympic Movement cannot change this. Change has to come from within.

'This has been one of Samaranch's finest achievements, together with the Seoul Olympics. Neither would have happened, but for him. *And* Samaranch has created financial stability for the Olympic Movement. Ending apartheid in society is not easy. Eusebio, Portugal's wonderful footballer, came from Mozambique. Portugal had discrimination, but not in sport. If South Africa can achieve this as a start, then there will be progress. Discrimination of one sort or another is not going to disappear overnight. Look at Britain. You don't find many blacks in the police, but if we looked at the playgrounds while we were in Birmingham for the Session, we saw integration. What counts is making the effort.'

Adefope knows what apartheid can mean in Britain. He remembers searching for digs in Glasgow and being told by landlords there was no room, when he knew there were vacancies, yet it has not left him bitter. There are white friends, including his bank manager, whom he visits every time he is in Britain.

Initial resistance to South Africa's regime of apartheid came with the Soviet Union protest at the Session of 1959 in Munich. Reg Honey, the South African IOC member, responded by saying that all South African competitors had been guaranteed a passport: the following year the team that arrived for the Olympics in Rome was conspicuously all white. Between then and the Games in Tokyo, attitudes hardened. The African militancy was being led by Chief Abraham Ordia of Nigeria, representing the Supreme Council, and additionally now by the South African Non-Racial Olympic Committee (SANROC), based in London. The IOC Session in 1963, scheduled for Nairobi, had to be switched to Baden Baden when the Kenyan government refused to allow South African delegates into the country. Rumours circulated that Brundage had threatened Kenya with removal from the Games in Tokyo, though this was denied. The Kenyan action was in line with the policy adopted at an Addis Ababa conference of independent African states. At the Session before the Winter Games at Innsbruck, in 1964, the IOC continued to fudge on South Africa's participation in Tokyo, though at this stage there was no confirmation whether or not South Africa intended to send an integrated team. In the event, they were barred on the grounds that their laws infringed the Charter.

In 1967, at the Session in Tehran, Frank Braun, president of the South African Olympic and National Games Association, attempted to talk his country back into the Games for Mexico the next year. Following the Session, Killanin was appointed to lead a Commission to investigate the sporting situation within South Africa. The trip was uncomfortable and controversial, the reception often hostile, while those liberal South Africans who wanted change revealed that they were regarded as agitators. Prime Minister Vorster told the Commission that he would not agree to mixed trials, and that there could be no mixed teams in team sports. One of the most extreme officials, Killanin was to write in his autobiography, was Frank Waring, the Minister for Sport, who was of British stock. Before Killanin's party departed, there were further insults. The Commission's report to the Session at Grenoble prior to the Winter Games of 1968 reflected both South Africa's intransigence and the cosmetic attempt, announced by Braun in Tehran, to produce an acceptable face and an acceptable team. On a resolution drafted by Australia, South Africa was voted back in.

This led to a unanimous decision, at a meeting of African nations in Brazzaville, Congo, to boycott the Mexico Games. This precipitated a special meeting of the executive board in Lausanne, prior to which it was leaked that the board would ensure a reversal of the decision of the Session at Grenoble. Honey, South Africa's IOC member, quaintly described the executives' decision to demand a second vote among the members as 'illegal and immoral'. The second vote decided against South Africa's inclusion: right-wing editorials in Britain condemned such vacillation. The debate would rage for the next 23 years.

In 1965, an all-white South African cricket party had officially visited England for the last time, and when Vorster refused the entry, in the late autumn of 1968, of Basil d'Oliveira, a South African-born Cape-coloured player selected for England's cricket tour party, the tour was cancelled: one of Britain's less equivocal acts in this long-running debate, taken in protection of *their* interests. It should be recalled that when the coloured cricket association of South Africa requested the England cricket tour party for a single match in South Africa during 1956, they did not even receive the courtesy of a reply.

In 1970, at the Session in Amsterdam, South Africa was expelled from the IOC. The same year, anti-apartheid sympathizers in England vandalized cricket grounds and threatened to disrupt the Springbok tour, which was cancelled. Arthur Ashe, the black American tennis player, was refused a visa to play in South Africa, which was banned from the Davis Cup. The Equestrian and Cycling Federations expelled South Africa; FINA, the swimming federation, following suit in 1973. In 1974, a British Isles rugby party toured South Africa; in 1976 the Republic would be expelled by international athletics. The previous year, Rhodesia had followed South Africa into the wilderness when the Session at Lausanne voted by 41 to 26 to withdraw recognition of the Rhodesian NOC, following a report of a Commission which had visited that country, led by Sylvio de Padilha of Brazil. A Rhodesian team had travelled to Munich for the Games in 1972, only to be forced into the rôle of spectators in deference to protests by other African countries about discrimination against blacks within Rhodesia.

The background to the African boycott of the 1976 Games in Montreal has been discussed in an earlier chapter. The next year, at the

Session in Prague, the members formally deplored those countries involved in the boycott, but imposed no penalty against them. The Prague meeting succeeded the unanimous decision by Commonwealth prime ministers, at a conference in Gleneagles, that there should be no future sporting contacts with South Africa. The agreement was signed by Robert Muldoon, the prime minister of New Zealand, which reduced African animosity provoked by the rugby tour which had triggered the boycott. What became known as the Gleneagles Agreement had questionable authority, as demonstrated by subsequent rugby tours by Britain to South Africa, in 1980, and by South Africa, to New Zealand, in 1981. An unofficial tour of South Africa by England cricketers in 1982 led to the players being banned from Test cricket for three years; a similar tour of South Africa in 1983 by West Indian cricketers led to bans for life.

That year I made my first visit to South Africa, and it was swiftly apparent that although the apartheid laws were still producing an intolerable division of peoples in day-to-day life, with punitive discriminations against non-whites, there was a massive move for change among white liberals and a majority of those aged under 35. I met men such as Professor Org Marais, who had instituted, ten years previously at the University of South Africa, a course in business studies for non-whites who lacked the academic qualifications for the university. Through his initiative, five hundred non-whites had already graduated in Business Administration. He himself had flouted the law by physically removing the segregation notices in the toilets. I went with Freddie Williams, the coloured 800 metres national champion, to a restaurant in Cape Town, where the proprietor, though having an 'international' licence which permitted all races to enter, refused to serve us. Williams, accustomed to such insults, merely smiled resignedly. Subsequently he left for Canada; and in 1991, representing Canada, he failed by only a few hundredths of a second to qualify for the final of the 800 metres in the world championships in Tokyo. At the 1983 national athletics championships at Stellenbosch, a 10,000 crowd repeatedly rose to their feet to applaud the winners, never mind if they were Williams, or the black Matthew Temane in the 5,000 metres. The first four in Temane's race were black; and a swarm of autograph-hunters, many of them under twelve, were indiscriminate in their choice of winners whom they asked to sign their programmes. When Williams, temporarily sick after his second big race in three days, went to the first aid room, he was caringly tended by white medics. Anyone could see then that South Africa was not just changing: it had changed. There was so much happening of which the rest of the world was unaware, however intolerable the laws, however severe the subjugation of the non-whites. A tide was in motion, among whites and blacks, as you could discover by chatting to Soweto office workers during their lunch break in any downtown Johannesburg cafeteria, that could not indefinitely be suppressed.

There were, of course, still the radicals, such as Frank Van der Horst, a civil engineer in Cape Town, living in a pleasant pink-washed villa with a superb view of the harbour on the side of a hill in a 'coloured' residential area. As secretary of the South African Council of Sport – a predominantly coloured, as opposed to black, administrative body in sport – Van der Horst was emphatic on the maintenance of the slogan: 'No normal sport in an abnormal society.' Van der Horst was working in collaboration with those such as Sam Ramsamy, the leader of SANROC in London, Jean-Claude Ganga and others, under the umbrella of the United Nations, on the continued exclusion of white South Africa – and thereby unavoidably of black South Africa – from all international sport. Yet eight years before the IOC were to readmit South Africa, I was reporting from Johannesburg a discussion with Cyril Kobus, the black general manager of the 95 per cent black National Professional Soccer League (NPSL). 'SACOS is very narrow-sighted, and does not accord the same freedom it demands,' Kobus said. 'They are hypocrites, and have a very insignificant rôle in our domestic sport. They are not affiliated in soccer to the non-racial governing body, and therefore cannot speak for the major sport of black South Africa.'

The 'No normal sport . . .' slogan was a fatalistic viewpoint, Kobus claimed. 'There is no excuse for inaction,' he said. 'We [NPSL] identify with Africa and the African Soccer Federation as our door to international competition. We are not saying because the situation here is abnormal that we are doing nothing about it.' Much the same situation existed in 1991: liberal, imaginative optimism by intelligent South African blacks, and restrictive politically orientated radicalism from SACOS, attempting to frustrate the IOC initiative; though by then Ramsamy had, with some discomfort, changed sides on the argument.

In 1986, the IOC were to oppose the 'South African Games', a multi-sport festival, coincidentally taking place concurrently with the government abolishing all race restrictions on hotels, restaurants, bars and accommodation. The mood within South Africa was accelerating. The boxing event of the Games had been cancelled because of intimidation by SACOS; but in the wrestling event, nine- and ten-year-old black boys were tumbling about on the sideline with white contemporaries, too young and innocent to be token stooges. Johnny Prinsloo, a white middle-aged maintenance worker with Iscor Steel, at Van der Bijl Park, fifty miles from Johannesburg, who was attending the event, said: 'When *I* was a boy I grew up side by side with the blacks. They were my pals, we swam together naked in the river. It was only later we were forced to grow apart.'

Johan Du Plessis, president of the national wrestling federation, who would be at the forefront of the readmitted NOC five years later, said to me: 'By hook or by crook I have a duty to get competition for my wrestlers. As a sportsman, I cannot change my government. Four years ago our four different [racial] associations amalgamated. Our fifteen thousand competitors, with 20 per cent of the seniors either black or coloured, are educated at all levels, and the profits from this tournament will primarily go to black communities.' When I wrote such truths back home in Britain, I was decried and even ridiculed by left-wing do-gooders who had not even been to South Africa recently, including such as the Bishop of Liverpool, the former Test cricketer David Sheppard, who never saw fit to challenge the apartheid between Gentlemen and Players at Lord's.

The Olympic Games at both Los Angeles and Seoul were marginally threatened, the first by the involvement, and the second by the possible involvement, of Zola Budd as a British runner. There was also the problem, in 1984, of an England rugby tour of South Africa, though this, in the event, surprisingly had no bearing. Nor did black Africa see fit to withdraw in protest over the inclusion in Los Angeles of Budd, who at the last minute, by deviously manipulated friendships and commercial opportunism, had gained a British passport. By 1988, the British Amateur Athletic Board was still behaving deviously, being of half a mind to uphold Budd's selection in spite of the fact that she had repeatedly continued to consort with *her* people in *their* land. She had wilfully failed to consolidate her acquired citizenship with permanent residence. She had previously been declared ineligible for England's Commonwealth Games team in 1986, though that decision was little more than an act of appeasement towards black African nations that were threatening to boycott the event in Edinburgh – and did so anyway, on account of the refusal by Prime Minister Thatcher to impose stricter trade sanctions on South Africa. In the summer of 1988, Budd panicked, or lost her nerve, and returned to the country to which she really belonged and from which morally she had never departed. By now the Lausanne African Summit had taken place, and suddenly black Africa and the Olympic Movement had engaged a forward gear that would carry them rapidly towards a revised perception of the South African problem.

The pressure from beneath had also continued, evident at the All-Africa Games in Nairobi in 1987. In his opening speech, President Daniel Moi had talked in the same breath of the justification of the boycott of Edinburgh the previous year, and of Kenya's decision to offer the African National Congress an office in Nairobi. Leading sports officials in Kenya for the Games admitted that the problems posed by the conflict between solidarity on the anti-apartheid issue and the genuine interests of sport were increasingly insoluble. So it felt to me, when watching Zimbabwe play Nigeria at hockey in Nairobi, part of a seven-nation round-robin tournament for the winner's reward of a qualifying place at the Olympic Games in Seoul. Supporting Zimbabwe in the small grandstand at the City Park Stadium were a group of cheerleaders, shouting themselves hoarse: 'Zim-baa-bway'. The supporters were exclusively black. The team they were cheering, other than one Asian, was all-white.

Part of the new logic regarding South Africa within black Africa was, it must be admitted, financially orientated. There was money available in South Africa, a share of which could contribute substantially not just to African sport – notably African football – but to African trade in general. The growing instinct within the African Soccer Confederation, to consider renewed association, was given impetus by the success of Cameroon, the African champions, at the World Cup in Italy in 1990. There was no point in Africa struggling for a place on the world map, and attempting to do so without one of the most powerful forces of black sport contained within the banned republic. Black African sports leaders had begun to accept the principle for which I had been lobbying for some years: that the readmission of South Africa, in those sports where there was a *genuine degree of integration*, could exert a powerful influence on the further liberalization of South African social conditions.

Following the 'summit' meeting of June 1988 in Lausanne, the route towards South Africa's readmission in July 1991 can be traced through a series of further critical meetings:

December 1988, Vienna: First meeting of the Apartheid Commission.
September 1989, Lausanne: South African National Olympic Committee (former deposed white NOC) meets Samaranch, who initiates a further appointment for SANOC with Keba M'Baye, chairman of the new Apartheid Commission.
October 1989, Lausanne: SANOC (chairman Johan Du Plessis, and general secretary Doep Du Plessis) have first formal meeting with sporting authority of black Africa, in the person of M'Baye.
November 1989, Harare: Non-racial South African sports bodies meet Sam Ramsamy and Fekrou Kidane, of the International Campaign Against Apartheid in Sport.
January 1990, Paris: First-ever meeting between Sam Ramsamy, leader of SANROC, with officials of SANOC, under liaison by Fekrou Kidane, adviser to the Apartheid Commission.
February 1990, Kuwait: United Nations Committee Against Apartheid in Sport, represented by its chairman, Ambassador Gbeho of Ghana, meets the Apartheid Commission, under the liaison of Kidane, the

IOC's observer at the UN Apartheid Committee. A resolution is agreed to invite the Association of African NOCs (ANOCA) to meet South African sports organizers.
November 1990, Harare: African Sport Representatives from ANOCA and the Supreme Council, with representatives of all five South African collective bodies: SANOC, SANROC, SACOS, the new National Olympic Sports Congress (NOSC, affiliated to ANC), and COSAS (Confederation of South African Sports, the governing bodies of all sports). A consultative committeee of South African sport is formed.
December 1990, Johannesburg: Unofficial visit of IOC executive board.
February 1991, Gabarone, Botswana: The formation, at the request of ANOCA, of the South African Interim NOC (INOCSA), comprising all five collective bodies.
March 1991, Johannesburg/Cape Town/Ulundi: IOC special delegation meets Prime Minister de Klerk, ANC leader Mandela, and Inkatha Zulu Freedom Party leader Buthelezi, with a concluding recommendation for provisional readmission of South Africa.
July 1991, Lausanne: Permanent readmission of South Africa agreed, 31 years after their last appearance in an Olympic Games.

There had been, in parallel, other meetings: between the National Soccer League, South Africa's non-racial, black-orientated professional league, and the ANC at the latter's headquarters in Lusaka, Zambia; and that of the South African Rugby Board, the former white-dominated body, in Harare, also with the ANC. Doors were opening. Central to the series of IOC-initiated meetings, besides the judicial wisdom of Keba M'Baye, the Apartheid Commission's chairman, had been Fekrou Kidane, the Ethiopian adviser to the Commission. The self-effacing Kidane is not only an astute reader of African politics and psychology, but a man of unlimited patience, tact and, above all, tolerance. When the history of African sports politics comes to be written, his discreet role will be seen to have been a determining voice of reason.

'Samaranch was the first IOC President who was really concerned with this issue, wanting to discuss it with the Africans,' Kidane says. 'He was the first to visit *all* the African states, to appreciate the problems of Africa, of the many underdeveloped countries. He is a simple person, contacted easily. When he sees problems, he will take action. You will not find an NOC in the Third World which has been refused anything by him.

'After his election, he helped with the formation of ANOCA in 1981 in Tokyo. Previously, the Supreme Council had operated as the co-ordinating body in Africa, but it was not a recognized organization, and had no position in the Olympic Movement. And Samaranch never refused a meeting with anyone on anything. He sees himself as being there to help. He called the Summit in June '88, the *first* time the Supreme

Council had been invited to an Olympic function, yet the Supreme Council is the body of sports ministers in Africa and it is difficult to be successful without them. When SANOC (Johan Du Plessis) asked to meet Samaranch in '88, he told them first to meet M'Baye, which they did with SANROC in Paris in January 1990. Samaranch started it all – that was the first time Ramsamy [20 years the leader of the boycott movement] had met SANOC. The IOC was helping to finance all the meetings. The Kuwait meeting was important, suggesting that ANOCA meet the South African sports organizations.

'Both Brundage and Killanin had been concerned about the South African issue, especially after South Africa was expelled, but they had done little. At the time of Killanin's visit in 1967, I was secretary of the Ethiopian NOC. There was a lot of support within the IOC for South Africa. In 1968 they believed South Africa should be given another chance. Ethiopia decided to boycott Mexico if South Africa was admitted, and was followed by 41 other countries. After a postal vote, the invitation to South Africa was withdrawn, and Ethiopia went to Mexico. [de Coubertin had wanted the universality of the Olympic Games, and he invited the Prince Regent of Ethiopia (then Abyssinia) to Paris in 1924. Comte Henri de Baillet-Letour of Belgium, who succeeded de Coubertin as President in 1925, said it was too soon for Ethiopia to have an IOC member.]

'Samaranch has said that the first duty of the President must be a willingness to speak with everyone, however big or small, down to the most junior journalist. Because people have confidence in him, they will consult him. And because he has met everyone, it is almost impossible to surprise him. The range of his interest in Africa, much of it unwritten, is extensive, even down to helping to buy equipment for the school in Kenya run by Kip Keino.'

The speed at which attitudes within Africa towards South Africa were being revised, indeed reversed, was leaving some outposts of the anti-apartheid empire ethically isolated. Scandinavia has always been at the forefront of support for the anti-apartheid movement, and in September 1990, the Fourth International Conference Against Apartheid in Sport was staged in Stockholm just at the time when rival bodies within South Africa were busy negotiating peace. It was apparent at the conference that some foreign ideologists were still intent on pursuing *absolute* political liberation within South Africa, at a time when Africans together with South Africans were seeking an interim solution that might keep international sport alive in advance of the establishment of one-man-one vote. Present in Stockholm was Mluleki George, the president of the newly-formed National Olympic Sports Congress, a body affiliated to the ANC and approved by Mandela. George was at the heart of rationalization among black South Africans, and he went as far as to say that he hoped this would be the last conference before apartheid was destroyed. Yet he insisted, on addressing the conference, that it would be dangerous to relax, for the time being, the sporting boycott during a push towards positive conclusions. 'Not all the changes taking place are due to a change of heart,' George said, 'but it is encouraging that so many whites have a willingness to merge. The objectives of NOSC are unity, development and preparation for the post-apartheid era. It would be invalid to claim that international readmission should be a reward for the existing regime. Our greatest problem continues to be the fragmentation of society caused by apartheid: not just between black and white, but between black and black. The situation is still far from what we require, and must be resolved.'

Ramsamy attended the conference to give the background to a recent ten-day visit he had made to South Africa, at the request of ANOCA, in order to produce a report for all interested African organizations, political and sporting, to be presented at Harare in November. Ramsamy said it was not a matter of whether readmission would happen, only when. He touched on the issue central to African thinking when he said: 'South Africa has abundant resources.' This was echoed in the statement of Jean-Claude Ganga, a member of the IOC's Apartheid Commission. 'I dream of organizing an all-Africa Games in Johannesburg as a celebration of African youth.' Such a sentiment would have been impossible twelve months before; some of the Scandinavians could scarcely believe what they were hearing. 'The issue is one of human relations,' Ramsamy said at the time. 'It has always tended to be seen as a political issue because it is only politicians who can make the decisions. The situation, therefore, depends on political development. I found (during my visit) that all organizations were overwhelmingly in favour of single, national, non-racial governing bodies for each sport.'

Reports from the Harare meeting of November 1990, between African and South African organizations, was so encouraging that Samaranch was able to announce, at an executive board meeting in Lillehammer, Norway – host city of the 1994 Winter Games – that for the first time in 23 years the IOC would officially visit South Africa. A delegation from the Apartheid Commission would hold meetings the following April, at the highest possible level with political and sports authorities from all racial parties, regarding South Africa's imminent return to international sport. Keba M'Baye was to head the delegation, and it was in Lillehammer that South Africa's return to the Olympic Games in 1992 for the first time became a matter of realistic speculation. The findings of the delegation were to be reported by the Commission to the IOC Session at Birmingham in June 1991. The delegation would be: M'Baye; Kevan Gosper of Australia, IOC vice-president; Ganga; Major-General Henry Adefope; Edwin Moses, gold medal winner;

Amadou Lamine Ba, secretary-general of the supreme Council; Kidane; and François Carrard, the IOC Director-General.

Samaranch was maintaining his principle that the South African problem had to be resolved by Africa. This was now happening, at a pace. 'It is possible that sport can be the test bed of social integration,' Kidane said in Lillehammer. 'History is moving so fast that we consider anything is possible,' M'Baye observed. It was the first IOC visit to South Africa since that led by Killanin in 1967, five years before he succeeded Brundage.

When the delegation arrived in Johannesburg, it was strangely noticeable that the South African press was initially inattentive. An absence from the Olympic Games of a generation of South African competitors and journalists had bred an ignorance of the authority now enjoyed by the IOC in its relations with many of the more prominent international sports. The South African press was predominantly locked into an international sports syndrome which responded primarily to the affairs of non-Olympic cricket and rugby. The ice-breaking arrival of the IOC left most South African papers unmoved – until the news conference on the day of departure. Yet the delegation found their reception from politicians enthusiastic. Following meetings with all five sports bodies in Johannesburg – now amalgamated as the Interim National Olympic Committee of South Africa – the delegation travelled to Cape Town, where President de Klerk made repeated references to 'the new South Africa'. de Klerk made evident his awareness that international sport could hold one of the keys to a stable South African future, and spoke of sport's 'electric effect on nation-building'. He confirmed the National Party's intention to abolish the last of the apartheid laws in June.

Following the conference in Cape Town, the delegation flew to Ulundi in Kwazulu to meet Chief Mangosuthu Buthelezi; and the following day, at an undisclosed destination, Nelson Mandela. 'Sport will hasten the process, and the progress, of rationalization,' Chief Buthelezi said. 'Sport can be a tool of change, an example to other cultures, for sport is as much a way of life for South African blacks as for South African whites.' Apartheid had denied black South Africa a thousand human rights, and among them had been the presence at the Olympic Games of one this planet's most handsome peoples: runners and throwers, boxers and wrestlers, of mythological strength and grace. 'Sport coaches people for higher office,' Chief Buthelezi said, 'and does so in such a way that the checks and balances which are there in democracy are made to work because people want them to work. There is so much aggression in South Africa, as a consequence of many decades of harsh racist rule, that anything that will help turn political competition into political co-operation is vitally needed. The lesson sport has for us is that competition is only permissible when it is played within the rules. There are rules of the game to be played in South Africa, and it is vital that South Africa's political leaders should borrow from the sports world the spirit with which competition becomes exhilarating....

'Everything in South Africa is going to be in crisis during the years that lie ahead, after a multi-party democracy has been established. That also includes sport. You cannot re-distribute sports centres. You can only add to them. The millions of blacks living outside convenient travelling distances to existing facilities will have to be provided with new facilities.... If the IOC and foreign governments begin insisting on *more* than a merely honest nationwide struggle to establish democracy, then we are going to be condemned to remain outside the international sporting community for as far ahead as one can see.' As de Klerk had said, while governments can change laws, sport can change minds.

The following morning, Nelson Mandela assured the delegation that he was willing to give full support to the actions and objectives of the new Interim NOC. 'His willingness to help enabled us to be free to continue along the present path,' Jean-Claude Ganga said on return to Johannesburg. 'His approval was essential.' Kevan Gosper said that all doors were now open, and South African sport could utilize its relationship with ANOCA. At a crowded press conference at Jan Smuts Airport, Keba M'Baye was able to announce the granting of temporary recognition to South Africa by the IOC – and by ANOCA – for the first time since SANOC was expelled in 1970. The temporary recognition was dependent on six conditions:

1) The abolition of the apartheid laws, as promised by de Klerk.

2) INOCSA to comply, in structure and action, with the Olympic Charter.

3) INOCSA to establish a proper constitution of its committee, and to encourage normalization of relationships between South African national sports federations and respective International Federations.

4) The pursuit of unification in sport on a non-racial basis.

5) Normalization of INOCSA's relationship with the Association of NOCs of Africa (ANOCA).

6) Continuation for the time being of the moratorium on international competition.

'Under circumstances of the recent past, and developments within South Africa, the IOC have the ability to show flexibility and compassion,' Kevan Gosper said. 'What we've done is to give South Africa an opportunity.' Many black South Africans and especially the South African Council on Sport (SACOS) were likely to remain cautious during the six-month trial period of temporary recognition. The radical/liberal *Weekly Mail*, with a circulation of 30,000, questioned whether abolition of the apartheid laws was sufficient for normalization of life in South Africa, yet the IOC's social intervention could go only so far.

Dr Willie Basson, chairman of the Confederation of South African Sports (COSAS), the assembly of governing bodies which had withdrawn from INOCSA the previous weekend because its members – including many non-Olympic sports – could not guarantee to uphold the moratorium, expressed concern about finance within the 'new' South Africa. 'It's not a question of South African sport returning to international competition,' Basson said. 'That is going to happen. The problem is the disparity in conditions between the five million sports activists and the twenty-five million without opportunity. Sport is going to need between two and three billion Rand [up to $1 billion], and how is that going to be possible in post-apartheid sport with zero national growth rate? We (COSAS) are less concerned with international sport than pursuing broad-base internal needs.' It would be important, he said, that INOCSA became democratically elected, and not an *ad hoc* committee created among officials with vested interests. 'INOCSA has a vital role to play,' M'Baye said. 'They can bring together all other organizations, and confirm adherence to the Olympic Charter.'

The cloud on the horizon was, and would continue to be, the politically motivated activity of the South African Council on Sport (SACOS), led by its chairman Harry Hendricks, who represented the opposite pole from Mluleki George. 'We [NOSC] were the first to talk of unification,' George said to me during the delegation's visit, 'and we were doing this at a time when SACOS and others were still insisting on the principle of "No normal sport in an abnormal society". Yet if we had continued this, when would unification have ever begun? We were the first to say that South African sport had to prepare itself for the future, for the freedom that was coming. We are no longer as radical as SACOS. Can we now carry them with us? That's very hard to predict. It is one thing to insist that normalization must be total, that everyone should have the vote in addition to the abolition of the apartheid laws. But if you wait too long, then by the time absolute freedom arrives, what will have become of sport? You will have problems. The compromise on principle – of not demanding *absolute* freedom and equality – can help to pull in the extremes of radicals on both sides. The thing that would prevent the compromise working is if we move too fast. I'm expecting a split among the whites. I don't think the AWB [the far-right conservative whites] will move with us. But if foreign sports tours begin again once the moratorium is over, will the AWB stay on the sideline? We, the non-racialists, believe unification must be achieved for the sake of sport. We must be honest: the conservative whites *and* the radical blacks. It's possible. I believe it's going to work.' Only time will tell; and when the IOC come to consider electing a South African member to their ranks –

the last having been Reginald Honey, who died in 1982 – then George, who was tortured as a political prisoner yet has led a counter-social revolution from within South African sport, will be one of the front-runners.

The decision by M'Baye's delegation, to grant temporary readmission, was duly approved by the IOC Session at Birmingham three months later; and in July, at a special meeting of the Apartheid Commission in Lausanne, the readmission was given outright recognition, immediately endorsed by Samaranch and the executive board, under authority delegated to it by the Session in Birmingham. M'Baye and his colleagues, encouraged by the evidence of an accelerating move towards the formation of single, non-racial governing bodies of individual sports in South Africa, together with removal of the apartheid laws in June, felt able to recommend this historic step. In line with Samaranch's principle, the decision had been taken by a preponderance of blacks: M'Baye, Adefope, Ganga, Lamine Ba, Kidane, Ramsamy, and, a recent addition to the Apartheid Commission, Andrew Young, the former United States Ambassador to the United Nations, former mayor of Atlanta, and a lieutenant of Martin Luther King during his human rights campaign. The recommendation of the Commission was:

> Having met with INOCSA in Lausanne on July 9, 1991, in the presence of ANOCA; and considering that, by virtue of the abolition of the laws of apartheid, INOCSA can from now on respect the Olympic Charter, has undertaken to do so, and has successfully embarked on the unification of sports in South Africa on a non-racial basis . . . that the IOC President and executive board formally endorse this effectiveness by proclaiming the outright recognition of the National Olympic Committee of South Africa and draw therefrom all legal consequences, *subject to review of its implementation in the light of (determining) events relating to sport in South Africa* [author's italics].

The last clause clearly gave the IOC an option of withdrawal, should political conditions seriously deteriorate. Meanwhile, within the hour, Samaranch had drafted a letter to Sam Ramsamy, INOCSA's president, confirming full recognition, while stressing the following urgent requirements:

> To intensify work towards non-racial unification of South African sport; to accelerate normalization between national federations and IFs, and of South Africa within ANOCA; to seek assurance from national and local government on non-discriminatory access to facilities; to pursue egalitarian, non-racial training of competitors.

The cloud, however, remained. SACOS had refused to attend the conference in Lausanne, though not withdrawing from INOCSA, and was pressing for the retention of trade sanctions and the international sports boycott. SACOS in the coming months would continue to disrupt attempts to create unified national federations, and was directly responsible for the failure of South Africa to be able to send a team to the world athletics championships in Tokyo at the end of August, despite elaborate attempts by the IAAF to facilitate their participation.

The motivation of the black Africans who had recommended the readmission was that which I had been pursuing for eight or nine years. 'Because there is not yet political franchise in South Africa,' Lamine Ba, the secretary-general of the Supreme Council for Sport in Africa, said, 'the democracy of one-man-one-vote that will now be operating in sports administration will be an example and a social force. *That* is why we accepted them. The biggest problem is in the minds of people, and the establishment on the ground of non-racial policies. The apartheid laws may have gone, but apartheid, in facilities and administration, will continue to some degree because of unavoidable economic discrimination. There has to be a change of spirit among whites, that there *is* a new situation, that training facilities must be available equally to blacks and coloured [Asian or mixed race] people. There is so much to achieve, such as the constitution of new clubs. The Organization of African Unity can help, but only when we know what are South Africa's priorities.'

In mid-1991, unified federations were being formed almost by the week. Football, basketball, boxing, tennis, table tennis: these and others were already fact, on the table awaiting ratification of their constitution. A unified athletics body, amalgamating former white, black and coloured governing bodies, was formed, but the coloured members, under pressure from Hendricks, would not agree to participation in Tokyo. The irony of this was that the SACOS-affiliated coloured athletics governing body, the former Board, had few athletes; for some years, more than 90 per cent of *all* South African athletes, of whatever race, had competed under the flag of the former white but now non-racial Union, which had initiated the formation, under its leaders Joe Stutzen and Gert Le Roux, together with Mluleki George, of the unified SA Amateur Athletic Association.

Meanwhile, Dr Basson, of COSAS, was saying: 'This [readmission] will be a catalyst for a sporting explosion, both among competitors and in commercial activity that has been internationally dormant for so long. The government will realize that sport is a vehicle into the outside world and to international respectability.'

On 26 July 1991, Jean-Claude Ganga, as president of ANOCA, wrote to Ibrahim Gambari, chairman of the United Nations' Special

Committee Against Apartheid, explaining the background to the IOC's decision, in the course of which he said:

> My [first] visit to South Africa gave me the opportunity for realizing that there had been many changes in sports. These had been felt in the composition of clubs, the utilization of facilities by all racial groups, as well as in the willingness of all sports leaders to work towards unification.... The fact that our brother Sam Ramsamy, who has been for the last twenty years the leading figure in the struggle against racial discrimination in sports in South Africa, is now chairman of the NOC, gives every reason to think the process will go along satisfactory lines. Everything is not yet perfect: one-man-one-vote is to come. What matters is that there are no more laws forbidding any South African to practise sport in any area. It is important for the UN to realize that sport is like religion, based on a sacred book, i.e., the sports regulations. . . . As soon as there is no racial discrimination in sport, there is no reason why South Africa should not be readmitted to the international sports movement ... Our struggle against discrimination has been so consistent that the international community will hopefully trust us regarding the decision the IOC has taken upon our request.

Another black African campaigning, through the channels of the IAAF, to pull South Africa back into the fold was Lamine Diack, a vice-president of the IAAF. He had been part of a separate athletics delegation which had visited the country, and it was particularly frustrating for him that the attempt to get South Africa to the championships in Tokyo met with failure. 'Athletics can be the way to help change the mind of South Africa,' Diack says. 'I know Hendricks, and his principles, but what is important to me is the youth of South Africa, the mass sports movement. We can maybe wait another six months, but we can't wait another fifteen years. If SACOS maintain their position, we shall ignore them, and I think that in a few years they will disappear [as a credible force].'

Yet the influence of SACOS on the coloured membership of sporting governing bodies continued to be disruptive throughout the South African summer of 1991-92, threatening the unanimity of the country's return to the Olympic Games in Barcelona. This was most damagingly so in athletics, in which a series of meetings between the three separate former governing bodies failed to produce agreement on a constitution that would facilitate affiliation to the International Federation. In December 1991, the former union – white body – unrealistically demanded 50 per cent of the voting power within a new triumvirate.

Although F.W. de Klerk, the premier, had paid fulsome lip service to the values of South Africa's readmission in June 1991, the national government subsequently had not allocated one rand extra towards the preparation of an Olympic team. The undercurrent of racial friction, which was bound to continue for some years following so long a period of inequalities, boiled to the surface once more when the new, integrated Olympic Committee announced that it would not use in Barcelona the revered springbok symbol nor the existing anthem and national flag; instead, the team would compete, as had Britain and others in 1980, under the Olympic flag and anthem. This was a diplomatic and understandable step by a committee under pressure from all sides, but was met with hostility by the whites of the extreme right. Hoping to stabilize the situation, the IOC decided to send a second delegation to South Africa early in 1992.

For no one was the frustration greater than Joe Stutzen, who as a Jew is well aware of the ramifications of discrimination. Yet for twenty years no one in the world of sport has fought harder for non-racial rights than he. Even when the departure of his team for Tokyo was torpedoed by a fax message from Hendricks, sent to Nebiolo in Tokyo, falsely claiming that South African 'athletes' were not unified, Stutzen refused to remain downcast; he had fought too long on behalf of black compatriots now to be deflected, even when a further attempt at pan-African unification by Diack – a proposed Unity Games embracing South Africa to be staged in Dakar and Johannesburg in October 1991 – was also forced to be postponed. As Charles Mukora, the IOC member for Kenya and vice-chairman of the Commonwealth Games Federation, observed: 'The debate has to become more open between politics and sport, because it is inevitable that suspicions are still there between people who have previously not been talking to each other. There are many pressures on South Africa's sportsmen, but they have to understand that development goes hand in hand with participation.'

Writing about the IOC's initiative, Andrew Young, who 25 years before had campaigned with Martin Luther King in Alabama against the racial intransigence of Governor George Wallace, explained what, to some Americans and many other non-South Africans, seemed an anomaly:

> There is no endorsement of apartheid here, no compromise with Olympic principles. . . . The newly-formed Committee (NOC) includes people of all races who have struggled all their lives against apartheid and who are well-prepared, with the support of the IOC, to train and field teams of all South Africans. South Africa must now begin to build an inclusive society. Nothing can make any more powerful impact on the attitudes of all South Africans than the emotional involvement with sports teams, that reflect the kind of pride and spirit the country desperately needs. The first South African to win an

> Olympic gold medal will become a national hero. Most nations have realized the importance of sport for multi-national unity and pride. We have seen it clearly with high school athletics in small towns in Georgia. . . . South Africa is far from an integrated society. The recognition of the new NOC was no reward for those elements in the country still trying to hold back progress. It was, instead, the creation of a new force for freedom and dignity for all South Africans. . . . Soon the youth of South Africa may be able to live out the drama and conflict of life on the athletic fields rather than on the battlefields. That day cannot come too soon. The IOC Commission on Apartheid hastened that day.

'On a visit to Atlanta early in 1991, I realized that South Africa's situation was much more important to Americans, with their mixed-race population, than in Europe,' Samaranch recalls. 'Americans were worried about the way the IOC was going. I happened to meet Andrew Young together with Jesse Jackson, and was able to convince Young, who is on the Atlanta organizing committee for the Centenary Games, that he should be a member of our Apartheid Commission. It was an important step. I had information that George Bush, knowing that Young was with us in Lausanne, was waiting in July 1991 for our decision on South Africa, before announcing his own lifting of trade sanctions. With Young's involvement on our Commission, there would be less opposition to the lifting of sanctions from American blacks.

'Of course I would have been happy for South Africa to have been in Tokyo for the athletics, it would have set the tone for the Olympic Games in Barcelona. The radical blacks in South Africa tried to keep postponing the decisions, pressing for the establishment of one-man-one-vote. But when our delegation met de Klerk, he stressed that we should not keep moving the goalposts when setting terms for South Africa's return. We were encouraged in our attitude by countries such as Kenya and Japan lifting their ban on South African sport during 1991. We realized that normalization in South Africa was moving faster in sport than in other social activities. I saw a television interview of Ramsamy in South Africa by three whites, after he had said that it would be obscene for South Africa to return too swiftly to international sport, and the whites had told him that *he* was the obscenity. Prejudices remain. Yet before the autumn of 1991 there were already 24 unified sports recognized by the new South African NOC. Keba M'Baye is intervening now in *all* the main problems that the IOC has, and is without doubt one of our most prominent members.'

Jean-Claude Ganga pays tribute to Samaranch's leadership in the IOC's search for a solution. 'He always put the Africans in the front line,' he says. 'The negotiations went smoothly because of him. I have fought this issue for twenty years, I think I have done my job for Africa. If I say it is good for South Africa to return, I do not think Africans will disagree. We didn't readmit South Africa so that they could compete in the Olympic Games, but because they now fulfilled the rules, because they are integrated. The release of Mandela was important, and the ending of the pillar laws of apartheid. It is not Africa that has changed, but South Africa. SACOS is a very small minority. *We* are ANOCA, we are the IOC, and we make our decisions. The withdrawal of SACOS from the NOC is not important. I told them in Harare in 1989 that if they wanted to wait until there were no black people in prison in South Africa, until there was no marijuana on the streets, they would only see that in heaven. There was discrimination in the United States years ago, and there are still some problems today. Once we had Nelson Mandela's support of Sam Ramsamy, however, we knew we could proceed.'

If the IOC still represents a moral philosophy, it is expressed by Louis Guirandou-N'Daiye, the Ambassador for Ivory Coast: 'There is a new generation within the IOC,' he says. 'I am closer to my IOC colleagues than to my brother, and it is this that can help kill apartheid. Olympism with a human face. Everyone can believe in our principle, in which race is no more than an address. I am not an *African* IOC member, I just happen to live there, a PO Box number. Maybe I'm dreaming, but I am against groups, against blocs. If you vote against me, I do not think you are voting against Africa. With a gentleman, we can disagree, and be friends. When I was Ambassador in Ottawa for five years, the Ambassador for South Africa was a personal friend, he was just another man. In Africa we need missionaries to send the message. IOC members can lead the way.'

Late in 1991 I enjoyed an informal dinner with Sam Ramsamy, an Asian, Mluleki George, a black, and Johan Du Plessis, an Afrikaaner: three South Africans united in peaceful persuit of sport. Such a dinner could not have been possible, in 1991, without the inflluence of the IOC.

13 Bidding

If an apparent solution to the South African controversy has left the IOC in a good light, the same cannot be said, unfortunately, of the present system by which host cities are elected for the staging of the Olympic Games. The charges range from, on the mild side, ignorance or regional prejudice, to, at the worst, commercial opportunism; and even, among a small minority of IOC members, and some candidate cities, corruption in the shape of financial demands or inducements. Even if such irregularities are reduced, they bring discredit on the organization and create an urgent need for modification of the electoral system which, in the plain words of Samaranch's wife Bibis, is 'a pain'.

During the winter of 1991-92, the executive board was urgently considering ways of adjusting the system, both to reduce expenditure by bidding cities and to eliminate any scope for corrupt offers or requests by cities or IOC members. A special committee of M'Baye, Gosper and Carrard was appointed to make recommendations, but at its meeting of December 1991, the board could reach no agreement. Those such as Flor Isava-Fonseca of Venezuela, the first women member of the board, vigorously wished to preserve all rights of individual members, but there was a clear move towards a two-tier system that would reduce the number of candidates to two or three before the final vote was taken, this to include IF and NOC representatives.

Now that being elected host city has become the most lucrative prize in the entire world of sport, with high profile coverage actively encouraged by the IOC, the scope for the usual weaknesses of human nature are extensive. Within less than a decade of Los Angeles being the only candidate for 1984, the pendulum had swung to the opposite extreme, with rival cities fighting tooth and nail to stage the billion-dollar Olympic festival. It was Los Angeles, ironically, that began this commercial roller-coaster, with its profit of a quarter of a billion dollars. By the time of the election in 1986 for the Games of 1992, there were six candidates for the Summer Games and seven for the Winter Games. Spending in pursuit of the bid had become grotesque, and, by the time the Centenary Games' host for 1996 was determined at the Session in Tokyo in 1990, was even worse. Samaranch was riding a train hurtling along without brakes or signals; yet, as he reasoned, 'It is a system I inherited.'

When Atlanta was elected for 1996 rather than Athens, which was viewed on historic grounds as the logical favourite, worldwide opinion of the IOC became alarmingly cynical. Atlanta, the home of the Coca-

Cola parent company and of the influential Turner Broadcasting, was said, however inaccurately, to have 'bought' the Games. This, as far as I am able to judge from the facts available, was far from being the case. Atlanta fought an excellent campaign, while Athens repeatedly shot themselves in the foot. The IOC's public relations, however, were so poor on their second-most publicized activity after the Games themselves, that nothing could immediately change the perception of a sceptical public. In the words of a former vice-president of the IOC, when the public saw a member of the IOC, it now wondered whether it was looking at a crook.

The perception of the IOC was further worsened in 1991 by revelations in *USA Today* of multiple financial malpractices involving conflict of interest in Olympic-related affairs by Robert Helmick, USOC president and executive board member. This was a severe embarrassment to Samaranch, who had specially sought Helmick's election to the board. It was revealed that Helmick had received in excess of $300,000 in legal consultancy fees and retainers in situations where such advice was clearly not for sale by an honorary Olympic official. Helmick had received fees for advising golf on possible inclusion in the Olympics and had been on the payroll of Ted Turner's Goodwill Games, even though that event was potentially in conflict with the Olympic Games. Criticism was compounded by the almost total absence of previous disclosure of such personal interests, though Helmick persisted in maintaining his innocence, saying he had not harmed the Olympic Movement, apparently unable to understand the conflict of interest issue.

Soon after the disclosures, Helmick resigned as president of USOC, but requested his executive board colleagues to await the outcome of an inquiry instigated by USOC. The report of this inquiry by Arnold Burns, a former deputy US attorney-general, seriously condemned Helmick on eight counts. Simultaneously, and independently, an inquiry commission appointed by Samaranch, and consisting of M'Baye, Hodler and Carrard, made investigations prior to the executive board meeting of December 1991. Helmick had provisionally been replaced as USOC president by William Hybl, yet continued, under IOC Charter regulations, on the committee of both USOC and the Atlanta Games organization. USOC, rather than condemn their own man, unsatisfactorily passed the buck back to the IOC. All Samaranch's achievements over twelve years were now at risk if he and the board failed to grasp the nettle and expel Helmick – the first such action in the IOC's history.

Helmick flew to Switzerland for the executive board meeting in Lausanne on 4 December, evidently still reluctant to resign, but during 48 hours prior to the meeting he was given to understand in lengthy discussions with his colleagues that his position was untenable. With his back to the wall, Helmick finally was obliged to resign his IOC membership, and a letter to this effect was slipped under Samaranch's hotel bedroom door in the silent hours of the night. A serious moral crisis had been resolved. The Charter, of course, could not be more clear. Rule 20, sub-section 1, paragraph 5 states: 'Members of the IOC must not accept from governments, organizations or other legal entities or natural persons any mandate liable to bind them or interfere with the freedom of their action or vote.'

Helmick never understood this, and his gross indiscretion had seemingly substantiated the view of those who alleged that Atlanta's election the previous year could have been rigged. This was an intolerable situation for Samaranch, having worked so tirelessly to raise the prestige of the organization. In the mid-1980s, he had welcomed the upsurge in enthusiasm among bidding cities, which was a reflection of the new financial security. Yet Samaranch was slow to see the dangers; by the time an ineffective series of administrative regulations were introduced, on the conduct of both IOC members and bidding cities, in the summer of 1991, the damage had already been done. The IOC was caught by the democracy of its own procedure: a semi-public vote among its 90-odd members at the end of a campaign that was now conspicuously conducted for up to four years by each bidding Committee. The IOC is no more immune to human weaknesses than any other organization; certainly not when the contemporary membership, unlike former times of aristocratic and privileged individuals, contains an increasing number of people of modest means, and still a few from totalitarian regimes for whom activity on behalf of the IOC represents their only opportunity for the good, or a better, life.

The problem for Samaranch, in terms of policy, is that the election of host cities has been built upon the democracy of the membership. 'You can always complain about the system, but historically the decisions haven't been that bad,' the Princess Royal has said. 'That's one side. The other is that anything that discourages throwing money around in the bidding system – for example, having the decision taken by the executive board – would be a good idea. Yet this is the last, maybe the only, decision which the IOC members are likely to take.' Determining the site for other major sporting events might be made by processes more open to manipulation than that of the IOC, but an absence of publicity means that the decisions seldom if ever come under public scrutiny.

So excessive had the expenditure become for the bid for the Centenary Games that, when a debriefing was subsequently held in Lausanne among the candidates, Paul Henderson, the leader of Toronto's bid, suggested stringent new regulations to the executive board. Henderson, a former Olympic yachtsman, and now vice-president of the International Yacht Racing Union, who has a prosperous business in plumbing, was rightly appalled that his Committee should pay three-quarters of a million dollars on their 'technical bid book' alone: a glossy presentation to the members, some of whom would do no more than glance through it. Following the debriefing, and observations from Robert Scott, the leader of the Manchester bid for 1996, and others besides Henderson, the IOC issued in 1991 new guidelines for candidates bidding for the Games of 2000. At the time of writing these included Berlin, Brasilia, Istanbul, Manchester, Milan, Peking and Sydney. The guidelines were:

- Air tickets for IOC members visiting bid cities to be supplied by the IOC, non-refundable to the individual, and reimbursed by the city to the IOC.
- A $200 limit on any gift, these to be primarily small souvenirs.
- No receptions, cocktail parties, etc. to be given, and no breakfast, luncheon or dinner beyond normal subsistence during maximum three-day visits.
- No boat, restaurant or club to be used for meetings, which were to be restricted to a single room or suite.
- Prior to the day of voting, no exhibition, demonstration or other event.
- Bid book documents on technical proposals to be on A4 format paper, other than maps.
- City delegations visiting conferences of IOC/IFs/NOCs to be kept to six members or less.
- Serious or repeated breach of these regulations to bring disqualification.
- No visit by cities to the country of IOC members where a member has already specifically visited that city.

Establishment of cure is admission of ailment. At the time this seemed like closing the stable door after the horse had bolted, and it was soon evident that the IOC still lacked the will to enforce the rules. Allegations of corrupt practices either by bidding cities or by a small minority of members might be exaggerated, yet the final responsibility for the proper conduct of its affairs must lie with the IOC, rather than with potential host cities whose enthusiasm it seeks. I have heard sufficient first-hand reports alleging that IOC members have charged for two or more separate first-class air fares when in fact travelling on one round-trip to believe that in a minority of instances this has happened. There are uncomfortable stories of insurance compensation claimed for alleged jewellery thefts from hotel bedrooms while on city-inspection visits. The advent of campaigns in which a dozen cities are simultaneously bidding for Summer or Winter Games has provided IOC members with both a burdensome responsibility, if they treat the matter seriously, and the scope for enjoying a constant globe-trotting existence. I would say, from personal observation, that the vast majority of both IOC members and of senior officials of bidding cities over the past ten years have conducted themselves honourably. Equally, I have not the slightest doubt that there are some who have sought improperly to exploit the situation to their own advantage.

Fifteen years ago, the staging of an Olympic Games was seen as a road to disaster; now, the level of television and sponsorship fees has turned it into a golden egg for any successful city, creating a platform for the development not only of multiple-sports facilities and venues, but for a basic infrastructure of road, rail, housing and airports. It is hardly surprising that candidate cities are now willing to spend anything up to twenty million dollars on the bidding campaign alone.

Helping to create this incentive has been the decision by Samaranch to permit the televising of the voting announcement. This showbusiness event, running for up to an hour, though admirable in raising the profile of the IOC and projecting the affairs of the Olympic Games to an ever-wider audience, serves as a justification for expenditure by the candidates. Moreover, the continuous exposure in the media, internationally, over a period of several years, culminating with the televised highlight, gives a projection that could never be bought by the same expenditure in straightforward television or press advertising. In other words, the IOC is a party to the extravagance. The television 'shows' that we have witnessed four times – in Lausanne (in 1986, for the Summer Games of '92), in Seoul (1988, for the Winter Games of '94), in Tokyo (1990, for the Summer Games of '96), and in Birmingham (1991, for the Winter Games of '98) – were dramatic and entertaining, yet represented something deeply wrong within the Movement. The process is seriously flawed, even if the cause is legitimate. It is a competition in which everyone but the winner is suddenly shot between the eyes when the President of the IOC opens an envelope in front of the cameras to announce the result. While the Committee, and citizens, of a single city leap in delight, start pouring the champagne and commence the reality of their city's structural conversion, defeated candidates are in an instant left numb with shock. Several hundreds of workers, many of them volunteers, are left with a sense of emptiness, frustration and betrayed optimism.

The IOC members gather to decide, without any set of rules or regulations to guide their consideration, and cast their votes sometimes ensibly, sometimes provocatively. The last two occasions – the votes for the Summer Games of '96 and the Winter Games of '98 – have in my opinion been especially damaging. On the first, it had been evident for more than a year that Athens, on many counts, was not the most practical candidate. The name of Athens should only have been allowed to go forward as an *unchallenged* candidate on the grounds of historic tradition. To have allowed Athens to be entered in open competition, with the possibility that it might be defeated, was, taking account of public perception, self-destructive for the IOC's reputation.

On the second occasion, the election in Birmingham in 1991 presented three candidates, Ostersund of Sweden, Salt Lake City of the United States, and Nagano of Japan, that were almost equally worthy for differing reasons: Ostersund was an outstandingly compact and attractive bid from a country that has repeatedly attempted yet never staged a Winter Games. Nagano, though still needing to construct most facilities, offered the chance for expansion of the Movement in the Orient, and what would be only the second Winter Games in Asia. Salt Lake City offered facilities for competition, accommodation and transport without previous parallel; yet they were up against the disadvantage of Atlanta having been a criticized nomination the previous year for the Summer Games as a *fifth* North American host in a twenty-year span. The outcome – Nagano, by four votes – was unbearably dramatic, wholly democratic, and utterly unfair on the two losers. It is already too late to prevent the Olympic family enduring this procedure in the vote for the Games of 2000, which will take place in even more lavish surroundings, with greater hyperbole than ever, at Monte Carlo in 1993. Samaranch has a duty to modify what is at one and the same time both a glorious coronation and a multiple public execution. Nagano were helped by a probable unofficial deal in which Chic Igaya of Japan withdrew as vice-president candidate, leaving Smirnov unopposed, in return for possibly five or six Eastern European votes.

'We have to follow the system by which our members take the decision, voting until one city receives an outright majority,' Samaranch said defensively following the Nagano election. 'Other federations, such as FIFA and the IAAF, do it another way, involving only their executive committee, or their council. As you know, we have looked at the rules regarding the campaign, and have made further alterations, concerning travel and expenditure. Maybe we have to go even further, and have even tougher conditions. One of the problems with bidding cities is that sometimes it is too much of a private enterprise, without the full co-ordination of local government. I believe that the bidding committee has a responsibility to advise their own population on the possibility that they may not win, whereas what happens much of the time is that the bidding committee explains only the positive advantages of the campaign – what can be achieved when the city is successful – and never discusses the chances that they may lose. That cannot be seen to be our responsibility. It is suggested that we should introduce a rotating system of geographic zones, to prevent different zones, Asia, Europe and America, simultaneously bidding against each other. But if we were to do that we would have to change the slogan that the Olympic Movement belongs to the world, that any city should be at liberty if it wishes to bid for any Games.

'Our responsibility, as the IOC, is to try to award the Games to what will be the best city in the interest of the competitors. Yet which is the best? Do you give it to a city which already has existing facilities and is offering these as a "gift" to the Olympic Movement? Or do you give it to a city which will utilize the opportunity to produce new facilities that would be a legacy to future generations of competitors? Each is deserving. If a city already has a profusion of facilities, that demonstrates an existing need for the facilities among the population and is a strong case for deserving the Games. To a degree, we are in a situation where whatever we do will be both right and wrong.'

Another of the ways in which the IOC made a rod for its own back, in my opinion, during the campaign for the Summer Games of 1996 – once the possibility to nominate Athens by unanimous acclaim had been waived – was not to have publicized the findings of the Evaluation Commission. These quite clearly indicated that, on technical merit, Athens was not in the category of either Atlanta or Melbourne. This was partly a public relations failure. The findings of the Evaluation Commission, even had they been disclosed after the vote, might have reduced the flak that whistled around the IOC's ears immediately their decision became known. Procedure repeatedly traps the IOC. Thirty years ago, when it took decisions, hardly anyone noticed until a month or a year later. Now, by its own design, its decisions are being revealed simultaneously, yet it is still attempting to conduct its affairs in the manner of an unaccountable private club.

Following the vote for Atlanta, Richard Pound, from Montreal, at the time a vice-president, said that the decision had been a philosophical watershed: 'The divide between those looking backward to 1896 and those looking toward the twenty-first century. It was not, as was suggested, a rejection of the traditional values offered by Athens, but two different influences at play.' Pound was one of those who had ventured to voice warnings about the administrative difficulties that could confront the IOC were Athens elected: finance, transport/pollution, security: all these were potential hazards for a tiny nation attempting to handle an Olympic family in excess of twenty thousand people. A year before the election, George Papandreou, a former Minister of Education heavily involved in the preparation of the Athens bid, Melina Mercouri, at that time the Greek Minister of Culture, and Nikos Filaretos and Lambis Nikolaou, the two IOC members, had admitted to me that cultural heritage and tradition could only be regarded as a bonus when it came to influencing voters, not as factors that could be the basis for their campaign. That was the theory; in practice, however, the Greeks, as if unable to help themselves, behaved right up to the time of the election as though they did have a *right* to host the Centenary Games. Simultaneously, the Greeks were as expedient in their motives as any other city. They saw in the Olympic Games an opportunity to cure the many ills of their cramped and polluted capital, and to gain the emotional support of the population for a programme of expenditure on infrastructure that was bound to impose sacrifices on a small country with limited resources. Moreover, when it came to moral issues, the human rights card that was heavily played by Atlanta, utilizing the personalities of Andrew Young and Anita DeFrantz, the IOC's first black woman member, was always likely to be as powerful, internationally, as the more sentimental, abstract appeal being peddled by Athens. The contribution to the modern Olympics by Greece is slight compared to Britain's initiation and nurture of many Olympic sports.

In the event, there were many factors that pointed to the decision not being commercially influenced by Coca-Cola; not least that, of the 28 votes that became available during rounds two, three and four, with the successive elimination of Belgrade, Manchester and Melbourne, only 15 went to Atlanta. That hardly smacks of vote-fixing. The Atlanta Committee, who, when their campaign had begun three years earlier, hardly knew an IOC member from a hotel porter, had fought their way to the front on five counts. Firstly, William Payne, their lawyer-president, Charlie Battle, another lawyer, and Ginger Watkins, a campaigning housewife, had been the essence of courtesy, modesty and efficiency; clearly projecting the message that the city's potential both in its facilities and its tourist accommodation, was outstanding. Secondly, the human rights factor would emotionally have polled votes throughout the Third World. Thirdly, eastern European and Third World members were *legitimately* attracted to North American prosperity, in the same way that, two years earlier, Commonwealth Games members had voted for Victoria, British Columbia, rather than for New Delhi, which would have been the first Asian host of the Games. Fourthly, the existing anti-Athens tide was magnified on the day by the Greeks' tactical blunders: Spyros Metaxa, the Athens chairman, had stated that Athens would never enter again if rejected; Nikolaou was heard to say as the Greeks left the conference room following their presentation that no further debate was now necessary; while news of a discourteous press conference had also filtered back to the IOC members during the luncheon break. Fifthly, there was resistance to a suspected preference by Samaranch himself for Athens. Marc Hodler, of Switzerland, said afterwards that Athens had got what they deserved, while Anthony Bridge, of Jamaica, felt that Athens had been pointing a gun at the members.

Andrew Young expressed the opposite of the view that would fill newspapers around the world the following morning. 'We hope we've taken commercialism out of sport by taking commercialism for granted,' Young said. 'With no financial problems, we can concentrate on Olympic ideals. If you are struggling for money, then you will struggle for ideals too.' The world's press was not at that moment listening to Andrew Young. Billy Payne said, amid the elation of hundreds of volunteer workers: 'Anyone close to the Olympic Movement would be able to discern that our bid has not been about money and sponsorship, but about people. We have conclusively established that it was not based on commercialism. It is just that we are fortunate to be living in prosperity.'

The round by round voting was:

Athens	23	23	26	30	35
Atlanta	19	20	26	34	51
Belgrade	7	–	–	–	–
Manchester	11	5	–	–	–
Melbourne	12	21	16	–	–
Toronto	14	17	18	22	–

From these figures it can be seen that nearly two thirds of the members present preferred *either* of the North American candidates to Athens – additional evidence that support had not been 'arranged' for Atlanta. For 22 members to have supported Toronto in the fourth round, when Atlanta and Athens had been level in the third, was a clear indication of independence of mind. Yet still the newspapers would cry 'fix'.

'The bidding process *is* showbusiness,' Lord Killanin reflects, 'and I suspect that Samaranch was worried about the Games having gone to Atlanta, returning to North America too much. I would have liked them to go to Australia [a common neutral view, including my own]. It is difficult for lesser candidates to pull in the votes. I remember Dennis Howell, who was leading the Birmingham bid for 1992, telling me that he had been promised twelve votes. I told him he'd be lucky to get two loyal Brits, and he was most annoyed!'

In early summer 1990, I had begun to hear indirectly of Samaranch expressing unofficial support for Athens, the first time when attending a seminar in Newport, Rhode Island. The same news reached Billy Payne, who a month before the election observed to Samaranch: 'If you are supporting Athens, then we withdraw.'

One member of the executive board at the time is known to have said to Samaranch that if he really did want Athens, then he had better remain President until 1996 so as to deal with all the problems that would ensue. Alex Gilady of NBC, a close reader of such situations, is of the opinion that Samaranch thought it his duty as President to try to deliver Athens; but that his lobbying was imperceptibly conducted around the world, never with fellow IOC members. Gilady also reflects on the arrogance of the Greeks – one of their committee apparently returned to the hotel the night before the vote, after entertaining (illegally) several IOC members at a Greek taverna, and asserted: 'The IOC members will never *dare* not to vote for Athens.' What the Greeks may not have realized was that many of those with technical reponsibilities for the staging of the Games were deeply anxious about the problems Athens might present. Gilady had said to Richard Pound; 'If you want people to vote for Toronto, give them two free tickets to go and stay at any hotel in Athens.'

Paul Henderson, leader of the Toronto bid, also suspected that Samaranch was siding with Athens, yet says: 'I always found him incredibly open, available, talkative. I felt he was always trying to be compassionate, that he cared. I felt that he was being like an uncle towards me. I knew as well as anyone that you can take no notice of what other IOC members are telling you beforehand, that ninety members will have promised four-hundred votes in different directions. In my opinion, the Evaluation Commission should reduce the candidates to a maximum of four about eighteen months beforehand, the IF presidents and the IOC should then reduce that to two, and the IOC members should take the final decision. There should be *no* promotion by cities until the list is reduced to four. I would also prohibit the IOC travelling on inspection tours and bringing guests or children, and I would ban *all* gifts.'

Perhaps the most relevant of all Henderson's proposals is that the voting figures should not be disclosed round by round, other than for the tellers to announce which city has been eliminated on the least vote. This, of course, would oblige members to decide on their first choice and stay with it from the first round, eliminating tactical voting during the early rounds – members supporting candidates initially to which they will not give their final vote.

'You never get what you deserve, you get what you negotiate,' Samaranch observes in a way definitive of his own style. 'It was not possible to say "1996 *belongs* to Athens"; you have to work for it. The IOC works in strange ways, unpredictable: one plus one is five minus three. It's a pity in such an institution that you can't be logical. When I went to Melbourne, the whole city was full of posters, you could feel that the bid was for the people. In Athens there was *nothing*. Atlanta were the most professional people, the essence of what public relations today should be. The key was their timing: they arrived at the peak of their campaign the day before the election, with a personal letter to the IOC members signed by George Bush. Toronto had been front-runners, but they peaked too early. Melbourne worked very well, and the way they lost votes on the third round, dropping from twenty-one to sixteen, was strange. It was a shame the Greeks were not united and did not present themselves in a better way. A city should not push the way they did. As President, I have to say I think it was a pity they were not elected. The one thing that could have united the country, all political parties, was the Olympic Games.'

Lambis Nikolaou claimed that the decision was a disaster for the IOC, that the IOC was corrupt. If that were so, then surely he and Filaretos should have resigned. Up to the present time, they have not done so. It seems unlikely that the proposal, raised several times in the past, for a permanent Olympic home within Greece, can ever again have credibility. Such a romantic hypothesis had been put forward to Lord Killanin in the 1970s by Constantin Karamanlis, the then Greek Prime Minister. Quite apart from practical questions of ownership, funding, distribution/accountability of profit or loss, use between Olympic Games, and maintenance – none of them addressed by Karamanlis – the proposal ignores one of the fundamental attractions of the Games: that they do move around the world. The idea that a permanent home in Greece would avoid the necessity of negotiating a deal with a varying complexion of foreign governments overlooked the question of the volatility of the government of the month in Greece.

If Payne and Young provided much of the dignity of the Atlanta campaign, Charlie Battle, another lawyer, provided the friendly informality that earned allegience wherever he went. For two years, it seemed, if you glanced up in an airport lounge or hotel lobby almost anywhere in the world, there was Charlie Battle. There was one week during the campaign in which, out of seven nights, he spent five in the air. He was constantly impressed by how informed, and informal, Samaranch always was, 'I'd been to an EANOC meeting in Malta on one occasion, and was joining Billy Payne in Lausanne, via Rome,' Battle recalls. 'It was over a hundred degrees [37 centigrade], and I was dressed in jeans and a T-shirt, no socks. When I went to collect my luggage at Geneva, there was Samaranch. Should I introduce myself and perhaps blow Atlanta's chances?! Yet he instantly remembered who I was, and started asking me questions about Malta. Wherever I met him, *he* tended to know the results of our baseball matches.'

If the quality of the IOCs decisions is publicly questioned today, it was ever thus. In 1966, when *The Times* carried a letter signed by 26 British Olympic medal winners requesting the transfer of endurance events at the forthcoming Games in Mexico City in 1968 to a new venue at sea level, Lord Exeter confirmed that the acclimatization/altitude factor in Mexico had not been discussed and probably would not be. When the IOC's membership – then including one king, two princes, four lords, four generals, two knights, one rajah, one grand duke and one sheikh – who had selected Mexico City, now met in Rome to determine a site for 1972, none would have an idea by what means they would determine between Detroit, Munich and Montreal. The seven communist members did not want Munich, while most of the others fancied a return to Europe, following consecutive Games in Asia and Central America. Detroit, incidentally, was bidding for the ninth time, so perhaps Sweden need not feel too unhappy about their contemporary failure to win the Winter Games.

Gossip within the Olympic Movement is as fascinating, or mischievous, as in any other walk of life. It did not help the reputation of Atlanta, for instance, that Andrew Young should be heard saying, the night before the election in Tokyo, that fifty votes for the morrow were *secure*: no doubt an innocent and optimistic remark. The rumours about Atlanta were no worse than they had been four years earlier surrounding the election for 1992 of Barcelona, Samaranch's home town. Yet again, a study of the voting pattern, with a minority of votes for Barcelona in the first two rounds, would seem to indicate that Samaranch's influence was not decisive. Throughout the Barcelona campaign, indeed, Samaranch had studiously refrained from any mention of any country. He has several times said to me that his feelings were divided equally between pride at his city being nominated and anxiety about the myriad of problems that he knew were likely to arise and could result in severe reflected discredit.

When he addressed the Session at Lausanne in 1986, prior to the vote for 1992, he revealed an understandable euphoria at the galaxy of thirteen cities contending for the two Games, Winter and Summer. 'For the first time in many years,' he said, 'we're going to have to choose for the designation from among six and seven cities on three continents. I would like to take the opportunity of thanking them all for this expression of confidence and faith in the Olympic ideal and in its future. We can only rejoice at this very tough but friendly competition, even though at the same time we regret that not all the continents are taking part to the same extent. That is one of the points to which we shall have to give our attention in the near future, if we really wish to ensure the universality of our Movement.'

His satisfaction came from a sheltered view. Public criticism of the $50m that had been spent collectively by the candidates on their campaigns, Birmingham's having been the least expensive among the Summer candidates, was already drawing contempt on the IOC at a time when there were many millions starving in the depressed areas of the world. Entertaining by Paris and Barcelona in the attempt to outmanoeuvre each other had been lavish indeed, while even Birmingham spent $25,000 in giving a dinner aboard a yacht moored at Vidy. That expense paled beside the marble floor of Barcelona's exhibition stand, allegedly costing six times as much. The year before, for the Session at Berlin, Brisbane had flown in all the way from Australia a dinner of Tasman Sea fish. The excess had already become grotesque, though there were moments of light relief; as when Tessa Sanderson, the black British javelin gold medallist at the Los Angeles Games, having been introduced to King Constantine, nowadays an honorary member of the IOC, on board the boat at Vidy, cheerfully called out ''bye, King' as she left. Duke Ellington and Count Basie she knew, and this presumably was some Greek bouzouki player. Constantine dined out on the story for months.

The contest for the Summer Games of 1992 was a two-horse race. Belgrade were not serious – though well-equipped with indoor stadia; Amsterdam were critically sabotaged by environmental protestors; Brisbane had more spirit, in the personality of their mayoress, Sally-Anne Atkinson, than substance; and Birmingham, commendably making the first British bid for forty years, undermined their chances by failing, through political prejudice, to establish a clear political line through to Prime Minister Thatcher and by claiming that they were going 'to give the Games back to the athletes'. Who, the critics asked, had taken them away?

Jacques Chirac, the French Premier, in a brilliant address, all but swept the IOC members off their feet, and had the vote been taken immediately, Paris might well have succeeded; never mind that their bid at that stage had nothing to offer but Paris, which, being French, they considered sufficient. Barcelona, in spite of a dismal presentation, nonetheless won, this probably being a political compromise. Confronted by French candidates in both Games, the members awarded the Winter Games to Albertville – a decision that was to prove laden with hazards – and gave Barcelona, making its fourth bid in sixty years, the Summer Games. While there was no doubt in my mind that Barcelona was the correct choice, many people – though not IOC members – would have preferred the innovative bid by Sofia, in Bulgaria, for the Winter Games. This was the voting:

Summer Games			
Amsterdam	5	–	–
Barcelona	29	37	47
Belgrade	13	11	5
Birmingham	8	8	–
Brisbane	11	9	10
Paris	19	20	23

Winter Games						
Albertville (France)	19	26	29	42	–	51
Anchorage (USA)	7	5	–	–	–	–
Berchtesgarten (WG)	6	–	–	–	–	–
Cortina (Italy)	7	6	7	–	–	–
Falun (Sweden)	10	11	11	9	41	9
Lillehammer (Norway)	10	11	9	9	40	–
Sofia (Bulgaria)	25	25	28	24	–	25

Samaranch had not slept for a week, and the night before the vote he rose at three and was having breakfast by five. The evening before, he had studiously not spoken to a soul, which many took to be an indication of what he expected of them. Alain Coupat, his former *chef de bureau*, recollects: 'Following the success of Los Angeles, Samaranch had lengthy talks with the Spanish Prime Minister regarding the candidacy of Barcelona. He talked to the King, to Pasqual Maragal, the mayor, to Leopoldo Rodes, a prominent banker and close friend. On one hand he didn't want to be a supporter, on the other he wanted to be sure they arranged their bid properly. His office at Vidy was often busy with visiting Catalans. Of course he helped them, but the biggest help was the number of candidates. Had there been only two, I think the membership would have polarized more around Paris, so it helped him when Brisbane and Birmingham came in.'

Samaranch admits that some members probably voted for Barcelona specifically because he *didn't* ask them – Gafner, Hodler, Siperco and others. 'For me, it would have been much better not to have had Barcelona as a candidate,' Samaranch says. 'I was involved in the committee at the beginning, and I had to remind them that it was not the Olympic family but only the IOC members who voted. They worked with a very small team: Rodes, Carlos Ferrer, Varela, Ignacio Masferrer and Kata Bosch. It was a good team.'

The work of Rodes was exceptional. There were occasions when he would fly overnight on Saturday to Latin America to join two or three IOC members at, say, a football match in Mexico or Brazil on Sunday, then fly home again overnight to be in the office on Monday morning. He estimates that in the course of the campaign he travelled to meet ninety IOC members individually an average of seven times each. 'Juan Antonio adopted a very distant position after the early stages,' Rodes recollects. 'I met him less and less often prior to the election. I'm quite sure he never asked a single member to vote for Barcelona, and he certainly didn't want to be Barcelona's counsel. When Barcelona gave a party at the LA Games, he saw it was being run by uninformed politicians. When we got home he invited me to dinner with Maragal, to bring me into the committee, and said we should concentrate on getting the necessary 46 members. I knew there were suggestions of money gifts to certain IOC members, and I went to see Maragal to demand if this was happening and to threaten my resignation. Maragal denied it. We did give small gifts, but tried to make them original and individual, and never the same gift to two people.'

Both Barcelona and Albertville would encounter a myriad of problems: Albertville because they started changing the venues originally proposed in their bid; and Barcelona because of a serious over-charging for accommodation in conjunction with an acute shortage of hotel rooms, plus design problems in the renovation of the Montjuic Stadium, originally constructed in the bid for the Games in 1932. There were serious problems for yachting, with high levels of sewage pollution evident in tests a year beforehand, though in many ways the Games in Barcelona promised to be efficient and spectacular. Two imponderables remained; the uphill climb over the last four kilometres of the marathon to the finish inside the Montjuic Stadium; and the open-ended threat of terrorism. For the second Games in succession, Samaranch would not be sleeping well until the flag was lowered and the flame extinguished.

It is essential that either Samaranch or his successor should tackle the question of the contract signed by elected cities. Three successive Winter Games hosts, Calgary, Albertville and Lillehammer, have radically failed to remain true to their bid book. The Calgary Games, in spite of persistently being labelled by Samaranch 'the best ever', were a chapter of deficiencies, primarily on account of the wilful reluctance of the Albertan cow town to accept advice. The ski jump was built on top of a hill, exposed to wind that repeatedly caused postponement; the bob run was exposed to dust that froze on the run; the alpine runs at Nakiska were poorly sited. Although the Albertville Games had technically efficient sites, and the opening and closing ceremonies a distinctive French élan, the travelling difficulties over a huge area were grossly inconvenient and exhausting, and will have made the IOC long for the ease of Salt Lake City. As for Lillehammer, at least three events had, at the time of writing, been moved out of town in what was initially presented as a compact bid. Such manipulation after election should not be permitted, on pain of severe financial penalty. The income from the Olympic Games is now such that the IOC, in conjunction with the IFs who control the running of their sports, are in a position to impose strict discipline.

The cost factor of bidding is defended by Ivan Slavkov, the IOC member from Bulgaria and twice chairman of the bid committee for Sofia: a bid which had the merit of introducing Olympic competition, as did Sarajevo, to a new region. Slavkov's initiative has brought him uncomfortable personal repercussions within Bulgaria, with accusations, motivated by envy, of alleged over-spending, when in fact the two bids earned his country extensive publicity. 'If Coca-Cola can spend $30m buying a place in the TOP sponsorship programme, why should a city not spend $5m on bidding for the Games?' Slavkov asks. 'Our two bids put Sofia on the map. For two campaigns, our expenditure was no more than $1.5m, with $1m from the government and half a million from overseas sponsorship. Everyone now knew where Sofia was.'

Scepticism about the voting system was further intensified by the perversity of members during the election of Nagano in 1991. Because a number of Latin-Americans, out of sentimental loyalty to the mother country, supported Jaca in the Pyrenees at the start, though clearly intending to switch when the voting became 'serious', this oscillation almost caused the early elimination of Salt Lake City. Such an outcome would have been a disgrace. Following further postponements of adjustment to the voting system at the Albertville Session, Samaranch indicated that it was likely to be agreed in Barcelona that round-by-round figures would not be disclosed to members – Henderson's proposal – and that IFs and NOCs would be given five collective votes each.

There is also extensive criticism, since Nagano's election, concerning allegations that the Committee does not own the land on which projected Olympic sites are to be built. The background on this has still to be resolved. Establishing such information is clearly beyond the competence of run-of-the-mill IOC members, and calls for even more vigilance on the part of the Evaluation Commission. The view of Dick Pound is that the membership should reduce candidates to three finalists, from knowledge provided by the Evaluation Commission, and that the final decision should be left to the executive board.

The more you analyse each aspect of the administration of the Olympic Games, the less justification there is for the continuing democratic function of the ninety-strong private club. In 1993, the election for 2000 is going to produce yet another almost impossible dilemma, with the probability of equally meritorious candidates from Asia (Peking), from Oceana (Sydney), from South America, never having hosted the Games (Brasilia, and possibly Buenos Aires), and from Europe (Berlin, Manchester, Milan and Istanbul). How can the IOC make a selection that will be seen to be acceptable? How, you may ask, can the Games be denied to Beijing and the world's most populous country? Sydney, Manchester and others will try to provide the answer to that.

14 Successor

> There is a longing among all people to have a sense of purpose and worth. To satisfy that common longing in all of us, we must respect each other. Young people are the pioneers of new ways. Since they face too many temptations, it will not be easy for them to know what is best.

Those words might have been written with the Olympic Games in mind, though they were not. They are from a man steeped in the wisdom that comes from an appreciation of the beauty of the forests and plains, the mountains and rivers, of the sun and rains upon which our life depends. He understood the challenges and hazards that confront every man. The writer was a North American Indian, the late Chief Dan George of the Coast Salish tribe, whose book, *My Spirit Soars*, is a poem on man's relationship with nature. The battle for survival of the native people and of their threatened historic culture was an unseen contest during the Winter Games in Calgary in 1988. For the Indians it was a race against time, against the material superiority of the white man, and the Indians' own non-acquisitive nature. The Games, appropriately, bred a kind of unity between the organizing committee and the Lubicon Lake tribe, who are grouped among the southern Alberta Indian population and had threatened disruption of the Torch Run. It never happened, and Treaty Seven, the southern Alberta reservations group of 23,000 aboriginals, collaborated throughout the Games' preparations with the organizing committee, and the Torch Run embraced 46 Indian reservations. 'The Games opened doors and took us into new areas,' Sykes Powderface, the Indian co-ordinator with the organizing Committee, said. 'It has always been our intention to resolve land claims peacefully with the government. And we wanted the Olympics to be partially for us.' What quiet moral superiority there was in such a statement from a people driven from the land that was their natural inheritance.

One of the fundamentals of sport is its simplicity, its closeness to human nature's instinct for exploration, for testing our capacity to excel, to survive and to relish the exhilaration that comes from a combination of mental and physical effort. 'The Olympic Games are under constant threat,' Sonny de Sales of Hong Kong, the chairman of the Commonwealth Games Federation, says. This has always been so, never more so than as the twentieth century draws to a close, whatever the tide of prestige the Games may be riding. Juan Antonio Samaranch, or his successor, and the members of the International Olympic Committee have, I believe, a greater responsibility and difficulty than ever to define the future structure of the Olympic Movement, precisely because its size and success have developed under Samaranch to proportions never previously experienced. They have to encompass, somehow, the realities of a multi-national business corporation while attempting to retain the ethical, abstract qualities without which the Olympic Games are meaningless, no more than just another sporting event. They have to sustain the spirit and example of the immortal Jessie Owens, the most legendary of all modern Olympic figures, who in his later years repeatedly appealed for the application of the ideals governing sport to every other field of human endeavour. 'In order to turn dreams into reality, it takes determination, self-discipline and effort,' Owens said. 'These things apply to everyday life. In sport, you learn not only the game, but things like respect for others, the ethics of life, how you are going to live your life and how to treat your fellow man.'

Without this relevance preached by Owens, sport in general and the Olympic Games in particular are without educational and cultural significance. There have been times in recent years when there has been reason to doubt whether those who administer sport are conscious of the responsibilities they hold. It is good to know that when debating these issues, informally, in March 1991, the executive board of the IOC was almost unanimous on what must be the priorities in the years ahead. Kevan Gosper, of Australia, put to his ten colleagues the alternatives: maintaining the Olympic tradition of honour and glory above all; or, by the turn of the century, allowing the payment of appearance money. A ballot was taken, including the president, and all bar one were stridently for honour and glory, Samaranch included. 'It is this quality that gives us our stature,' Gosper reflects, 'when we come into a country and meet heads of state and other dignitaries; that is what keeps men such as Keba M'Baye, a chief justice, dedicated to our administration.' The same issue was raised by Dick Pound on another occasion with similar reaction.

The dilemma for the IOC, and for whoever is its President, is that keeping control of an organization as vast as the Olympic Movement requires varied qualities within the membership: idealists and abstract thinkers, hard-headed businessmen, people long experienced in the technical requirements of the International Federations, and those wise in the personal relationships that are basic to the successful running of National Olympic Committees. I am convinced that in the long term the IOC must radically revise the structure and membership of its organization, if it is to be able to handle satisfactorily the complex demands placed upon it. Historically, the most significant quality attached to membership has been intellectual independence. Although it can be said with justification that the membership during Samaranch's twelve years

– during which there have been 52 members elected – has become more in tune with the times, it could not be truthfully said that they are all either intellectual or independent. That is hardly possible in a body ninety strong. The majority certainly have a sense of *constitutional* independence, personified by no one better than Anton Geesink, the former judo gold medallist of the Netherlands. Geesink is independent almost to the point of academic detachment, but because the IOC has now become a predominantly executive-run body, the scope for the practical application of independent intelligence is less than ever before. In one sense, therefore, the ideal qualifications for membership are a disqualification for practical influence. Run-of-the-mill members have only a marginal bearing on the majority of decisions that are taken. Those who have the strongest impact nowadays are necessarily thrusting specialists, excluding rare instances of exceptional intellectualism, such as that of M'Baye.

'I have to be independent, by nature,' Geesink says. 'Therefore, I set about creating my own sports foundation. I approached the big companies, not for money for myself, but to contribute to the running of an IOC office in the Netherlands, so that I can restore the Olympic culture. When I began, the NOC was little more than a travel agency working once every four years. Now, I have the financial backing of fifteen companies. I have never needed to ask for a penny in expenses either from the NOC or the IOC, even when I visit candidate cities bidding to host the Games, so as to maintain independence. I have a good life, but a simple life: rich in the way I am able to work.'

Samaranch is all too aware of the delicacy of the IOC's situation. In one of his more recent addresses, to a symposium at Matsumoto in Japan in 1991, on 'Human Society and the Olympic Movement in the Twenty-First Century', he said: 'The Olympic Movement is enjoying enormous prestige and plays a central rôle in the peaceful development of human society and education. However, the scale and importance of this prestige and social rôle creates within Olympism and sport a vulnerability . . . we have to study the way we want sport united with culture to develop in the years to come. . . . Olympism is a philosophy which, by blending sport with culture, seeks to create a way of life based on the joy found in effort, the educational value of good example and respect for universal ethical principles.'

Does Samaranch have the ability, and energy, if he serves another four-year term of office – or would any successor – to hold the Olympic movement on the rails? Having helped achieve a development unimaginable twelve years ago, Samaranch and his colleagues have a Leviathan on their hands, yet without an administrative structure able to handle the many different pressures created, primarily by the extent of the wealth now generated by the Olympic Games. 'He is a bit of a curate's egg,' Charles Palmer observes of Samaranch. When Palmer lost his position as chairman of the British Olympic Association in addition to his removal from office with the International Judo Federation and GAISF, Samaranch, with a typically altruistic concern for sport, maintained the involvement of this Englishman by appointing him to the Programme Commission. 'Many of the younger members think Samaranch is excellent, but some of the older ones are less happy,' Palmer suggests. 'What is the Olympic Movement? I disagree to some extent with having the most high profile competitors [professionals] involved, regardless, particularly those who compete in their sport for prize money. What is best for the movement? That it is incorruptible, or that it should bring the whole world of sport to the Games? There are some smaller countries there now who could never previously have been there. Is that better, to be able to raise an Olympic team, than to build a hospital? I am sure Samaranch's intentions are for the best, for the benefit of the movement. What he *thinks* is best. I hugely admire his dedication and self-discipline, his concentration, the way he finds time for everything.'

The simultaneous admission of professionalism into the Games and an increasing number of new small NOCs carries an in-built contradiction: the shift towards more extended professionalism will make it even harder for competitors from the under-developed world to keep pace, let alone catch up, with the leading nations. This will inevitably create further frictions within the IOC. The mistaken belief of the smaller Third World countries is that what they need is more aid from the Solidarity Fund, yet this can hardly do more than dent the surface of the problem. What African governments and others should realize is that in the long term they need not so much to try to pull out a plum, by special treatment of a single athlete or team, but to invest in a coherent schools sports programme. The traditional closing remarks of the senior IOC member, HRH The Grand Duke of Luxembourg, at the session of 1991 at Birmingham, pointed to this dilemma:

> The Olympic Games, which must not be confused with the world championships, must be open to athletes from all countries, including developing countries and smaller ones. We are all perfectly aware that for the time being we cannot exceed the figure of ten thousand athletes and that we can send only competitors prepared for high level competition in order to avoid 'Olympic Tourism', which would be incompatible with the rôle of this great festival of sport. In order to arrive at an acceptable solution, we must find a compromise between the immutable principle of universality and the need for a high standard of competition.

'The future management of the range of institutions Samaranch has introduced is going to be tough,' Gosper says. 'The extent to which he has opened up the Games could be dangerous: there is the possibility that the Games will be for full-time athletes only within another ten years. Thus, having totally opened the Games, he would ultimately have narrowed them.' Gosper is sure that payment for medals in the Games is the wrong road, and has suggested that guidelines should be set for NOCs on financial rewards. Samaranch said that the IOC should not set rules in areas they cannot control, but agreed to the production of guidelines. In 1992, for instance, the Unified (Russian) Team was paying $3000 to a gold medal winner.

Samaranch finds himself in a position not dissimilar from that of George III with the American colonies: monarch of an ancient kingdom with established traditions of authority and power around the world, but confronted with forces developing at a speed beyond control. 'I have said to Samaranch that I believe in him and will support him,' Vazquez Raña, president of the Association of NOCs, says, 'but does he know where he is going? I've done everything I can in sport, and have problems with *everyone*. The foolish are often those who have no problems. It's the same in business: those who succeed are criticized. We need to protect the Olympic philosophy, to take care of the Olympic Games. I myself have money, certainly: but I see that everything is turned to money, and that is not positive. We need money to raise the level of sport nationally and internationally, but we must not reach the point where only such as the United States, Japan and Germany are winning. We cannot compete with IF world championships, we are a different concept. We have to retain that fundamental.'

Many of Samaranch's most influential colleagues are acutely aware of the deep water towards which the IOC ship is inexorably heading. 'We have been building a position that will become almost unmanageable for the IOC President, Samaranch or his successor,' Peter Tallberg, a member for Finland, chairman of the Athletes Commission and president of international yachting, says. 'I doubt if I would put my name forward as a candidate [as successor], because it means trouble not only for you as an individual but for your country. Holding the position promotes both. But there is no one currently within the IOC, in my opinion, with the breadth of power, the scope or the diplomacy to handle it, no one with Samaranch's skill, though he didn't have it to begin with. And now it will need more. Jacques Rogge of Belgium is intelligent and might ultimately be such a figure. I think it would be wrong to have a president from a major nation, because he or she would be seen, and seem, to be associated with the perceived government position. I think, however, that the authority of the IOC should be kept as it is at present – though what happens when there are 250 NOCs? How will their voting power be disposed? The Olympic movement is moving away from political blocs to ethnic blocs. If the Commission for the Olympic Movement were given more strength, then it should carry the voice of the athletes. If I had wanted to achieve more power, I would have tried to turn the Athletes Commission into a union.' Ashmini Kumar is another who doubts whether the IOC can find a successor able to cope.

Two events of 1991 highlighted the degree to which forces within the Movement striving in different directions were bringing the unity, on which Samaranch has staked so much, close to breaking-point. The Session in Birmingham showed divergence on two major issues: the election of a host city for the 1998 Winter Games, and of Mario Vazquez Raña as IOC member for Mexico in succession to the retiring Eduardo Hay. The meeting of the IOC executive board with the council of the IAAF, immediately prior to the athletics world championships in Tokyo, produced a confrontation over rising demands to the IOC on finance and power from the most prominent sport in the Olympic Games.

In Birmingham, the IOC had a narrow escape, in my opinion. If another three members had joined the 42 who were content to see yet another Games in North America – what would have been the sixth in a 22-year span – further damage would have been inflicted on the reputation of the Olympic Games as a global event. Following the election of Atlanta for the Centenary Games the previous year, victory now for Salt Lake City would have been seen publicly, however inaccurately, as abject surrender to the dollar. In the third round of the voting, Ostersund of Sweden, facing the obstacle of a third consecutive European Winter Games after Albertville and Lillehammer, polled a commendable 23 behind Nagano (36) and Salt Lake City (29). Sweden's support then divided 10-13 for the respective yen and dollar rivals, to give the compromise Japanese candidate a 46-42 majority, and the second Winter Games to Asia. The decision and the controversy behind it contained several complications. Firstly, there is not a directive to guide the IOC members on any rotation between one continent and the other; and secondly, there is a mounting demand among IFs to be included in the voting process, Summer or Winter, in view of the level of technical factors that now govern the successful staging of an Olympic Games. The IOC rank and file, anxious to protect their independence, are reluctant to yield to IF demands, yet it is rational that the respective voices of the two associations of Summer and Winter federations should be heard, and indeed should have a vote. This thorny issue is being debated by a sub-committee of the executive board, consisting of M'Baye, Gosper, and François Carrard, the Director-General. (Samaranch reflected on the likely outcome at the conclusion of the previous chapter.)

The resistance of the rank and file to the election of Vazquez Raña – related in an earlier chapter – sprang from the same trait of independence, the view that Vazquez Raña as president of ANOC was 'one of them rather than one of us'. This is, I believe, an illogicality, which I will come to in a moment.

In Tokyo, during a five-hour grilling of the IOC executive board, prior to the IAAF championships, the IAAF demanded the following: an increased share of Olympic Games revenue; a guarantee of voting involvement in host city elections; IOC membership as of right for its president, currently Primo Nebiolo; uniformity in random drug testing as a qualifying condition for every Olympic sport, with uniform suspension penalties. (A partial solution to this, agreed at the Albertville winter games, is discussed subsequently)

The income of the two Olympic Games over the four-year period from 1989 to 1992, from television and all marketing, will be $1.84 billion, roughly twelve times the income projected for the IAAF for 1992-1995. The IAAF $140 million does not include its share of the gross Olympic television rights. The IOC's own residual income from the four-year period will be $120 million, or 7 per cent of the overall total. For the IOC to give the IAAF, the governing body of the principal Olympic sport, a larger slice of the cake would require either a cut from its own funds or deduction from another source. The 93 per cent of the total is at present divided between two Olympic host organizing Olympic committees, the participating NOCs through the Solidarity Fund, and the IFs via the two associations of winter and summer sports. The IOC could point to the fact that the IAAF at present altruistically takes only an equal share of television rights with every other summer sport and should perhaps reconsider this division. The IAAF, on the other hand, had a good case: the split of Winter and Summer Games into alternate even years, from 1994, further absorbs the available market, reducing the amount of global sponsorship/advertising available to world championships. It would be difficult to deny the IAAF on this issue, yet that could start a dangerous domino reaction among other ambitious federations such as basketball and volleyball.

A dynamic tension has existed between the IOC and the IFs throughout much of the 46 years since the Second World War. At the Session in Athens in 1961, the Soviet Union proposed that presidents of IFs should automatically qualify for IOC membership. This was a predictable, politically orientated attempt to 'democratize' the IOC, and would be subsequently supported by UNESCO, seeking voting rights for NOCs. There was less support than expected among 22 of the then 26 Olympic federations that met in Athens, many presidents considering that they had more power operating outside the IOC than within it. The creation of power in the three arms of the Movement is symbiotic. By the time of the Congress at Varna, Bulgaria, in 1973, the IFs were increasingly flexing their muscles. It was significant that all 26 federations attended the Congress, whereas there were 27 absentees among 74 IOC members, and 58 were missing from among 131 NOCs. Because their needs in staging events on a regular basis have always been more clear-cut, the IFs have always had a sharp awareness of the balance of power. The degree of absenteeism at Varna was indicative of the amateurish attitude that still existed among the IOC and NOCs. Though amateurism for the past century has always been upheld as a virtue, the shortcoming of the amateur has too often been that of inefficiency. This was to a degree true until the time Samaranch arrived in Lausanne. The IOC was still as insulated from reality, in business administration, as any provincial rowing club.

Sensitive to the demands of IFs and NOCs, Lord Killanin created at Varna the Tri-partite Commission, with equal representation of the three arms, and further decided that the Commission should become permanent, under his chairmanship. The effect of this for a time was to satisfy the IFs and NOCs that their needs were being heeded. Yet they were still without constitutional power. Samaranch, as already related, had determined on his election to undercut the power-seeking Thomas Keller, president of GAISF, by the formation of the two associations of Summer and Winter Olympic Federations. Samaranch's presidency was to be a tale of strategic cunning behind the scenes while paying tribute, publicly and repetitively, to the principle of unity. Addressing the GAISF Congress in Monaco in 1991, Samaranch stated: 'The Olympic Movement is free from any form of rigid structure and is run by those organizations which subscribe to its ideals. Its three pillars are the IOC, the trustees of the Movement; the International Federations, which put into practice the Olympic precepts; and the National Olympic Committees, which disseminate our ideals in their respective countries. The Olympic Movement is a continuous creation.' The spontaneous tensions having enlarged by the time of the Congress at Baden Baden in 1981, it was agreed that the Tri-partite Commission should be extended, with more representatives from each arm, together with representatives of other organizations where necessary. Samaranch adroitly recreated the Commission as the Commission of the Olympic Movement, continuing the process of appeasement by involvement, without concession of direct power. Samaranch the diplomat was clever with words, many of his speeches shrewdly written by Alain Coupat, his *chef de bureau*. The speeches around the world paid genuine tribute to those pursuing the ethics of Olympism and endlessly stressed the need for unity and the mutual advantages of shared strength. The latter was in part a legitimate philosophy, part lip-service to the IFs and NOCs. Samaranch was all too aware of the perils of disunity that stalked the IOC: the underlying threat was always there. It was evident, for instance, in the statement of allegiance issued by Vazquez Raña on behalf of ANOC at the time of the Soviet boycott in 1984. 'The Games are not just the property of the International Olympic Committee,' Vazquez Raña said, 'but of mankind as a whole.' Five months prior to this statement, it should be recalled, Samaranch had failed in a move to gain *ex officio* membership of the IOC for Vazquez Raña and for Primo Nebiolo, president of athletics and of the Association of Summer Sports (ASOIF). Outwardly as optimistic as a child at play on the beach, Samaranch picked his way through the minefield of personal relations with almost unsleeping awareness of the scheming and ambitiousness of others. Addressing the Session in Tokyo in 1990, for example, he said: 'Immobility and rigidity have never been a sign of health. Change for change's sake, in constant haste and improvisation, is not desirable either. We must be aware of our twofold responsibility: of preserving our ideals and of adapting ourselves. . . . Everything stems from the basic union which we have been able to create between the IOC, the IFs and the NOCs. Without this union, the Olympic Movement would cease to exist.' Union, however, was decreasingly acceptable for the two 'outsider' arms of the Movement, which sensed their own power without having an opportunity to apply it.

It is a warning shot across the IOC's bow when Jacques Rogge, the multi-lingual surgeon/yachtsman from Belgium, who is president of European NOCs, and is by nature non-confrontational, feels entitled to say: 'The IOC should not regard the Olympic Games as its own personal toy. Each IF and NOC has as much right to a say as anyone. Of course, there has to be leadership, and that is rightly the IOC's.' There are currently 33 members of the Commission for the Olympic Movement: they have their say, but their influence is limited. A statement from the Tri-partite Commission, published in March 1978 with undue self-importance, had defined the foundation, objectives, legislation, organization, development and future of the Olympic Movement, and concluded:

> The division of responsibilities between the IOC, IFs, NOCs and other sports confederations should be confirmed and implemented, and their unity of action and their solidarity should be strengthened, at the same time hoping that the study of the project for a supreme body representative of all world sport as a whole should be continued.

The conception here was for a kind of 'World Sports Council'. The United Nations is immediately brought to mind, with all the limitations that have been experienced by that well-intentioned organization, ultimately without real power. Samaranch's achievement has been his conception for the IOC – at least partially fulfilled within the boundaries of its administrative authority and its moral leadership – as such a world body. The spectacular growth of the IOC, in social/political prestige, in financial security, in its influence outside sport, as shown by events in South Korea and South Africa, is due to Samaranch's exceptional will, energy and anticipation of the way events would turn and rivals would act and react. The prestige would not have been gained, nor would the Movement have held together, had he not been prepared to travel three million kilometres: not merely visiting all but a handful of NOCs over a period of twelve years but attending *every* important international event of every major sport, no matter where its venue, in addition to endless trips to the major centres of political power – America, the Soviet Union and the Far East – during periods of Olympic crisis. Samaranch's reward is now to discover that he has created an empire beyond his own grasp. 'The IOC could be a rudderless ship,' Dick Palmer, of Britain, reflects. 'That is why I have the greatest admiration for Samaranch, who up to now has been able to control the machinations of the Commission for the Movement.' But for how long?

Lord Killanin, unsurprisingly, doubts whether the IOC is dispensable, leaving aside the fact that, technically, the IOC *owns* the Olympic Games. History will show how far the IOC was ill-advised, in the later part of the twentieth century, not to enlist the kind of competence that had become essential to its efficient function. When Samaranch sought the election of Peter Ueberroth, the most commercially-aware operator in the IOC's experience, other than Horst Dassler, Samaranch was resisted by his own members. Ueberroth was condemned, as was Dassler by many, as being too clever for his own good. At the same time, the IOC, the IFs and the NOCs were only too happy to accept all the financial advantages that flowed from Dassler and Ueberroth and which helped create the present strength.

Raoul Mollet, one of the originators of ANOC, is categorical on the direction that the IOC should take. 'The IOC *must* have businessmen,' Mollet says, 'even though they may then lose some traditional independence. The IOC as it stands is obsolete. Samaranch currently has an underground fight against Havelange from soccer, and Nebiolo from athletics. Within a different system, such IF leaders would be included. My proposal would be for the present, elected IOC to be reduced to fifty senators, together with, *ex officio*, the IF presidents and representatives of ANOC and the continental associations. I believe that the Olympic philosophy is valid for all sport, that such games as rugby and golf should be included. Why not? I warned Samaranch about the "Commission syndrome" [the impotence of Commissions], but he insisted that they were a reward to IOC members not on the executive board. Up to now Samaranch has been able to see into the future because his information network has been so good. Of course there has to be a body defending the Olympic philosophy, the IOC, but at the very least the Commission for the Olympic Movement ought to have legislative power.' During my discussion with him, Mollet did not say whether he would put his recommendations, as radical as anything yet done by Samaranch, to the Congress in 1994.

Conscious, perhaps, that the structure of the IOC membership and the supposed inalienability of the Charter were the most difficult of all to alter, Samaranch has skilfully managed, up to now, to embrace the rival IF/NOC factions while keeping them at arm's length. Early in his presidency, official recognition was granted to ANOC and to continental associations; this had a dual purpose of making them feel wanted while exercising the age-old policy of divide and rule. The bottom line of the dilemma for Samaranch or whoever succeeds him – for the IOC itself – is quite simple, at least as viewed from the proximity of my position as a journalist over the past 36 years. In any multinational business organization – accepting that the Olympic Games are now a corporate business as much as an ethical concept – it would be thought unrealistic not to have on the executive board the heads of major subdivisions, such as the most prominent, finance-generating sports or the organization providing the competitors. Can the IOC seriously expect to invite the IFs and NOCs to collaborate in the creation of a billion-dollar event without giving them *any* direct administrative authority? The Charter is conspicuous for specifying the superior jurisdiction of the IOC in all matters, while nowhere conceding any *rights* to the IFs and NOCs, merely underlining their responsibility. No multinational corporation could expect to survive so exclusive and private a constitution. Dick Pound, a Montreal lawyer and a central figure in the IOC's commercial development as Samaranch's chosen lieutenant, is quick to point out a fundamental difference: a corporation has the power to dismiss any executive official not considered to be performing satisfactorily. A corporation is not a club of self-elected members basking in mutual appreciation. It must be doubtful how long the IOC can continue along this path, however desirable such an idealistic principle as de Coubertin's may have been a century ago. The principle suggested by Mollet – in effect demanded by Nebiolo with involvement of IF presidents – was partially embraced, amid controversy, at the Session prior to the winter Games at Albertville. The members approved – though reluctantly, being aware it would open the door for Nebiolo, whom many opposed for varying reasons – the appointment by the IOC President of two discretionary members, irrespective of nationality: on the grounds (a) of the person's elected office or (b) on their personal qualities and experience, there to be no more than two such members at a time, and the-member to retire upon the removal of the office as in (a). The voting was 75-0, following extensive debate with some thirty speakers. There were five abstentions, led by the Princess Royal, and including Mary Glen-Haig, Anita DeFrantz, Pirjo Haggman and Philipp von Schoeller of Austria. Older members with doubts, such as Maurice Herzog of France, eventually voted in favour out of loyalty to the President. 'I trust him', reflected Herzog. Younger members, such as Thomas Bach of Germany, the former fencing gold medal winner, and Dennis Oswald, president of international rowing, voted on the sense of the principle, rather than being influenced by factors of personalities. In my opinion, it is as important *not* to oppose an issue of principle because of personalities as it can be at times to do so. I feel that the Princess's stance put Britain out on a limb, on an issue that she might have known was likely to be heavily supported; on which, therefore, protest would have short-term credit and possible long-term disadvantage for Britain and its interests, such as Manchester's bid for the 2000 Games. Samaranch duly nominated Nebiolo in his capacity as IAAF president, a month later; predictably, there was immediate collaboration from the IAAF on recognition of South African athletics, scheduled to be approved in May. Alarmingly, Nebiolo also began pressing not only for increased Olympic revenue for athletics, but the unacceptable innovation of stadium advertising and bib-number sponsorship.

Raymond Gafner, a recently retired Swiss member, who retains the position of administrative delegate and is another originator of ANOC, has lived uncomfortably with the conflict of IOC principles for more than twenty years. 'The IOC now has many risks,' Gafner says. 'Some of them have been there for a long while. Brundage proposed to the executive board in 1971 that I and five others should be expelled! [This was on the issues of eligibility and relaxation of the financial restraints imposed on training.] Brundage was in place too long: every move that was not in line with him was now treachery. I had always said that I could not accept that we [the IOC] should teach young people that hypocrisy was the first qualification of sport: that if you were not caught, you were not guilty. The same happened subsequently with drugs. If you want to promote sport and have money, you have to move with the times. A century has gone by. I like to think sport is not a profession, but it is necessary to devote your time exclusively for several years. Certainly, *some* athletes are paid too much, but if competitors are giving *all* their time to sport, that does not disturb me. If we look beyond sport, coincidentally, the Catholic and Jewish religions have never exactly been pure. Without money, the IOC cannot exist. Having the money is *not* the problem. I have supported the financial growth, but the question is whether you are serving sport or using sport? What we have to try to do is to use sport to serve sport. The value of sport in present society is still to embrace victory and defeat equally, to respect the rules and to make friends. Progress can always go too far in every activity of man, but if man didn't have the heart to progress and adjust and survive, we would not still be here. Samaranch's strength is that he has been able to handle the complexities of the world. His arrival, with hindsight, was vital. He has had a political feeling, and he has steered the Movement through the political waves, keeping its independence and not being a subsidiary. Brundage thought the IOC was *another* world. Samaranch's conception has proved to be correct. However, I think it is important to maintain "clean" stadiums, free of advertising, to uphold de Coubertin's original policy. By the year 2000, we may have over two hundred NOCs, and some will have the economic power for an independent life, independent attitudes. What is the correct number of competitors, given that we already have ten thousand for the Games? So many problems lie ahead.'

Samaranch, so often pragmatic, believed that it was more practical to have Nebiolo at the boardroom table than banging angrily on the door outside. Those who feared Nebiolo's power should have reflected that he has only six years to run to retirement age of 75; and as Pound observed, the IOC has the votes to resist his demands. The request for a larger share of Olympic revenue is reasonable, but the idea of stadium advertising is damaging to the exclusivity of TOP sponsors, causing 'clutter'. Now he is in the 'club', Nebiolo has to be sure he is rowing the boat, not rocking it.

'When the IOC feels it may be losing power, you have to go step by step cautiously,' Samaranch says. 'Maybe in the future we will have more *ex officio* members full-time, though I still consider it is a better system when members are elected. A difficulty with *ex officio* appointments can arise when other organizations change *their* elected officers, producing a lack of continuity within the IOC and possibly divergent attitudes.' Dick Pound believes it is unwise to allow the IFs to gain a dominant hold, having been 'put to bed' with the deflection of Keller and GAISF by the creation of Winter and Summer associations. Pound thinks that what makes the Movement work *is* the existence of a healthy tension, but considers Samaranch has erred in allowing the IFs again to become too strong. Samaranch, in his defence, has attempted to limit this factor by the normal election to the IOC, where possible, of IF presidents and general secretaries: at present eight. These included Havelange, from football, but not, until the 1992 concession to the IOC president, Nebiolo. Killanin's view is that the IOC is better without them, speaking from the experience over many years of having Lord Exeter simultaneously as a member, as president of athletics and chairman of the BOA. (Exeter always claimed his permitted *three* pairs of free Olympic Games tickets!) It was often unclear, Killanin recalls, which body Exeter was representing when he spoke. Samaranch's view, correct in the opinion of progressives, is that it is advantageous for IF presidents to be involved, and that is why he had unavailingly proposed Nebiolo and Vazquez Raña as *ex officio* members in 1983-84, they being the respective presidents of ANOC and ASOIF (Marc Hodler, president of the Association of winter sports, had been an IOC member since 1963). The proposal was opposed from the floor by, among others, Gunnar Ericsson, a member for Sweden since 1965 and a strong traditionalist, who is currently on the executive board. Ericsson's objection was that *ex officio* members would, by definition, represent organizations, whereas the IOC, by definition, is independent. The Princess' objection in 1992 was, and remains, that the rule-change was insufficiently clearly worded, both on definition of appointment and on termination. She also objected to the proposal being presented to the Session as being a vote of confidence in Samaranch.

Primo Nebiolo became president of athletics in 1981, a man of evident ambition, and his appointment as president of ASOIF was at the time part of Samaranch's policy of divide and rule. Nebiolo, enhancing his own reputation, decided that ASOIF would split their share of Olympic television revenue equally between all 23 sports; archery thus suddenly had the same income as athletics, the latter having previously taken 20 per cent of television allocation, with the other sports dividing the remaining 80 per cent. Simultaneously, Nebiolo was dramatically expanding the structure of the IAAF. To the newly created World (continental) Cup (1977) and World Championship (1983) were now added championships for juniors, marathon and road-running, and a Grand Prix, primarily staged in Europe, that rationalized the previously random and unnecessarily opposing invitation meetings. Whereas the reputation of athletics had previously been dependent on the Olympic Games, effectively the sport's world championships, now it was developing in many directions, financially and competitively, for which much of the credit was Nebiolo's. The sport might never replace soccer as number one in the world – Nebiolo's stated ambition – and many coaches might express alarm at the physically damaging burden upon athletes from the multiplication of events, yet athletics was unquestionably now big business.

Nebiolo's situation was complicated in 1987 by a scandal at the world championships in Rome when an Italian long-jumper, Evangelisti, was falsely awarded a bronze medal through manipulation by officials controlling the pit. Nebiolo unwisely procrastinated on the appointment of an inquiry, which eventually disclosed the details and led to the life suspension of those involved. During this period Nebiolo lost his position as president of the Italian NOC, and voluntarily resigned as president of the Italian Athletic Federation. The Evangelisti scandal rebounded upwards, and there was widespread speculation about whether Nebiolo could hold his positions as head of IAAF and ASOIF. A little-known detail of the Evangelisti affair is that Nebiolo, a former long-jumper, and his wife have lived with the disappointment of having no children, and over a period of years he had developed a relationship in which the young Evangelisti, in the opinion of well-informed Italians close to the situation, had become in effect a surrogate son. Evangelisti willingly relinquished his medal in 1987 when he learned of the error, and it was rightfully passed to Myricks of the USA. For the next two years there were moves to replace Nebiolo as president of ASOIF, initiated by Thomas Keller, Francesco Gnecchi-Ruscone of Italy, then the president of archery, and others. Alternative potential presidents were, first, Peter Tallberg and then the Princess Royal; but from a position off-stage Samaranch persuaded Tallberg not to stand, on the grounds that he had been appointed Finland's commissioner for Expo '92, the world trade fair in Seville; and at a subsequent meeting, at Budapest in 1989, at which there was substantial support for the Princess Royal, the long arm of Samaranch stretched from Lake Geneva to the Danube to persuade ASOIF members to back off. Without a clear mandate, the Princess Royal did not stand, and in return Nebiolo was persuaded to introduce a system of limited presidency by which he will retire in 1992. Samaranch was convinced that if Nebiolo were voted out of office by ASOIF, he would quickly try to re-establish a division of the television money favouring athletics, thereby generating more widespread controversy. Now Nebiolo has re-awoken the sleeping dog.

'In the spring of '89, at an ASOIF meeting in Barcelona, Gnecchi-Ruscone and Keller pushed me to stand,' Tallberg recollects. 'The meeting was concurrent with an executive board meeting, and Samaranch asked me over a private lunch to let Nebiolo sort out his situation. There were many criticisms, such as the minute books being out of order. I proposed to my ASOIF colleagues that a vote should be postponed until the autumn meeting in Budapest. It was there that Nebiolo organized a letter signed by each federation, requesting voting rights on the election of host cities. Chatrier, from tennis, Oswald, from rowing, and I did not sign. The equestrian federation signed, even though the Princess Royal was against it. Nebiolo was pressing for a response to this letter from the IOC at the Session in Tokyo in '90. In 1991, Nebiolo was wanting to change the constitution back to what it had been, so that he might stay in office after '92. Ruben Acosta, the president of volleyball, again wanted me to stand as an alternative candidate. Yet I am due to retire from the yachting union in '94, besides which I wonder whether, for negotiating purposes on a share of television and sponsorship money, it is better for ASOIF to be led by a non-IOC person.'

Here is the contradiction that Nebiolo, on his side of the debate, ought to have considered: in the pursuit of power for the IAAF, might he not exercise greater influence while remaining outside the IOC, never mind his overbearing belief that his position rightfully demands a place inside? At the heart of this question is whether Nebiolo is primarily working on behalf of the Olympic Games or of athletics. If the latter, and if he is not worried about divisiveness, then undoubtedly he has more strength outside. As an IOC member he will merely have one vote among ninety, and will have the obligation to honour above all the interests of the Olympic Games. From the IOC's viewpoint, it would seem to me that there is the prospect of *less* conflict by the admission of *ex officio* members – with a limited term of office and the possibility of replacement within their own organization – than by almost wilful provocation of excluded senior figures. The instinct of older members, such as Gafner and the emotionally-charged Flor Isava-Fonseca of Venezuela, has been for the IOC to pull its head down, let the flak fly overhead, stand firm on principle and to hell with the consequences, in the unshakeable belief that virtue and ethics will finish on top. This is an admirable view, though experience shows it is not always the way the world works. Robert Helmick, prior to his resignation as president of USOC, said to me during the 1991 Pan American Games in Havana: 'To have elected the president of ANOC, Vazquez Raña, to the IOC this year is good – it adds expertise – yet there is a feeling within the IOC that if too many are brought in from the IFs, the situation will get out of control: that the IOC will become a representative body rather than a college of cardinals that can weather crises and depressions.'

Nebiolo, who has that Latin characteristic of longing for love and respect because of, or even in spite of, his conduct, has remained unrepentant in his quest for what he believed was legitimate. There are moments, such as the ceremonial award in 1991 of one of Japan's highest public honours, when Nebiolo can seem transported by a sense of the virtue of leading the most important Olympic sport, emotionally overwhelmed like a small boy engulfed by acclaim at his birthday party; yet in the next breath Nebiolo can be as calculating as any, and there are those who consider it not impossible that he may attempt to impose an under-23 qualification for the Olympic Games as in football. Many observers are equally sure that this would lead quickly to his being disowned by the IAAF, and as Samaranch says: 'I cannot imagine an Olympic Games without athletics, or athletics without the Olympic Games.' Nebiolo over the years has growled in my ear, in his intimate way, even when I have been less than complimentary. He is ceaseless in his attempt to take his sport, and himself, where he intends; though I believe he will be less powerful within the IOC if the members have the will to stand up to him. 'When Samaranch asked if it was possible for the IFs to help him more, I did my best with the creation of ASOIF,' Nebiolo says. 'I did it because I understood his reasons, and because I felt close to him. His proposal to have the presidents of ANOC and

ASOIF on the IOC was a simple idea: two men from the pillars of the Olympic Movement who would better represent those two bodies. I think it failed at the time because of personal jealousies. In Italy the constitution allows the president to appoint six senators for life, so why could not something like this be a feature of the IOC? Someone in Samaranch's position needs close senior advisers. It is hardly a new principle. As president, Samaranch has had honest objectives, he has reformed the president's role, like the chairman of a major company. He has understood that you cannot lead effectively unless you have total involvement. He has tried to give importance to all members of the IOC and to increase the importance of the Games. Now everyone is proud. Samaranch's achievement is at the expense of self-sacrifice; he has travelled the world not because he enjoys it, but because it unites the Movement and sets an example for everyone. The Vatican he has created can truly be the Vatican of the sporting field. I am not often an admirer, but he has created something great and he has my complete support.'

That was not quite how it seemed to Samaranch at the conclusion of the executive board meeting with the IAAF council in 1991 and it led to the proposal on discretionary members first mooted in a letter from Lord Killanin, the retiring president, to Samaranch in 1980.. One of the reasons for Samaranch devoting ten days to attending the world championships was an acknowledgement of the difficulties that may arise with the IAAF. There are some who see in Samaranch, at the age of 72, signs of unfamiliar nervousness, as though he no longer has the conviction of his own instinct. He will need to analyse that instinct, and the long-standing reliability of his own judgement, before he decides whether to offer himself for another four years' service. 'Being in power for many years, like Brundage, can cut you off from reality,' Alain Coupat says. 'There is a tendency to get separated from affairs or, like Killanin, to delay decisions for fear of making the wrong one. A tendency to solve matters temporarily, and leave the problem for your successor. That might be happening to Samaranch, though it is perhaps early to judge. A way in which he's been clever is to let someone else carry the criticism for doing essential jobs, for testing innovative ideas that are bound to be unpopular. In this he found a willing candidate in Dick Pound, a young and at the time little-known Canadian advocate.'

When Samaranch was elected, Pound, who had been an IOC member for only two years and had been busy supporting the rival candidacy of James Worrall, acted with typically disarming directness. He wrote to Samaranch saying that he would like to support him, but thought there were problems which Samaranch should consider. Samaranch replied politely, after a long delay, querying what the problems were.

'News of decisions of Executive Board elections were reaching me,' Pound recollects, 'before they were heard by senior IOC members or before they had been made. I thought that was insulting. A few months later he asked for a private meeting with me, and after the Congress in '81, again asked me what I would like to do to help. This led to him suggesting I should run for the executive board, even though I'd been a member only for four years. Samaranch said to me, "I know what I do well, and I need to know what I *don't* do well." So I listed twenty points or so: you should travel on the coach with members more often rather than in a personal car, your wife should attend the tours for other wives rather than go shopping, and so on. He later said he thought the memo was valuable. In the end I ran for the board in '83-'84, and with his help was elected. I've been pretty close to him ever since, and in the past couple of years I have sensed that he is less able to be discerning on the information he receives, tending to react to the last view he has heard. Some days he's as nervous as a witch, on the negotiating of television contracts, for example [which Pound has supervised for eight years], saying, "Telephone me even if you have nothing to say!"

'He'd asked me to handle television in 1983, partly because he knew this would irritate Monique Berlioux, who was then still the Director and had negotiated previous deals. He kept me away from Europe, on television, and still does, because he doesn't want ripples with the European Broadcasting Union. What EBU pays has gone up, but is still less than the market value.'

Pound will be among the leading contenders to replace Samaranch, whenever that happens, though the personnel are likely to vary considerably according to whether the moment comes in 1993 or 1997. 'It would be very difficult to sit in his chair,' Alexandru Siperco of Romania says, 'and that's why I think there is at least a chance that he will wish to stay. There is no comparison in the IOC between now and before he became President. He has made us an organization of world stature. Previously it was only a little more than an English club, leading its own life with one event every four years. Now, the Olympic Games are not the sole action, he leads a huge Movement, helped by a much larger income. He succeeded in getting past the *reticence* of the IOC. From his travels, he knows personally most of the world and is recognized all around the world.' Samaranch has set standards that will be a daunting task for anyone to attempt to emulate. Anselmo Lopez, the director of the Solidarity Fund, recalls how, during Samaranch's formative years in Spain, he regularly worked until 10 or 11 at night and expected the same of his colleagues. 'It was difficult for me to combine my voluntary work with Samaranch, on behalf of sport, with my own business,' Lopez says. 'I'm not prepared to believe as yet that his revolution is finished.'

François Carrard, the Swiss advocate who became IOC director, has found his new responsibilities a fascination. 'Samaranch has a strange nature,' Carrard observes. 'Sometimes he's too impulsive, at others he's nervous. He breathes the information network of the media, misses nothing and has a permanent long-term view. I expected him to give me some lessons, and perhaps to be annoyed, yet I'm learning from him every day. He has a will of iron.' Considering the extent to which Samaranch is attuned to press and television, it is surprising that he did not anticipate the inevitable reaction to the election of Atlanta for the Centenary Games and make some provision in counter-publicity. Public relations is one of the IOC's most serious weaknesses. 'There was no strategic communication or plan to handle either the Atlanta election or Ben Johnson's suspension,' Michael Payne, the marketing director, reflects. 'The knee-jerk reaction by the media over Atlanta was predictable, yet the IOC was able to do little in damage limitation, nor was there any contingency plan when the Johnson story broke at three in the morning. It was fortunate that the IOC was able to turn round such a potential disaster into something comparatively positive.' John Boulter of Adidas observes: 'The building up of the bidding campaign, televising the ceremony, has got out of control, and I think Samaranch knows this. It urgently needs reining in. There is a fine line between running an organization from the kitchen table, the way it used to be, and going over the top.'

Whether Samaranch stands again depends on several factors, his health being the first. Apart from a minor gastric problem a year or two ago, he is fit, thanks to his daily exercising and circumspect diet. Bibis, his wife, thinks that his health at the moment would not stand in the way. He must consider, secondly, the possibility of serious opposition – unlikely at the present time, unless Barcelona were to be fraught with difficulties that inevitably would reflect upon him – and, thirdly, whether he feels capable of handling the many obstacles that lie ahead. There are conflicting temptations: to retire while at the top, with an exceptional record, or to remain President for the Centenaries of both the formation of the IOC, in 1994, and of the Games themselves in 1996. 'He's really good when there's opposition, something to fight,' says Michèle Verdier, the IOC media director, who has watched him from close quarters. 'Yet he knows when you are in power that you're so alone. He protects himself in public life and relies on his family life to give him sustenance. What's been interesting is how little his enemies really know him. For those working close to him, he's human and highly sensitive, adjusting easily, drifting from one person to another, to absorb opinions. He has been a conductor, realizing the importance of every player.' Where, Killanin and Dick Palmer ask with the same voice, does the IOC find a comparable executive director-type President? There are many, not least Berlioux before she left, who criticized the level of the IOC's expenditure under Samaranch. Having travelled with him, in one form or another, more than 100,000 kilometres – a mere fraction of his total – I can testify that he spends little if anything on self-promotion. His expenditure is in pursuit of convincing people and organizations throughout the Movement that the IOC cares for their interest, though certainly there are luncheons or dinners, for gatherings of ten people to a hundred or more around the world, some of which could be said to be expendable. Yet, as Verdier says: 'The President cannot rule from the seat of a bicycle. We now have enough money to treat people well. The criticism is more a human reaction than anything else.'

Pound believes that the years leading up to Seoul took more out of Samaranch than he realized; that since then he has tended to lean more on the executive board to help him achieve the decisions he wants, and that there might be a price to pay on short-term solutions having a long-term commitment. Pound wonders whether Samaranch *really* wanted the election of Ueberroth, possibly fearing him as a potential challenger. Evidence suggests Samaranch was nervous that a rival might have emerged for the election at the Session in San Juan, Puerto Rico, in 1989, though as Pound argues, every member elected to the IOC should be capable of being President: if the *right* people are being elected. In Gafner's opinion, though having no vote, he would welcome another English-speaking President, because it would switch from Latin-Spanish domination in international sports administration.

My opinion is that Samaranch may now decide to run again; that he has been provoked by various criticisms and sees a further term of four years, if his health is sound, as vindication of his qualities to lead an ideological body. Killanin points to the danger, as with Margaret Thatcher, the former British Prime Minister, of running beyond one's capability, suddenly to find that public opinion has cruelly shifted. The alternative view, held by many including Rogge, is that Samaranch owes it to the IOC to continue, being at present the only one capable of handling the impending problems. Personally, I suspect Samaranch is enjoying the job less, and that if he stays, by request, it might be only until after the Congress in 1994. At the Albertville session, Maurice Herzog announced that a majority of members wished him to continue. Samaranch did no more than show gratitude.

At least a dozen members have, or have had in recent years, either the ability or the potential support to make them candidates for the succession. In alphabetical order they are: Franco Carraro (Italy), Carlos Ferrer (Spain), Kevan Gosper (Australia), Robert Helmick (USA), Zhenliang Hé (China), Un Yong Kim (South Korea), Keba M'Baye (Senegal), Prince de Mérode (Belgium), Richard Pound (Canada), Jacques Rogge (Belgium), The Princess Royal (GB), Peter Tallberg (Finland), and Mario Vazquez Raña (Mexico). Of these, three at least can be discounted. Carraro is an able man who, for whatever reason, has turned inwards towards his political life in Italy. 'He had all the qualities to become very powerful,' Samaranch says, 'and it was disappointing when he more or less left sport for the Ministry of Tourism, following which he lost most of his opportunity with both the IOC and FIFA. He's lost the opportunity he had.' The failure of de Mérode to gain re-election to the executive board at the Session in 1991 indicates a lack of support from the rank and file. A man of charm and dignity, without the need to seek personal prestige, he could have emerged as a neutral choice while east-west tensions remained serious, but that period has seemingly passed. Helmick is no longer there.

Zhenliang Hé is a man of ethical and intellectual stature, his electability conditioned by the political situation of China, the last major communist stronghold. With a mixed Asian view about the suitability of Hé as a potential president of the Olympic Council of Asia, for the same reason – he withdrew his nomination, for the second time, in 1991 at the meeting where the son of Sheik Fahad was elected – it is unlikely that he would seek to stand for the IOC job, and certainly not in 1993, when Peking is a candidate city for the Games of 2000. Peter Tallberg, who failed in a first attempt to gain a place on the executive board in 1991, might have more support if the IFs were involved in the voting. He has a particularly rounded qualification with his experience as president of yachting and of the Athletes Commission, but it is unlikely that he could find sufficiently realistic support among Third World members. Carlos Ferrer, a Barcelona banker, is the strong, silent type like Samaranch, who had the opportunity to get to know the electorate during Barcelona's campaign to win the Games of 1992. It must be unlikely, however, that the IOC would elect successive Spaniards.

A possibility for The Princess Royal, remote yet nonetheless real, could occur should the IOC find that the only objective means by which to replace Samaranch satisfactorily would be to appoint a salaried chief executive. The IOC would then need a figurehead president; and the Princess, with her background as president of both an IF and an NOC, could be seen as an acceptable, neutral and incorruptible compromise. 'An international mediating role is precisely what I do best,' the Princess has said, without projecting herself. 'I'm a professional fence-sitter, and one of the things other people find hard to understand is that you're not plugging some political line or opinion. The whole thrust of one's existence has been to sit and listen and not voice opinions very much.' The Princess's aura may have lessened with her prominent abstention in Albertville, which suggested an absence of briefing. Jacques Rogge, only elected in 1991, could hardly be a candidate within two years, might be so in six and certainly within fourteen; he has the most rounded qualifications of all. Like Samaranch, he is highly conscious of the need further to modernize the IOC, and is emerging fast as a positive thinker. One of the reasons some members were hesitant about the election of

Vazquez Raña was the estimation that he could quickly become a presidential candidate, should he 'call in' the many debts owed, from his favours bestowed as head of ANOC and the Pan American Sports Organization. It seems unlikely that he could summon that support in the short term, yet through the machinery of the National Olympic Committees and the PASO, he could operate a campaign more widespread than anyone else apart from Kim.

That leaves four: Gosper, Kim, M'Baye, Pound. Kim has extensive friendships through his presidency of GAISF, and his work in the creation of a brilliant Games in Seoul, though the latter was hardly visible. His self-effacing, almost secretive nature make him comparatively difficult to get to know, and it may well be that the IOC is not temperamentally ready for its first Asian president following six Europeans and one American. The same question mark could apply to the first black African to be a candidate, Keba M'Baye, whom Pound, a rival, regards as 'a fantastic chairman and the presidential type'. It is remarkable that M'Baye should at this moment be the foremost figure within the IOC, when he had been on the point of leaving in 1980 because of lack of responsibility. 'He's intervening in all the main problems we have,' Samaranch says, 'and is without doubt one of our most prominent members.' M'Baye's lofty intellectualism and neutrality are exactly the qualities that could make him the perfect interim president, able to guide the rapid emergence of his own continent and the rest of the Third World. The Europeans, however, would probably block him; and he is already 68.

Richard Pound and Kevan Gosper are two of a kind, yet very different, both former Olympic athletes: Pound a swimming finalist in 1960, born in 1942 and elected in 1978; Gosper a 4 x 400 metres relay silver medallist in 1956, born in 1933 and elected in 1977. Widely regarded as the front-runners to succeed, they have contrasting characters, though both, like Samaranch, are personable and approachable.

Gosper's strength is administrative. He has a senior position in a prominent multinational company, Shell, which has given him experience of high-level decision-making in three continents, and is an idealist who at the same time recognizes the practical realities of the modern age. His move to an office based in London has facilitated access to Olympic functions, and as an Australian he represents no political power base. 'Gosper is very open to all people,' Samaranch says, 'though I don't know the extent of support he would get from the members, even though he is one of the most obvious candidates. He knows business and knows the world, yet he is protective of traditional principles.'

Pound can be enigmatic. Michael Payne says he is the only man he knows to play chess in three dimensions. If Pound has the quickest wit among the members, and an impressive record in the establishment of the new financial strengths, he also tends to be intolerant of fools – and to show it. There are members who, with justification, can feel intellectually inadequate in his presence. His strength is that he is not afraid to tackle controversies openly, on the one hand, but on the other hand can give the impression that he will accept an option for its convenience. Being instantly positive in his opinions, he is apt to form likes and dislikes among his associates, which are apparent. It is characteristic that he has been happy to bear some of the criticism that would otherwise have been directed at Samaranch. 'He's used me to be his tough guy,' Pound reflects. 'Somebody has to be, and I don't mind, it doesn't bother my nature. In that rôle, you have to play the character, because Samaranch doesn't send out people who can't pull the trigger. I'm seen as tough and non-political. He can't say *no*, and needs someone who can. As President, you have got to be Pope and populist; the latter is an acquired skill.' Samaranch thinks that Pound's position as a candidate will depend upon his re-election to the executive board at the Session in Barcelona in 1992. 'If he fails, that would be a bad sign,' Samaranch says. 'When I gave him power I don't think he was calculating on acquiring influence, and I hope he'll be back on the board, we need these kind of people. Maybe he could be more diplomatic.'

M'Baye, Gosper and Pound, with Kim as the outsider, are in my opinion the runners if there is to be an election in 1993. All have their qualities: Kim's the most complex, M'Baye's the most profound, Gosper's and Pound's the most practical. Should Samaranch's popularity decline during the next year – he has much at stake in the success of the Barcelona Games and in his attempt to restructure the IOC – the one candidate with the nerve to run against him would be Pound; and it must be doubtful if Samaranch would wish to face a contested election. What is beyond doubt is that the events of the next eight years might swamp any of them, or Samaranch, should he continue. The demands of the job created by Samaranch's excellence have become almost intolerable. The requirements of the next twenty years and beyond, as I have attempted to explain, require such major alterations that they would appear impossible for a body as amorphous as the IOC, in which almost every one of ninety-odd members has a differing opinion on what might be best, other than retention of their own unique and privileged status. It is that status itself which is the core of their problem.

Samaranch, it is possible, might be happy to retire at the top, if not remaining from a sense of duty: content with, optimistically, a successful Games in his home city, and the opening, in June 1993, of his cherished project, the Olympic Museum in Lausanne, now being constructed to the design of Pedro Ramirez Vazquez, the Mexican architect and IOC member, in an exquisite position overlooking Lac Léman and Evian on the distant French shore. The museum is costing between $35m and $40m, and Pound, pragmatic lawyer/accountant, questions whether the IOC will be able to afford the $12m per annum running costs. Museums are expensive institutions. 'As a major organization, you have to have administration and finance properly organized,' Gosper reflects, 'but you've also go to put in place some permanent pillars for the future. It's not enough to have a Games every two years, you have to have a house in which to exhibit your culture. The running cost will be manageable in relation to the cash flow now existing in élite sport. Without the museum, what would be the visible soul of the organization?'

All Killanin's archives are already there, sealed until after his death. They include bizarre items like the letter from Lord Porritt, former member for New Zealand, complaining that Lance Cross, later to be knighted, was not a suitable candidate because he was professional, and appeared at Games wearing a blazer with the emblem of NZ Radio; Porritt perhaps overlooked the fact that his own membership should never have been permitted as, contrary to the Charter, he was resident outside the country he represented, living in England for many years following the Paris Games of 1924. The museum, João Havelange of Brazil says, will serve as an example to everyone in sport of what the Olympic Games and the IOC represent. The museum has yet to be given a name. Three of the most symbolic names in the history of the Olympic Movement are those of Baron Pierre de Coubertin, Jesse Owens and, now, Juan Antonio Samaranch. Considering that the existence of the museum owes almost everything to the current President of the IOC, his name might be the most appropriate of all. The IOC, under the guiding force of Samaranch, is the most universal social instrument of peace in our time.

Glossary of Acronyms

AIPS	Association of International Sports Press
AIWF	Association of International Winter Sports Federations
ANOC	Association of National Olympic Committees
ANOCA	Association of National Olympic Committees of Africa
ASOIF	Association of Summer Olympic International Federations
BOA	British Olympic Association
CONI	Italian National Olympic Committee
COSAS	Confederation of South African Sports
EANOC	European Association of National Olympic Committees
FISU	International Federation of University Sport
FIFA	International Federation of Football Associations
GAISF	General Assembly of International Sports Federations
IAAF	International Amateur Athletic Federation
IOA	International Olympic Academy
NOCSA	South African National Olympic Committee
OAU	Organisation of African Unity
OCA	Olympic Council of Asia
ONOC	Oceania National Olympic Committee
PASO	Pan-American Sports Organisation
SACOS	South African Council on Sport
SANROC	South African Non-Racial Olympic Committee
SANOC	South African (former) National Olympic Committee
USOC	United States Olympic Committee

Protocol List of IOC Members

	Date of election	
1	1946	Grand-Duke Jean of LUXEMBOURG
2	1947	Raja Bhalendra SINGH (India)
3	1951	Giorgio de STEFANI (Italy)
4	1955	Alexandru SIPERCO (Roumania) Vice-president 1982-1986
5	1959	Syed Wajid ALI (Pakistan)
6	1960	Ahmed D. TOUNY (Egypt)
7	1961	Wlodzimierz RECZEK (Poland)
8	1961	Hadj Mohammed BENJELLOUN (Morocco)
9	1963	João HAVELANGE (Brazil)
10	1963	Marc HODLER (Switzerland)
11	1964	Prince Alexandre de MÉRODE (Belgium) Vice-president 1986-1990
12	1964	Major Sylvio de Magalhaes PADILHA (Brazil) Vice-president 1975-1979
13	1965	Gunnar ERICSSON (Sweden)
14	1965	Mohamed MZALI (Tunisia) Vice-president 1976-1980
15	1966	Juan Antonio SAMARANCH (Spain) Vice-president 1974-1978 President 1980-
16	1966	Jan STAUBO (Norway)
17	1968	Agustin Carlos ARROYO (Ecuador)
18	1969	Louis GUIRANDOU-N'DIAYE (Ivory Coast) Vice-president 1980-1984
19	1969	Virgilio de LEON (Panama)
20	1970	Maurice HERZOG (France)
21	1971	Vitaly SMIRNOV (U.S.S.R.) Vice-president 1978-1982, 1991-
22	1972	Pedro RAMIREZ VAZQUEZ (Mexico)
23	1973	Roy Anthony BRIDGE (Jamaica)
24	1973	Manuel GONZALEZ GUERRA (Cuba)
25	1973	Ashwini KUMAR (India) Vice-president 1983-1987
26	1973	Juge Kéba MBAYE (Senegal) Vice-president 1988-
27	1974	Mohamed ZERGUINI (Algeria)
28	1976	Matts CARLGREN (Sweden)
29	1976	Dr. Kevin O'FLANAGAN (Ireland)
30	1976	Peter TALLBERG (Finland)
31	1976	José D. VALLARINO VERACIERTO (Uruguay)
32	1977	Bashir Mohamed ATTARABULSI (Lybia)
33	1977	R. Kevan GOSPER (Australia) Vice-president 1990-
34	1977	Niels HOLST-SORENSEN (Denmark)
35	1977	Lamine KEITA (Mali)
36	1977	Shagdarjav MAGVAN (Mongolia)
37	1977	Philipp von SCHOELLER (Austria)
38	1978	Professeur René ESSOMBA (Cameroon)
39	1978	Hon. Tan Seri HAMZAH BIN HAJI ABU SAMAH (Malaysia)
40	1978	Yu Sun KIM (North Korea)
41	1978	Richard W. POUND (Canada) Vice-president 1987-1991
42	1981	Vladimir CERNUSAK (Czechoslovakia)
43	1981	Nikos FILARETOS (Greece)
44	1981	Pirjo HAGGMAN (Finland)

45 1981 Zhenliang HÉ (China)
Vice-president 1989-
46 1981 Flor ISAVA-FONSECA (Venezuela)
47 1982 Franco CARRARO (Italy)
48 1982 Phillip Walter COLES (Australia)
49 1982 Ivan DIBOS (Peru)
50 1982 Mary Alison GLEN-HAIG (Great Britain)
51 1982 Chiharu IGAYA (Japan)
52 1983 Faisal FAHD ABDUL AZIZ (Saudi Arabia)
53 1983 Anani MATTHIA (Togo)
54 1983 Roque Napoleon MUÑOZ PEÑA (Dominican Rep.)
55 1983 Pal SCHMITT (Hungary)
56 1984 Princess Nora of LIECHTENSTEIN
57 1984 David S. SIBANDZE (Swaziland)
58 1985 Major Général Henry Edmund Olufemi ADEFOPE (Nigeria)
59 1985 Francisco ELIZALDE (Philippines)
60 1985 Carlos FERRER (Spain)
61 1985 Prince Albert of MONACO
62 1986 Dr. Un Yong KIM (South Korea)
63 1986 Lambis W. NIKOLAOU (Greece)
64 1986 Anita DEFRANTZ (U.S.A.)
65 1986 Jean-Claude GANGA (Congo)
66 1987 Ivan SLAVKOV (Bulgaria)
67 1987 Anton GEESINK (Netherlands)
68 1987 Slobodan FILIPOVIC (Yugoslavia)
69 1987 Seluli Paul WALLWORK (Western Samoa)
70 1988 H.R.H. The Princess ROYAL (Great Britain)
71 1988 Fidel MENDOZA CARRASQUILLA (Colombia)
72 1988 Tay WILSON (New Zealand)
73 1988 Ching-Kuo WU (Chinese Taipei)
74 1988 Ram RUHEE (Mauritius)
75 1988 Marat GRAMOV (ex-USSR)
76 1988 Sinan ERDEM (Turkey)
77 1988 Willi KALTSCHMITT LUJAN (Guatemala)
78 1988 Major General Francis NYANGWESO (Uganda)
79 1988 Borislav STANKOVIC (Yugoslavia)
80 1989 Fernando Ferreira Lima BELLO (Portugal)
81 1989 Walther TRÖGER (Germany)
82 1990 Philippe CHATRIER (France)
83 1990 Carol Anne LETHEREN (Canada)
84 1990 Shun-Ichiro OKANO (Japan)
85 1990 Richard CARRION (Puerto Rico)
86 1990 Gen. Zein El Abdin Mohamed Abdel GADIR (Sudan)
87 1990 Dr. Nat INDRAPANA (Thailand)
88 1990 Charles Nderifu MUKORA (Kenya)
89 1990 Col. Antonio RODRIGUEZ (Argentina)
90 1991 Denis OSWALD (Switzerland)
91 1991 Dr. Jacques ROGGE (Belgium)
92 1991 Mario VAZQUEZ RAÑA (Mexico)
93 1991 Thomas BACH (Germany)

Games of the Olympiad

Year	City	No.	NCOs	Competitors
1896	Athens	1	13	295
1900	Paris	2	21	1077
1904	Saint-Louis	3	12	554
1908	London	4	22	2034
1912	Stockholm	5	28	2504
1920	Antwerp	7	29	2591
1924	Paris	8	44	3075
1928	Amsterdam	9	46	2971
1932	Los Angeles	10	38	1331
1936	Berlin	11	49	3880
1948	London	14	58	4062
1952	Helsinki	15	69	5867
1956	Melbourne	16	67	3342
1960	Rome	17	84	5396
1964	Tokyo	18	94	5586
1968	Mexico	19	113	6626
1972	Munich	20	122	7894
1976	Montreal	21	88	6189
1980	Moscow	22	81	5923
1984	Los Angeles	23	140	7066
1988	Seoul	24	160	9417
1992	Barcelona	25		
1996	Atlanta	26		

Winter Games

Year	City	No.	NCOs	Competitors
1924	Chamonix	1	16	294
1928	Saint-Moritz	2	25	464
1932	Lake Placid	3	17	252
1936	Garmisch-Partenkirchen	4	28	689
1948	Saint-Moritz	5	28	689
1952	Oslo	6	30	894
1956	Cortina d'Ampezzo	7	32	820
1960	Squaw Valley	8	30	666
1964	Innsbruck	9	36	933
1968	Grenoble	10	37	1293
1972	Sapporo	11	35	1128
1976	Innsbruck	12	37	1281
1980	Lake Placid	13	37	1283
1984	Sarajevo	14	49	1490
1988	Calgary	15	57	1759
1992	Albertville	16	64	1802
1994	Lillehammer	17		
1998	Nagano	18		

Olympic congresses

1894	Paris
1897	Le Havre
1905	Brussels
1906	Paris
1913	Lausanne
1914	Paris
1921	Lausanne
1925	Prague
1930	Berlin
1973	Varna
1981	Baden-Baden
1994	Paris

Index

Picture Acknowledgements
The author and publisher are grateful to the following for permission to reproduce photographs:

Agerpress 25; Allsport/B. Stickland 21; IOC 3, 4, 5, 6, 16, 23, 26, 29; IOC/Locatelli 15, 28; IOC/PI 7, 30; IOC/Riethausen 17; IOC/Strahm 27; IOPP/J. Puusa 9; NOPP 18; OPA 31; Popperfoto 10; Mark Shearman 11, 12, 13; Sporting Pictures 19, 20, 22; Unipress Hong Kong 14.